11049838

For
Browns Fans
Only!!!

By Rich Wolfe

©Rich Wolfe

Printed in the United States

No part of this book may be reproduced, stored in a retrieval system, or transmitted, in any form or by any means, electronic, mechanical, photo-copying, recording, or otherwise, without the prior permission of Rich Wolfe. Disclaimer: This book is not affiliated with nor endorsed by the Cleveland Browns or the NFL.

Published by Lone Wolfe Press, a division of Richcraft.

ISBN: 0-9729249-2-2

Cover Design: Dick Fox
Photo Editor: Dick Fox
Cover Copywriter: Dick Fox
Interior Design: The Printed Page, Phoenix, AZ
Author's Agent: T. Roy Gaul

The author, Rich Wolfe, can be reached at 602-738-5889 or at www.fandemonium.net.

Page Two. In 1941, the news director at a small radio station in Kalamazoo, Michigan hired Harry Caray who had been employed at a station in Joliet, Illinois. The news director's name was Paul Harvey. Yes, that <u>Paul Harvey</u>! "And now, you have the rest of the story...... ➡

DEDICATION

To Crazy George Schauer

Few people in America have influenced children
in a more positive way than Cleveland's Pied Piper of Sports.

Acknowledgments

What a blast it has been doing this book. Wonderful people helped make it a reality starting with Ellen Brewer, my indispensable side-kick of many years in Edmond, Oklahoma; ditto to Barbara Jane Bookman in Falmouth, Massachusetts; and the good guys at Wolfegang Marketing Systems, Ltd.—But Not Very: Jim Murray, John Counsell, Jack Reilly, and Jon Spoelstra. Let's not forget Wonder Woman, Lisa Liddy, at The Printed Page in Phoenix and another Wonder Woman out west, Carol Reddy, also in Phoenix.

How about a big thank you to Ira Rosen and Dave Nemec and Sharon Tully. A tip of the hat to all those interviewed who missed the cut—we just ran out of time. Three chapters were cut indiscriminately due to space limitations. We'll do it again next year. But the biggest thank you, the deepest bow and grandest salute to Richcraft's own, Randy Adams, the sage of Carmi and a real pleasure to have on board…a hard worker and a good guy.

Preface

"God love 'em, God bless their hearts." When those words are spoken in certain parts of West Texas, many people believe that the speaker—at that point—has carte blanche to say whatever nasty things he chooses about those people…as if God will forgive slander if the proper preface is spoken first.

So, too, with Browns fans. In this book they'll share their memories, their thoughts and their dreams. They'll even talk about Bill Belichick, Art Modell, Butch Davis and Kellen Winslow. In regard to the latter, God love 'em, God bless their hearts.

Now, I have a terrible confession to make: I've never been to a Browns game and, actually, I have spent very little time in Cleveland… but from a distance, Browns fans have amazed me over the years.

Several years ago I tried to interest publishers in a series of books involving fans of certain teams. They laughed; said no one would be interested in other fans' stories.

When I became my own publisher five years ago, I knew I would test this idea. The first book, *For Yankee Fans Only*, sold tens of thousands of copies. the second, *For Red Sox Fans Only*, sold out immediately as did its rather substantial reprint. *For Cubs Fans Only* not only became the best selling book in the history of the Cubs, it sold over four times the previous record. It is my feeling that the football fans books will do even better and there was never a question that the first book on NFL fans would be the Cleveland Browns. My interest in Browns fans started in college listening to Cleveland area classmates talk about the Browns, followed by two couples from Cleveland that I met in Acapulco in the late '60s who told amazing stories about their love for the Browns…the list goes on but it became apparent that Browns fans are special. The pride they exhibit for their hometown and their team is truly remarkable, particularly given horrible setbacks in both areas.

Now is a good time to answer a few questions that always arise. The most often asked is, "Why isn't your name on the book cover, like other authors?" The answer is simple: I'm not Stephen King. No one knows who I am, no one cares. My name on the cover will not sell an additional book. On the other hand, it allows for "cleaner" and more dramatic covers that the readers appreciate, and the books are more visible at the point of sale.

The second most frequent query is, "You sell tons of books. Why don't they show up on the best seller list?" Here's how the book business works: Of the next 170 completed manuscripts, 16 will eventually be published, and only one will ever return a profit. To make the *New York Times Bestseller List*, you need to sell at least 30,000 copies nationally. Sales are monitored at certain stores, at big book chains, a few selected independent book stores, etc. My last nine books have averaged well over 60,000 units sold, but less than 15,000 were sold in bookstores. Most are sold regionally, another deterrent to national rankings. While I'm very grateful to have sold so many books to the "Big Boys," I'm a minority of one in feeling that a bookstore is the worst place to sell a book. Publishers cringe when they hear that statement. A large bookstore will stock over 150,000 different titles. That means the odds of someone buying my book are 150,000-1. Those aren't good odds; I'm not that good of a writer. For the most part, people who like Mike Ditka or Dale Earnhardt—previous book subjects of mine—don't hang around bookstores. I would rather be the only book at a hardware chain than in hundreds of bookstores.

Example: My *Remembering Dale Earnhardt* hardcover sold several hundred thousand copies, mostly at Walgreens and grocery chains; places not monitored for the "best selling" lists. I sold the paperback rights to Triumph Books, Chicago. They printed 97,000 paperbacks—all sold through traditional channels. My hardcover did not appear on any bestseller list. Meanwhile, Triumph had a paperback on Earnhardt that made number one on the *New York Times* nonfiction trade list. Go figure. Also, I never offer my books directly to Amazon.com because I can't type, I've never turned on a computer and I keep thinking that Amazon is going out of business soon. For years, the more customers they recruited, the more money they lost…so sooner or later, when the venture capital is gone, the book-keeping shenanigans are recognized, and the stock plummets, look out. Meanwhile, maybe I should call them.

Since the age of ten, I've been a serious collector of sports books. During that time—for the sake of argument, let's call it 30 years—my favorite book style is the eavesdropping type where the subject talks in his or her own words—without the "then he said" or "the air was so thick you could cut it with a butter knife" waste of verbiage that makes it so hard to get to the meat of the matter. Books such as Lawrence Ritter's *Glory of Their Times* and Donald Honig's *Baseball When the Grass Was Real*. Thus, I adopted that style when I started compiling oral histories of the Jack Bucks (a Cleveland native) and Harry Carays of the world. I'm a sports fan first and foremost—I don't even pretend to be an author. This book is designed solely for other sports fans. I really don't care what the publisher, editors or critics think. I'm only interested in Browns fans having an enjoyable read and getting their money's worth. Sometimes a person being interviewed will drift off the subject but if the feeling is that Cleveland fans would enjoy the digression, it stays in the book.

In an effort to get more material into the book, the editor decided to merge some paragraphs and omit some of the commas, which will allow for the reader to receive an additional 20,000 words, the equivalent of 50 pages. More bang for your buck…more fodder for English teachers…fewer dead trees.

All that Browns fans need these days is a patient spouse, a loyal dog and a good quarterback. As for the Steelers and Ravens: God love 'em, God bless their hearts.

Go now.

Rich Wolfe

Chat Rooms

Chapter 1. There's No Expiration Date on Dreams **11**
   EXPERIENCE IS WHAT YOU GET WHEN YOU DON'T GET WHAT
      YOU WANT 12
   BRONCO FANS ARE PROOF THAT HELL IS FULL AND THE DEAD
      ARE WALKING THE EARTH 14
   IN TEXAS, DO COWBOY FANS ROOT FOR THE DEFENSE
      OR THE PROSECUTION? 18
   I SAW IT ON THE RADIO 24
   WHEN DAD PUT HIS FOOT DOWN... 26
   HE COULD HAVE BEEN A BUCS FAN BUT THE DOG BEAT HIM
      OVER THE FENCE 29
   SHORT STORIES FROM LONG MEMORIES: 32

Chapter 2. The Old Man and The Wee **45**
   THESE SEVEN SIGNS ARE THE TEN REASONS SHE'S HOOKED
      ON THE BROWNS 46
   A COOL FAN FROM HOTLANTA 50
   DO SIAMESE TWINS PAY FOR ONE SEASON TICKET OR TWO?? 54
   WHY DOES HAWAII HAVE INTERSTATE HIGHWAYS? 57
   I DO AND I DO FOR YOU KIDS AND THIS IS THE THANKS I GET: 61

Chapter 3. Sweet Home Cleveland **69**
   ACTUALLY, THERE ARE A LOT OF BUSINESSES LIKE SHOW BUSINESS . . . 70
   MARRIAGES ARE MADE IN HEAVEN... SO ARE THUNDER AND LIGHTNING . 73
   MUNICIPAL STADIUM: THE FIELD OF SCREAMS 75
   A LOT OF OLD PEOPLE LIVE IN FLORIDA...WITH THEIR PARENTS. 80
   BROWNS FEVER: NO CURE 83
   YADA, YADA, YADA 87

Chapter 4. Baltimore: The Last Refuge of Scoundrels **97**
   IF YOU'DA BEEN THERE, IF YOU'DA SEEN IT, I'LL BETCHA YOU'DA
      DONE THE SAME 98
   DOWN AT THE CORNER OF WHAT AND IF 101
   HOW ABOUT A SHOT OF THE TRUTH? MAKE IT A BOTTLE, I'M BUYIN' ! . . 114
   LOYALTY OUTSIDE THE WALLET. 118
   UPON FURTHER REVIEW: 121

Chapter 5. Today We Ride **135**
   WASHINGTON: FIRST IN WAR, FIRST IN PEACE, LAST IN THE NFL EAST . 136
   ROOTIN' FOR THE BROWNS WAS LIKE FLYIN' TWA FOR THE FOOD 138
   HE LIVES IN PHOENIX—"THE VALLEY OF THE SUN"…IN SUMMER,
       THEY SHOULD CALL PHOENIX "THE SURFACE OF THE SUN!" 142
   DON'T EVER SIT BEHIND THE POPE AT THE MOVIES…IF HE'S
       WEARIN' THAT HAT! 146
   IT WAS A FOOLPROOF PLAN, AND THESE WERE THE FOOLS
       THAT PROVED IT! 149
   BEER: MORE THAN A BREAKFAST DRINK 154
   TWO BROTHERS ARE STEELER FANS…THERE MUST HAVE BEEN
       A MIX-UP AT THE HOSPITAL 157
   THIS GUY'S FROM PITTSBURGH. NOT THAT THERE'S ANYTHING
       WRONG WITH THAT! 161
   'TIS BETTER TO TRAVEL WELL THAN TO ARRIVE FIRST. 165

Chapter 6. Put Me In Coach **177**
   WIT HAPPENS. 178
   SOMETIMES, GOD JUST HANDS YOU ONE. 181
   NOSTALGIA'S NOT WHAT IT USED TO BE 186
   IT'S NOT HOW BIG YOU ARE, IT'S HOW GOOD YOU ARE! 189
   CHEVY CHASE ONCE HOSTED THE OSCARS…HENDRIX ONCE
       OPENED FOR THE MONKEES…THE BROWNS ONCE FIVE-PEATED.
       THERE ARE SOME THINGS YOU JUST CAN'T MAKE UP. 201
   MEMORIES, LIKE HEROES, NEVER GROW OLD 203

Chapter 7. Fandemonium **217**
   IT'S LIKE PLAYIN' HOOKY FROM LIFE. 218
   WE HAVEN'T SEEN ANYTHING THIS CRAZY SINCE THE
       MICHAEL JACKSON INTERVIEW 220
   SOME PEOPLE FEEL THAT ART MODELL WAS THE BACKBONE OF THE
       CLEVELAND BROWNS. OTHERS WOULDN'T PUT HIM THAT HIGH. . . . 222
   DO YOU KNOW WHERE VOLKSWAGENS GO WHEN THEY GET OLD?
       THE OLD VOLKS HOME. 226
   CALLING BILL BELICHICK "BILLY" IS LIKE CALLIN' ATTILA THE HUN, "TILLY." . . 231
   THERE'S NO "I" IN TEAM BUT THERE'S AN "M" AND AN "E" 234
   A ROCKYTOP TENNESSEE WALTZ WITH SOME NASHVILLE CATS 238
   SO SAY YOU ON, SO SAY YOU ALL 242

Chapter 1

There's No Expiration Date on Dreams

Growin' Up With the Browns

EXPERIENCE IS WHAT YOU GET WHEN YOU DON'T GET WHAT YOU WANT

MARK BLOOM

Mark Bloom, a science writer in Colorado Springs, was born in Akron and graduated from Kent State in 1976. He attended to his first Browns game in 1963.

Very early, I remember being so impressed with the size of the stadium—it was enormous. I'd never been to an event that had so many people. The first time I went, we parked the car, and walked in, and I could smell the hot dogs and the food. It was exciting to me, and I saw lots of people wearing Browns paraphernalia. As we were walking through the concourse, trying to go up to where our seats were located, I knew I was going to see a football field, but all I was seeing were corridors and crowds of people and remember thinking it was dark. We suddenly merged into the light. Then, I saw the field and saw the players down there throwing the ball around and practicing. I remember that moment as being very exciting when I first saw the field and the players, live and in person as I came out of the darkness. It's the vastness, the size, and the atmosphere of it that was totally different than staying at home and watching on TV.

When I lived in Ohio, I remember going to Pittsburgh games. A lot of Pittsburgh fans would come to Cleveland. Now that I'm older, I think there is more drinking and taunting between the two sides at those games. I don't remember that as a young child. Maybe fans were a little better behaved way back then.

Most of my memories predate the Dawg Pound. When I was in Little League, our town had a Little League parade every year. They would try to get some quasi-local celebrities. The one year I remember best, several of the Browns players rode through town in a car. We would march in the parade in our team uniforms and met Gary Collins, Dick Schafrath, and Paul Warfield. Paul Warfield looked like he had graphite arms…strong. I stood in a short line with some of my friends and we had the players sign our baseball caps, which was kind of dumb because over the summer, we would wear the hat and sweat would make those signatures disappear…so I had their autographs, but they went away.

When I was ten, I started getting really hyped up on Cleveland football. I was a big fan of Jim Brown. My friends and I would all go to school and talk about the players and the game. This one kid was more or less bragging that his father was a doctor and that he was the doctor for the Cleveland Browns—for the team. We were really impressed with that. We would ask him if he got to go to the games. He said, "Oh, yeah, I go to all the games, and I know all the players." We were so jealous of this kid. Here he is telling us he has all this connection to the players, and that he gets to sit on the bench and had all these great stories. I said, "Gee, could you get me Jim Brown's autograph?" He said, "Oh, yeah, that'd be no problem." I was really excited then, knowing I was going to get Jim Brown's autograph. So, Monday comes around. I see him at school and run right over and say, "Were you able to get Jim Brown's autograph?" He said, "Yeah." I thought, "Oh, man, this is great." He pulls out of his pocket this yellow paper with blue lines on it that we used in school—the one we used when we first learned how to print and write. He gives it to me. It's all folded up. I open it up and look on the paper and written in pencil, in just the sort of printing that we're learning in school, and staying nicely within the lines, it says, "To Mark, from Jim Brown." It was all in capital letters, in pencil. I was 10 years old, but I knew darn good and well that it was not written by Jim Brown. In a way, I felt sorry for this kid because I knew that it was clear that he was just trying to be popular with the guys so I didn't call him on it. I just thanked him for it and later threw it away.

BRONCO FANS ARE PROOF THAT HELL IS FULL AND THE DEAD ARE WALKING THE EARTH

DAN JARVIS

Dan Jarvis was born and raised in Cleveland. He moved to Albuquerque, New Mexico 40 years ago where he is a stucco contractor and plasterer.

T he childhood diseases of the Cleveland Indians and Cleveland Browns are burned deep—run very deep. In 1957, I was nine years old, and discovered Jim Brown. I was more of an Indians fan up to that point and was lukewarm as a Browns fan. Then Jim Brown came on the scene, and he became my idol. It was Rocky Colavito in baseball and **JIM BROWN** in football. I had a healthy idol worship for both of those guys.

They televised a lot of the Browns games in those days, especially the away games. As a kid, I remember watching many of the games just to watch Jim play. I would listen to the rest of them on the radio. I was such a fanatic, that I used to chart all of his statistics—how many times he carried the ball, how far he ran, how many yards per carry, how many passes he caught, how many times he touched the ball. I was just a Jim Brown fanatic. That introduced me to the Browns.

I don't think it's the same with today's kids. I don't mean to judge them in any way, but I think it's the circumstances. When I grew up, radio was a big factor in listening to sports. If you weren't able to watch it on television, you listened to the radio broadcast. Kids today can pretty much see everything live. Even on the computer now, you can get game feeds, get replays, do whatever. I'm not sure as much of

> **The only person to score back-to-back fifty-point games in the history of Long Island High School basketball is JIM BROWN, the NFL legend.**

the imagination that I had as a kid that goes along with being a fan, things that you perceive and imagine, is the same. Everything now is pretty much real and *in your face*. I don't know if that's an explanation.

Sometimes you get false heroes. Today there are a lot of false heroes out there. These kids will cheer for a guy and idolize a guy. Then he'll do something in his private life, or even sometimes on the field, that you would think would turn some of the kids away from these athletes, but sometimes they idolize them even more for their crazy behavior. When we were younger, we weren't privy to their off-field life. That was just as well, as it turns out. Now I get more information than I want.

I was nine when I went to my first game—Jim Brown's second year. Then, I went to a game or two every year for the next several years. I remember the football doubleheaders they used to have during the exhibition season in Cleveland. I don't know if anybody else ever tried it, but they would actually play two football games in a day— just like the **DOUBLEHEADERS** for baseball. That was really getting your fill of football. Of course, the exhibition season meant August or early September so the weather was pleasant, and you could sit there all day. As a kid, that meant six hours of football and snacks. It would always be Cleveland against somebody pretty good and then two other teams that would pique the interest of the crowd. Sometimes it would be Cleveland against the NFL champion from the year before, and then two other pretty good pro teams. It was called an NFL Exhibition Doubleheader. They did that for two or three years, and then it went by the wayside. They were sure fun while it lasted.

In March, 1954, the Lakers and the Hawks played a regulation, regular season NBA game using baskets that were 12' high rather than the usual 10'...the next night they played each other in a **DOUBLEHEADER.** True facts, believe it or not! ...In 1944, the Chicago White Sox played 43 doubleheaders. last year they played one.

As a kid, my uncle had some inside connections. He would always wait after the game was over. He knew what door to wait at, where the players would come out. I got many autographs, just stood there and watched many a conversation between the Indians and Browns players after games. The average 10-year-old kid didn't get to see that. I saw Jim Brown in a lengthy conversation with my uncle and another guy one time. That was pretty exciting, and it really got me hooked even more and more…and made me want to go back to the stadium more and more. We went every year until we moved to Albuquerque in the early '60s. Dallas was a pretty new team, only about two years old, at that time, but you could slowly feel Albuquerque moving in their direction because they were the closest pro team to the people here.

It's hard for the Browns to maintain their new fan base right now. There are kids, young people, out in the middle of America who don't live in a major league city so they end up picking a team to show their allegiance to. They usually pick front-runners…so I don't think the Browns are picking up a lot of young fans. A lot of the Browns fans now are of the older base that are still hanging on. I hope that changes quick. I've been here in Albuquerque for over 40 years and no way would I have switched to any other team, at any time, under any circumstance. That was not an option. I don't care how bad we would have got.

Look at the Indians. They're never any good, and I'm still a die-hard Indians fan to this day. And, even a couple of my kids are their fans, too. They had a chance to choose whatever they wanted, and the poor kids are Indians and Browns fans.

When I was in the military, I enjoyed strutting my stuff, showing my colors, supporting my team, listening to games on Armed Forces Radio. Some of the games would be a two-month delay. But, if your team was featured, you dressed up in your colors. Being in the military, we would grasp for anything that would remind us of home. Everybody knew my loyalties were for the Browns and Indians so that whenever something like that came up, there would always be friendly rivalries with the other guys you were stationed with. Those times were special. I was stationed on Midway Island, isolated duty, but we were able to get sports feeds and football games. We had the

AFC champion game between Cleveland and Dallas. The broadcast was a month after the game had been played. We already knew the outcome, but we had a big party. Even some of our military mates who weren't Cleveland or Dallas fans would pick fights. We'd have this huge rivalry with a lot of beer and a lot of yelling—just something to cheer for.

We have a lot of Backers clubs here and overseas. Almost all of us get involved in charity work. We have a charity golf tournament every year for an educational foundation, and this year we raised $7,000 in one afternoon. Many, many of the Backers' organizations do something for the local community. As noble as it is watching football and drinking beer every week, we do go beyond the call of duty and get involved in the community. Not only the strength of numbers of the amount of Backers' groups we have, but the fact we get involved separates us from any other professional fan organization, and, especially, a football organization. All our groups do something, whether it's raising dog food for the local dog shelter, on up to golf tournaments like we have. It's one thing we're known for.

The formula for the NFL Quarterback Rating System is actually a recipe for chili

IN TEXAS, DO COWBOY FANS ROOT FOR THE DEFENSE OR THE PROSECUTION?

TOM McDOWELL

Retired from the Air Force after 26 years, Tom McDowell is enjoying his retirement at the end of a country road near Leander, Texas. He was born in Cleveland in 1933.

During the summer of '46, the two radio stations I listened to were WERE and WJMO, in Cleveland, because they had soft easy-listening music. They talked about the new team because the Rams left. They ran off to Los Angeles so we didn't have a team.

Mickey McBride, the owner of the Checker Yellow Cab was a big Notre Dame fan. He went to Chicago and got a Cleveland franchise for the All-America Football Conference. He wanted to get the Notre Dame coach, Frank Leahy. The priest that was in charge talked him out of taking that famous coach, but he did say, "Well, you're from Ohio. You should know Paul Brown." So, Mickey McBride wound up hiring Paul Brown. He had to go to great lengths because Paul was still in the Navy. This was in the summer of 1945.

There was a contest to see what they were going to call the new team for Cleveland. McBride put up a $1,000 war bond for the winner. My application that I put in was for the Kodiaks, those great big bears from Alaska. Chicago had the black grizzly bear as their mascot. I thought if they're going to talk about a big ferocious football team, it should be something like those big bears. The Kodiaks are bigger than grizzly bears.

In September of 1946, I went to see the Browns play the Miami Seahawks. The Browns wore all white uniforms, with white helmets, white shirts, brown numbers with the orange on the left-hand side called 'drop-shadowed.' It was the best looking uniform they ever had. They only wore it in '46. This was before they had color television. They just barely had black and white television—that was still real grainy and snowy.

I had a paper route for the *Cleveland Press* newspaper. I saved a dollar out of my earnings. I took the Payne Avenue streetcar from East 55th Street and went down to West 3rd. That cost me a dime. It cost a quarter for kids 12-and-under to get in. I fudged a little bit, even though I was 13. I got a hot dog and a coke for twenty-five cents each. I had to keep a dime for the street car to get back home. I saved a nickel for a candy bar the following day. The Browns beat the crap out of the Seahawks, who played that one year and then folded.

The NFL was against the Browns. What they did was they lined us up with Greasy Neale and his Philadelphia Eagles. The Eagles had won the NFL championship in 1949. They were the World Champions. We had a night game with them. We also played a night game in the pre-season against the Bears and beat them. To even make it harder, they wouldn't let us wear our white helmets. Morrie Kono, the equipment manager, had to go out and get paint—he got the burnt orange paint. The real colors for the Browns are burnt orange and seal-skin brown. They've always been burnt orange. It wasn't until '60, when color television came out that they went to the bright orange. It had been just a pumpkin orange, a burnt orange. Anyway, we only played that one game with the orange helmets and the reason was that the NFL at the time used an all-white football with a black stripe around each end. They didn't want to confuse anybody's helmet with the ball. *It's an NFL rule that you can't play sneaky.* Of course, on the other hand, they didn't make the Chicago Cardinals, who wore white helmets, change their helmet colors 'cause they didn't have any night games. That was the only game—the rest of the year for '51 they continued to wear the white helmets in league play. During the day, the ball was brown with yellow stripes.

Cliff Lewis was our first quarterback, not Otto Graham. But you've got to understand there were only 30 people on that football team. Those guys played both ways. In some of the games, you saw Bill Willis do a lot of tackles. The reason was Bill Willis was a right offensive guard, but he also played linebacker when they switched to defense. They didn't have a real two-platoon system in those days until later in the '50s when they switched to having more people. Groza was the kicker, and the back-up left tackle.

I was at the game when the Browns won their first NFL championship. I sold sodas or hot chocolate, depending on the weather. Kids couldn't sell at night. You've got to understand it was right at the end of the Second World War. Everybody had to do a lot for that war effort. We would take our wagons to school every Friday morning. After we went into home room, they took our names and then we were off all morning. We would go around and collect grease and bundled newspapers and metal toothpaste tubes, material like that. In those days, they still had the old paper/rags men. These guys would get an old horse and a wagon—just bums—but it was the only job they could hold. They would go around the neighborhood yelling out, "Paper. Rags." You would get maybe ten cents for a bundle of old clothes that were worn out and had holes in them.

The Jehovah's Witnesses had a big convention in 1944 down at the Lady of the Lake, the old Muni Stadium. I saw kids going around selling cokes. The next year, I was twelve and wanted to vend. I asked one of the kids and he said, "Just go talk to one of the vendors." So what you did, you went and talked to a vendor and told him who you were. They talked to you a little bit and found out you were honest. They jaw-boned you. $2.00 for a case of Cokes. You went and sold the case of Coke for $6. Coke only cost a nickel a bottle. The case was worth more than the soda. You could probably do three cases during a good baseball game. I sold for the Indians during the summer, and then when the Browns had day games, I would sell for them. I worked as many games as I could get to. You got into the ball game for free, plus you made money. And, you could stop when you were pouring a Coke and watch the game. They sold beer at the games back then, but the kids couldn't sell it—usually they had a big, fat black lady selling it—they always had the good stuff. They had the hot dogs and the hamburgers. They didn't have the pirogue things at that time. They did have Polish sausage. You could get a Polish sausage for about thirty-five cents, where a red hot was just a quarter.

The crowds were sellouts then. They'd have as many as they could get in Muni Stadium. The Muni was built as a WPA project by the government back in 1931. It put a lot of people to work during the depression. Of course, I was a depression baby. I remember standing in line—they didn't have food stamps—for a bag of dried apricots.

Because the Browns didn't play as many games as the Indians, they would draw bigger crowds. Finally, the Indians were working their way up—**LOU BOUDREAU** and **BOB FELLER**. You've got to remember, too, about the blacks and the whites. There were very few black players in either baseball or football. But the first two guys that Paul Brown recruited were Bill Willis and Marion Motley. Jackie Robinson didn't come along at the Dodgers until a year later—about the same time Larry Doby did for the Indians.

Back in '46, there was the first Cleveland tragedy. You know all the hard luck we've had. The first tragedy actually was that we had a terrific team, and we had the very first girl cheerleaders of any professional sport. What it was—Paul Brown was a coach at Massillon Washington High School back in the thirties. The band director who had the Massillon Show Band was named George "Red" Bird, an old guy. When he found out that Paul was going to be mixed up with the new team, he went with Paul and formed an all-girl band with about 25-26 girls in the band.

George Bird had these girls, these majorettes, who came out like a storm. The first day game they came out of the Indians dugout. Everybody was all quiet with just a little bit of mumbling going on…and, BLAST, these girls come out. They even had a glockenspiel. It was about the third or fourth game in. After games, the kids

> **LOU BOUDREAU**'s daughter was once engaged to 1962 National League Rookie of the Year, Ken Hubbs of the Cubs. Several years after Hubbs was killed in a plane crash, she married Denny McLain of the Detroit Tigers.

> **BOB FELLER**'s catcher in American Legion Baseball was Nile Kinnick, later to become the 1939 Heisman Trophy winner from Iowa.

could go down on the field, run around, play football, throw stuff around. The ushers didn't care. One of the girls had left her hat—her shako hat—in the dugout instead of putting it on her head and wearing it in to change her clothes. I saw it and contemplated, "Should I take this home as a souvenir or give it back?" I went on down the hallway, which was a tunnel thing, and saw this guy in a uniform that looked like theirs, a cream-colored thing with striping—it was George Bird. He said, "Well, thanks, kid. By the way, shake hands with Paul Brown." He looked in the hat and saw a name. And then he pounded on the door and yelled for her. She came out, and he said, "Here, you need to take care of your equipment. This kid brought it back to you." So, she gave me a kiss. She was kind of a cute girl…but, I was only 13. I wasn't really into girls at that time. Later, when we lived up in the projects, the Browns would come out and do charity work or public relations work, and Bill Willis came out to where we lived near 110th and Woodlawn. That was back in 1950 when I was in high school.…

It was fall of '46, and women and men both wore hats in those days. The women would have these brown felt hats. One time, Paul Brown was sitting behind this woman who had on a brown felt hat with these burnt orange flowers with white baby's breath on it. He thought that would be a good color.

You see, they never had even settled on a name. He had said, "No, we can't have the Panthers 'cause there was a 1921 team that had failed—it went belly up. I don't want to have anything to do with being a loser." So, he put another bond up. They had already given the first guy a thousand dollar war bond, but he put up another bond. This time it was overwhelming that the team should be called the Browns. Paul said, "No, I don't want a team named after me." They told him that it wouldn't be named after him, it would be named two ways—it was the Brown Bombers, meaning the B-17s that flew Europe and/or Joe Louis, the Brown Bomber, the great fighter.

The people were so tired and sick of that war. You've got to understand that during the war, men worked seven days a week. They let them off for four hours on Sunday morning to go to church because it was a big Catholic population. Then, after church, they had to go back to the machine shops and plants and make up the time to get the production out. This is why the Rams never drew a lot of people because people were exhausted. There wasn't a lot of bowling. There wasn't a lot of any activity. It was come home, drink a beer, go to bed, get up and go back to work again. The money was good because they were getting paid regular wages and overtime. That was terrific…after the depression. There was black smoke over the Flats every day—the steel mills pumped it out, pumped it out. We milled so much steel. They made so many tanks out there at the tank plant. There was a big VA hospital.

So, Sears Roebuck—it was still Roebuck's at that time—had a bunch of damn pixies hiding behind mushrooms and crap like that—just doing things and running around. Well, in the *Cleveland Plain Dealer*, they had the ball scores right on the front page. The Indians logo was **CHIEF WAHOO**, with a small picture of an Indian chief. Well, they didn't have anything for the Browns so the Browns were shown with the Brownie Elf Fairy thing. A sketch artist at the *Plain Dealer* actually invented the little pixie-fairy thing holding a football. There had been nothing to do legally with the Browns. In fact, Modell said, "I don't want to have anything to do with it." In 1968, they got rid of it. It had never been any kind of an official thing.

I know about the 'overcoat' game. At the end of the war, you could get an Army overcoat for five bucks. It was great. I had one in Air Force blue, and we used it as a blanket when we first got married. When we played the Yankees in '46 for the championship, there were three-quarters of the people dressed in those Army overcoats and scarves over their head and even had their Army galoshes. The called it the "Great Overcoat Game." That's where the musical majorettes really did it up good.

In a 2002 *Sports Illustrated* poll, 83% of <u>NATIVE AMERICANS</u> declared in favor of Indian mascots and team nicknames. Among tribal leaders, that figure was under 50%.

I SAW IT ON THE RADIO

CRAZY GEORGE SCHAUER

Cleveland native, George Schauer, is the Pied Piper of basketball. His incredible ball-handling show, combined with his "Don't Drink," "Don't Do Drugs" and "Stay in School" messages have thrilled millions of kids from Vancouver to the Five-Star camps in Pennsylvania and endears him to thousands of educators in North America.

For me, the Cleveland Browns were all about Gib Shanley. He was larger than life. When I was a kid, if you tuned in at the middle of a Browns game, you could tell if the Browns were winning or losing just by his voice. He was the best announcer I ever heard in any sport. It was colossal the way he painted the game for you on the radio. In 1964, when I was 12 years old, a lot of the games were blacked out, so we you had to listen to them on the radio. I can still hear the Gibber now. "Here comes the Browns—Collins set right, Warfield out left. Ryan back to pass. Here's Collins…. Touchdown, Browns! Or, "Here's a pitch to Jim Brown, sweeping right, 15—10—he's on the move, still moving, he's in the end zone. Touchdown, Browns!. "Jim Brown, up the middle…." When I was a kid, every year in October, we'd rake the leaves up into a big pile. We'd play, "Jim Brown up the middle," and dive in. Jim Graner was Gib's partner. They were both super. When they played the '64 championship game, a lot of people went to Erie to get it on Channel 61 in black and white. I turned it on, and all we could see was snow because it was such bad reception. I had the radio at my ear….

Kosar grew up in Boardman, and he beat the 49ers on Monday Night Football where he drew the play up in the dirt right on the ground like the sandlot. Belichick sent the play in, and Kosar said, "No, we're doing this." That was the end of that relationship. I never saw a guy do so much with so little as Bernie Kosar. In a race with a turtle and a pregnant woman, he'd come in fourth. He just was so smart— with impeccable timing. He threw sidearm. Most of the times when the receivers caught the ball, they had to lay out on the ground to catch it. It wasn't going to be intercepted. He never hung his head when he walked off the field, win or lose…never.…

I had a Deluxe Tudor Electric Football Game. It had the vibrator to make the guys shake. I'd put a vibrator box underneath each end so it would really shake. I had one team painted as the Browns and the other team the Packers. Of course, my Browns always won. I fixed the legs so the Packer players would dance in circles. Walter Roberts would go straight for a hundred-yard return every time.…

The first time I went to Cleveland Stadium I was shocked. I had to pee so bad. I went into the bathroom, and there was a river of urine about three inches deep on the floor. People went in the sink. It was disgusting.

…When the Browns scored a touchdown, you could see total strangers, black and white, hugging each other, high-fiving. I remember the Monday Night Football game when Don Cockroft kicked the field goal in overtime to beat the Patriots. I was in the bleachers where you could get in for six bucks. I got sick to my stomach from marijuana fumes floating through the air that entire game. The police just turned their backs the other way. I ran into Don Cockroft at the Hartville Flea Market last summer. I said, "Don Cockroft, you kicked that field goal against the Patriots." The guy started shaking his head and said, "How'd you remember that?" "I remember everything. You looked like you were a lot bigger. You're just a little guy." He said, "Yeah, but my leg is strong." I said, "How come you had a square toe?" He said, "Hey, they had to give us some kind of advantage." I asked him, "How come you didn't kick soccer style?" He said, "I was one of the last traditionalists." He just lined up and boomed that sucker.

I liked Paul Warfield. That guy would float through the air. He was the Michael Jordan of football. He was unbelievable…

The curse of Cleveland started when Modell fired Paul Brown. Then, Trader Frank Lane traded Colavito. That was the end of the baseball when they traded Colavito. That curse will never be reversed.

WHEN DAD PUT HIS FOOT DOWN...

MICHELLE COCKROFT STICKNEY

What's it like to have a famous football player for your dad? Most of the time, it's wonderful according to Michelle Stickney of Colorado Springs. Her father is Don Cockroft, Browns kicker from 1968 to 1980.

My dad, Don Cockroft, was playing for the Browns when I was born in 1970 and played until I was 11. When I was young, I wasn't too 'into' football, but I liked to see daddy on TV. I remember my mom would always call my name as my signal to look up at the television when he was on. I was usually drawing him pictures to give him upon his arrival back home, rather than actually focusing on the whole football game. Some of my fun memories are going to the airport to meet the team, getting to see him get off the plane with all those guys, watching for his face and not really caring who else he was with. We sometimes went to the stadium, but, oftentimes, I would prefer to stay at home with a babysitter than to go sit out in the cold. When I did go, I was much more interested in the band and in the popcorn. As I got older, I would take my Walkman and a book. Mom would have to poke me and say, "Michelle, your dad's on the field." We didn't get special treatment back then. We sat in the stands with everybody else and dealt with the elements and the beer and all that good stuff.

Everybody in my schools knew my dad was a Browns player because I was the child who left half-way through the year or arrived half-way through the year every season. We would always come home to Colorado for off-seasons. If the Browns had a good day on Sunday, then, I had a good day on Monday. If the Browns didn't do so well on Sunday, then, I usually heard about it on Monday. The ribbing was fine until my dad's last season, and then it got to be a little more brutal. All my friends were great, but it was other kids who weren't always as pleasant if, for example, he missed a field goal that could have won the game, which didn't happen very often, thankfully. That's why he played for so long. In the rare case that it did happen, that was a difficult morning. I wasn't that huge of a football fan at the time—I am now. After my dad was out of football, I began to realize that the people around us were famous. Then, when they would call the house or be around, it began to hit me a lot more. During the time dad was involved, they were just the people he worked with. It didn't seem like a big deal to me. When some of my friends had their little-girl crushes on teammates, I just couldn't quite understand that.

Dad had to stay at the training camps, so on family days, we would go visit him. I was very excited about being able to go to places like Hiram and Kent State to see daddy. They'd have an ice-cream maker there so we'd get to have ice cream. We'd get to see all the kids we hadn't seen since last season. It was difficult when a player was traded off, and you didn't get to see him or his family again. You always wondered if your family would be next and what would happen then. There were quite a few people we were close to that we watched come and go very quickly. It's like the military. Being here in Colorado Springs, we're surrounded by military personnel. You get close to somebody, and then they're gone very quickly. That part was difficult. The actual lifestyle of growing up in Colorado and then partly in Ohio was good. In Colorado, I went to a three-room school house where there was no gym or cafeteria. We were way up in the mountains. I'd go from that to Cleveland Public Schools. I had two totally different atmospheres every year so I think I've grown up very well-rounded thanks to dad's position on the Browns.

It was a fun way to grow up. There were neat experiences that you typically might not have. One vivid memory was that dad would always sign autographs for people. Regardless of where we were, unless we were in the middle of a church service, he would stop and take the time. I remember once we were at a Kenny Rogers concert. Somebody discovered he was there, and the line went all the way from whatever row we were in all the way out the door during intermission, and he couldn't get up to go to the bathroom. That was very typical. He wouldn't tell people "no." He really wanted the fans to feel appreciated.

My dad was named one of the classiest guys in football, and he held true to that. He was very full of integrity and not caught up in all the glamour of the job. When he played, the players weren't dancing around on the field and doing all that hoopla. They went out there, did their job, and then came home to their family. That was a good time to be in football. They might make more money now, but I feel he played at the right time.

The world was different the last time the Browns won the title... for one thing, it was flat.

HE COULD HAVE BEEN
A BUCS FAN BUT THE DOG
BEAT HIM OVER THE FENCE

JIM SZILAGYI

Jim Szilagyi, 36, has lived in the Tampa Bay area for 29 years. He drives a UPS truck in New Port Richey, just north of Clearwater.

When I was four or five years old, I remember being at my uncle's house where my dad, my uncle and my grandfather were watching Browns games. Kids pick things up, and I guess that's where I picked up Browns fever, and I've just stayed with it. My dad passed away when I was six years old. I moved down here when I was young so I didn't get to go to any games. I watched the games on TV and kept up with them. My uncle who had watched games with my dad also passed away. For my 18th birthday in '86, my aunt flew me up to Cleveland to see the Browns in a playoff game. That was my first Browns football game.

The only game I ever saw up there was that day at the Dawg Pound at the old stadium. It was everything that I ever thought it would be. It typified Cleveland. It was really, really cold. I thought it was great going to the game. We left with about four minutes to go in the game, and the Browns were down by 10 points. It was so cold, and we were just miserable because they were losing. It seemed pretty much insurmountable—you got that feeling that there's no way they'd come back.

We left the stadium, and as we were leaving, people had their little radios with them. There's parking around the stadium, but a lot of people would go to Terminal Tower, now it's called Tower City. That's where you get on your rapid transit to take you off to the rural areas so you can get your car. It was really cool, because you got home really quick. Anyway, we were walking back to the Terminal Tower at the time to catch our train back to our cars, and, as we were walking, we heard that the Browns had just scored. We looked at each other and we were trying to overhear another guy's radio. We didn't know whether it was a touchdown or a field goal. We just figured, "Okay, they scored." But, we had been walking for over five minutes, and there had only been four minutes left in the game when we left, so we figured with timeouts, there could be less than a minute left.

By the time we got to the Terminal Tower, which was probably about a ten-minute walk, we heard that the Browns were lining to up kick a field goal to tie the score. At that moment, we ran inside the Terminal Tower to see what was going on, and this is where it was really cool. When we got inside, it was like a mall. There were a few stores down there, and, to me, it was like the rebirth of the city.

Before, Cleveland sports had been just terrible, and the city had a bad rap, but when we got down there and started watching, all the businesses shut down, the police that were down there, everybody—we were all huddled around two very small black and white TVs that were setting out. There was nobody in McDonalds. There was nobody in the stores. Somebody could have just gone in there, opened the cash registers and got away with everything. The police—and everybody—were watching the TVs. Later, when the Browns kicked a field goal and won the game, for anybody in Cleveland, it was just like we won the Super Bowl. It was incredible. I imagine it was great down at the stadium, but I wouldn't have traded being there for that—the people and the way everybody reacted to it.

I looked around and thought, "This is a moment that you keep with you. It was really special." People were hugging. Even though the Browns didn't even make it to the Super Bowl, it was great. The Browns had been just terrible for so long. The city was just a shambles, sports-wise. To me, that's what started people going back to see Cleveland sports, and getting back into it....

Two years ago, I took my son to his first Browns game—in Jacksonville. He was five years old at the time. We were booked into the same hotel as the Jaguars were staying. My son had just learned how to write letters and numbers so he asked me how to spell 'Browns.' As we sat in our room, he took a pen and a pencil and wrote down, "Go Browns," on little pieces of paper, and he went out into the hallway and was stuffing these underneath doors. Little did he know that behind some of those doors were Jaguar players. It was really interesting. We were riding up in an elevator with Kyle Brady, the tight end, and two other guys—I don't know who they were. They were carrying their big playbooks. My son was all dressed in Browns stuff. He looked up at them and goes, "Go Browns." And, he started barking. I'm a big guy, but these guys were just huge, and I was like, "Oh boy!" I hope they didn't get offended, but they just smiled, and it was pretty cool.

In Tampa, the fans are bandwagon jumpers. When the Bucs are good, the fans are there. When the Bucs are bad, there's nobody there. Boston was whining about the Red Sox. In Chicago, they're whining about the Cubs. But, there's no city that has been through a drought as long as Cleveland. You can go to the Indians. The Indians had great teams back in '95—'96. They go to the World Series, and they lose it on a two-out home run. Then you go to the Cavaliers—you go to Michael Jordan's shot. Over a team that had Mark Price, Brad Daugherty, Larry Nance from **CLEMSON**—a stacked team. There's no city that has been so close and been denied so many times. The last time the Browns won was before me. The Indians were in 1954. And, the Cavs have never, so…. It's been almost fifty years for any championship team in Cleveland. There's no city that has done that. No city has been in such a drought as Cleveland has.

The fans stay loyal and that's part of it. It's what feeds the fire. Any team, give them a championship, and they'll be gods. I've never seen one, and it's getting to the point where there's not going to be many people left in Cleveland who have seen a championship.

There's always hope. If Boston can win the World Series….

> **When CLEMSON University plays in a bowl game most of their fans pay their tabs with $2 bills to show their economic impact…and increasing their chances of a future invitation.**

SHORT STORIES
FROM LONG MEMORIES:

I was a Cleveland Rams fan first. I went to the championship game in 1945 when the Browns played the Washington Redskins. I was 10 years old and can remember it like yesterday because it was real cold, and I had my first taste of hard liquor…at age 10 to help keep warm during the game. I was very disappointed that Bob Waterfield and company were moving to Los Angeles until I heard there was going to be a new football team and a new league called the All-America Conference. They would be called the Cleveland Browns after Paul Brown, who I knew something about because he had coached at Ohio State and Massillon High School.

I was 11 years old when the Browns started up. They spoiled me…they hardly ever lost. They won the championship of their conference in '46, '47, '48, '49. It got to the point where the league was suffering because the Browns were so dominant that everybody knew they were going to win. In 1950, they became part of the National Football League. I never missed a game. When I went with my dad and my uncle, we sat in the stands, but when I went with my cousin, who is my age, we sat in the bleachers. I spent a lot of time in those bleachers at old Municipal Stadium. The cost was 50 cents… fifty cents to watch an NFL football game! I have a 1946 bobblehead wearing the original, old, old helmet with the C/B on it—Cleveland Browns. It got broken in the 1994 earthquake, but I managed to put it back together, almost like new, and I treasure that thing.

——MARSHALL BASKIN, 69, Los Angeles

I remember going to a Browns game with my father on a cold winter day. I was around 10 years old, and that was in the days of Otto Graham. Paul Brown was the coach. I remember the people in front of us being very loud and boisterous and drunk. Throughout the game, they kept yelling, and my father and I enjoyed later reminiscing about them. One guy kept yelling out, "Put in George, Paul." George Ratterman was the backup quarterback. Otto must have been having a bad day because this guy just kept yelling at the top of his voice….

I've lived in Boston, Berkeley and other places all over the country, and we'd go to the highest mountain to try to pull in a signal so we could listen to the Browns games. I always was a fan, but I hate to go to the games. I'm more of a television or newspaper fan. Actually, football is a very brutal sport, and if it went away, I wouldn't care, really. It's awful. It speaks badly of our culture…but I do like the Browns and the Cavs and the Indians, no matter where I go.

——GENE BEECHER, 68, Fort Louden, Pennsylvania

Growing up in Painesville, **DON SHULA**, former coach of the Dolphins, went to my high school. He's older than I am, but he had been a customer of my family's furniture business. During the Miami Dolphins undefeated season, the Browns were one of the teams that almost beat the Dolphins. Don Shula actually gave my grandfather two tickets to the Miami-Browns game in Miami. Shula sent a nice letter to him, and I have kept that letter. It was cool that we 'almost' saw the Browns ruin their undefeated season.

When I was in college, my father had these 45-yard line upper-deck seats. He would always take his wife to the games. I wanted to get into the game, and I had a buddy I always used to go with. He and I had this deal going on where my father would go in and slip the usher a $10 bill before he sat down and say, "My son may come. If he does, can you help him out if there are any seats around the 45 in the upper deck?" That was the beginning of it. Then, I would wait until a minute before kickoff, and buy tickets from a scalper for a really cheap price, walk in, slip the usher another $5. So, for a couple of seasons in a row, I'd sit right next to my father. I'd only pay $15 or $20 bucks for my ticket.

——SCOTT BROWN, season-ticket holder from Washington, D. C.

Mark and Michelle Shack are brother and sister, and we lived across the street from each other. When Michelle and I were in grade school, Mark enlisted in the service and went to Korea. The funny

> When **DON SHULA** retired, he had more victories than over half of the other NFL teams had total wins.

story is that Mr. Shack, who drove a truck for a building supply company, was a bartender in the evening. Some of the Browns used to come in there. This would have been in the '60s. He made friends with some of them. One of the players invited Mr. Shack, his wife and Michelle and Mark over for dinner the day after Christmas. When they got to their house, the player's wife was totally loaded and passed out. Most of the people had left already. The player felt really bad because Mr. Shack had brought wine and a gift. The player said, "I want your son to have this." It was a football that the Browns had all signed. It had Jim Brown, Paul Brown, all the great players from the '60s, completely signed. When Mark had gone to Korea, Michelle and I were in about third grade, and we were learning to write in cursive. We found the ball...so, now, underneath Paul Brown's name, it says, "Michelle Shack, your sister." Under that name, it has my name. So, we both *signed that football*. To this day, Mark brings that football out and says, "Look what you did to my football!"

———PAULA FOGEL-DUCKSWORTH, Bedford Heights, Ohio

It was Christmas, 1943, and I was a junior in high school, George McKinnon, my high school football coach, had gone to Northwestern and was friends with Otto Graham. He said to the entire team shortly before Christmas, "Listen, if you guys are going to need any appliances for your parents, toaster, blender or whatever, give some consideration to coming down to this store. I'm working there. It's owned by Otto Graham and Jim Hegan." Jim Hegan was the star **CATCHER** of the Cleveland Indians for many, many years. We had two of the top Cleveland sports stars scuffling to make a few extra bucks for their families at Christmas time. They were temporarily renting this storefront where they could sell appliances. It was right on Euclid Avenue, the main drag, but it was a few blocks up past where the big, heavy foot traffic was—so people didn't necessarily know about it. You would think today, if somebody wanted to do something like that, they could get all the publicity they would want.

> **Former Colorado Rockies Manager Jim Leyland was once a second-string <u>CATCHER</u> for Perrysburg, Ohio High School. The starting catcher was Jerry Glanville.**

A carload of my teammates went down to the store on a Saturday, to do our coach a favor, and maybe even to get a gander at Otto and Jim. As we walked into the store, the only other people in the store were George McKinnon, Jim Hegan and Otto Graham. Can you imagine that? They probably didn't even make any money at it, but they were trying. Can you imagine a starting quarterback and a starting major league catcher who would have to get a Christmas job today?

Today, the pay scale is so out of kilter. You get a mediocre shortstop who can hit .240 in the big leagues, and he's going to make a million and a half to two million dollars a year. You get a broken-down, left-handed reliever, who has a losing record, and he's going to make more than a million bucks a year. It's just preposterous. Baseball is in trouble. It's the only sport in which you can outright just buy the title every year. How can you call that competitive? It's a monopoly. It's ridiculous. Fortunately football doesn't let that happen. They've succeeded with parity so handsomely that there are 8-8 teams in the playoffs. We'll never have another dynasty like the Cleveland Browns. Nobody will ever be able to put a team together from scratch like Paul Brown did at the beginning.

Your best players are going to leave you. You won't be able to afford them. You'll be able to afford one or two, but you won't be able to afford three or four or five. They're definitely going to move on. It's ridiculous. I don't know how you build the kind of loyalty when the cast is changing every year—"Oh, is he playing for us now?" "Where's so-and-so now?" How do you build those loyalties? I don't know. Those of us from Cleveland will hang onto our Browns, Indians and Cavaliers.

——EMIL DAVIDSON, 68, Los Angeles

Back in '45, I joined the Navy when I was 17 years old and went to boot camp at Great Lakes. We went to see the Great Lakes football team play, and Paul Brown was their coach. In '45 the old Cleveland Rams won a championship, and moved to LA. The Browns came in '46. I did see the Browns first game in 1946 against the Miami Seahawks. I sat in the bleachers for twenty-five cents. That game was played in the Cleveland Stadium, the old Municipal Stadium. I went to many games there to watch the Browns play. I froze with that wind coming off the lake, but when you're young, you don't care. We watched all the games—but the game I still remember is that first one.

I'm 77 years old. The day is going to come when I'm going to sit back, at 80-85 years old, and the Browns win a Super Bowl, and I'm going to get there. The year they were ready to go to the Super Bowl, and they played Denver at Cleveland—that game is called 'the Drive.' Where my wife was working, they were going to take up a collection to send me to the Super Bowl to see the Browns. …she didn't tell me that until after the Browns got beat on The Drive and The Fumble…. When they started playing, Otto Graham was making $8,000 a year and some of the players were making $5,000. Otto Graham lived in a third-floor apartment house on East Boulevard. Today—my God—they don't even have to play, and they make a million dollars. I think that's turning off people.

——**TOM DECHANT**, Texas resident since 1969

I was only 12 years old when they won the '64 championship game. I remember being in my upstairs bedroom, lying on my bed, listening to the radio. I had all my football cards out and had my Browns pennant on the wall. I felt that was a high point of my 12 years, being a part of it when the Browns won the championship. I was so afraid they would lose to Baltimore.

My favorite player, as a kid, was running back, Leroy Kelly, #44. A couple of years ago I wrote a textbook, in which I created some characters with different takes on the environment. One was a hunter. One just liked to go out and watch birds. Another one wanted to develop the area for farmland. I named one of the characters in the book Leroy for Leroy Kelly.

——**DAVID HANYCH**, Colorado Springs

As far as the Browns, I was just a kid when they first started. I would have been 13 years old and can remember sitting on my front porch steps when we lived on Lorain Road and listening on the radio to the very first preseason game the Browns ever played. It was against the Miami Seahawks. This was in 1946. The Browns won—fairly substantially…. Cleveland, in those days and in those years, was a very, very, very hot town. The best year for Cleveland sports was 1948. The Indians won the World Series. They set attendance records, in doing that, at Cleveland Stadium. They had some crowds down there in the 85,000 to 87,000 range. The Browns, in 1948, won every single game. They went from 1947 to 1949—mid-season, each one—without losing a game. So, '48 was a heck of a year for Cleveland.

A friend and I used to take the North Olmstead bus downtown, walk over to the stadium. He and I sat in the bleachers, which is now called the Dawg Pound. The tickets were fifty cents. They played teams in the All- America Football Conference, they played— well the San Francisco 49ers were there. They had the Los Angeles Dons. There was the **NEW YORK YANKEES.** There were a whole variety of teams that came and went. The Baltimore Colts were also in the AAFC, but I don't know if it was the same Colts that went on to the NFL. But the 49ers and the Browns definitely did—they both started in the All America Football Conference…. There was no break between the Rams leaving and the Browns coming into town. The Cleveland Rams won the championship of the NFL in 1945 in a snowstorm in Cleveland Stadium. I never got involved with the Rams for some reason, but the Browns seemed to grab me.

When they were deciding on a name for the team, they had selected the Panthers, or something like that, and it was decided that the Panthers wasn't good because somebody else already had it. There were two stories going around—as recently as a few years ago. One story was that they were named for Joe Louis, who was known as The Brown Bomber, out of Detroit, a prize fighter. The other story is that they are named for Paul Brown. It seems like pretty much everybody now agrees that they were named the Browns for Paul Brown because the Panthers name fell through, and they just said, "Well, let's just make it the Browns." The Joe Louis story was kind of a phony, but that persisted for quite a while. Now, they couldn't be called anything but the Browns! They *are* the Browns!

——RAY DEWEY, composer of "Touchdown, Cleveland Browns"

> In 1952, the **NEW YORK YANKEES**—an NFL team— moved to Dallas and were called the Texans. They scored their first touchdown as the Texans when New York Giant punt returner, Tom Landry, fumbled on the Giants 22-yard line. Do not confuse with Lamar Hunt's Dallas Texans of the AFL, later the Kansas City Chiefs.

I can remember, as a kid, watching Jim Brown and John Wooten ride through the city of Cleveland after some event. I remember when Ernie Davis, from Syracuse, was drafted by the Browns, but he died from leukemia and never got to play. The city was all excited about having Davis and Jim Brown in the same backfield. Jim Brown would be driving through our neighborhood and would stop the car and talk to us. We would just lose our mind. You'd never see players today do that.

As a kid, I got to go to games at the old stadium. I remember selling programs at the very first Monday Night Football game, which was played in Cleveland. We were selling programs outside of Gate B, and we watched Keith Jackson and **HOWARD COSELL** walk past us going into the stadium.

We would sell programs before the game, and, at the end of the first quarter, we would turn in our unsold programs and money, and we would be able to go in and sit in the bleachers to watch the games. The bleachers were all blue-collar people. Tickets only cost about six bucks. At that time, the bleachers were predominately black from one end to the other. Most of these people worked for Ford Motor Company and GM. It was like one big family. Everybody knew everybody else. People would bring in food, and it would be passed up and down the rows and shared by everyone.

One time the Browns were playing the Dallas Cowboys. Don Cockroft kicked a field goal into the bleachers. Three weeks later, an article came out in **_SPORTS ILLUSTRATED_** about kickers of the

> **When former ESPN and current NFL Channel anchor Rich Eisen was in college, his stand-up comedy routine included reading "Letters to Penthouse" using HOWARD COSELL'S voice.**

> **_SPORTS ILLUSTRATED_ was first published in 1954 and its first swimsuit issue was in 1964. The _Sports Illustrated_ Swimsuit Issue has 52 million readers, 16 million of them are females… 12 million more than normal.…In 1955, SI selected horse owner William Woodward as their Sportsman of the Year. Woodward's wife shot and killed the unfaithful Woodward before the issue went to press. SI then selected World Series hero, Johnny Podres.**

NFL. On the centerfold, was Cockroft kicking this field goal into the bleachers. There we were—a couple of high school friends and me—right underneath the goal post. That was a big thrill for us because all of our high school friends were so excited about us being in Sports Illustrated. We were celebrities there for a while.

———CURTIS FRANKLIN, 48, Cleveland

I always liked to hang around with trainer, Leo Murphy. He had been with the team since 1950. He always had a cigar in his mouth and a funny story to tell.

Duty with the trainer was always more interesting than washing sweaty uniforms. Once after practice, Murphy asked me to help him with tight end, Milt Morin, who was having some back problems. And, it was no wonder, if you ever saw him catch a pass at midfield and then just look for defensive backs to run over. After practice, Murphy used to take a hypodermic needle and extract fluid from Morin's back. He asked me to help press on his back to facilitate the process. Morin joked about it. He told me that he had so many holes in his spine from needles that if he took a deep breath and fingered the holes, he could play his backbone like a flute. The first time I helped Murphy do this with Morin, I was horrified. I said something like "Ewwwwww!!!" Later, Murphy took me aside and said I should never show any emotion or say anything bad when examining an **INJURY**. He said despite the fact that these guys were giants, they could be real babies when hurt.

A month later, the Browns were playing the Steelers in a little tune-up scrimmage in front of a huge crowd. After one play, offensive guard John Wooten was still down on the field. Murphy told me to come with him. We jogged out there and knelt down beside Wooten. He looked terrible, like he was in shock…or worse. Even though it scared me, I remembered what Murphy said about injured players and

> Almost every good football team at any level in America is one play away (injury) from being average.… Average time lost due to injury in high school football is six days.…Healing time due to injury to a high school cheerleader is 29-days.…Among the sixteen most popular college sports, spring football has the highest injury rate.

keeping my mouth shut. Finally, Wooten motioned for Murphy to lean in closer and whispered in his ear. After a few minutes, we helped him get up and limp off the field with Murphy and me on either side. The crowd applauded his courage. Later, I asked what Wooten said. "He just told me he got kicked in the groin," Murphy said.

——MICHAEL HEATON, son of sportswriter Chuck Heaton, on hangin' with the Browns as a teenager.

I grew up hating Pittsburgh, "Pittspuke!" I still hate Pittsburgh. I remember the Turkey Jones hit, slamming Bradshaw down. I remember going to a Steeler game as a high school kid, sneaking into the old Municipal Stadium. There was a guy from Pittsburgh there who said to me, "Do you want to fight?" He kept giving me grief and kept pushing me. Finally, some man, a Cleveland Brown fan, stepped in front of me and him. I thought I was going to get my butt kicked, but he said, "Hey, leave the kid alone." The Steeler fan then realized he was going to have to let it go....Going to Miami of Ohio, I really got to hate Cincinnati just as much—the arrogance of Cincinnati, the Queen City, and all that stuff, and Kenny Anderson. I remember the Darden hit on **MCINALLY**, just laying him out. I remember Bernie Kosar's first pass back in '86 in the last game. The first play from scrimmage he threw an 80-yard bomb that almost got a touchdown. I thought we were going in and win the game...were going to take it to them.

——JOHN KARLIAK, 40, Psychiatric Crisis Counselor

Where I grew up, obviously there were not a lot of Browns fans or interest. The 'Wish Book,' the Sears catalog, at Christmas was my bible, as a little kid. I was always looking through it for the sports stuff. They'd always have Eagles, and Cowboys, and whoever had made the playoffs. They'd have pajamas and tee shirts, but only for a few teams, and *never* the Browns. But that one year, the Kardiac Kids,

The NFL—since 1968—has given every player the Wonderlic test (a human resources test measuring the ability to acquire and use job knowledge). In a recent year, 118,549 non-NFL people took the test and only four had a perfect score of 50. In the first 30 years, the only NFL player with a perfect score was Pat McINALLY of Harvard. McInally starred with the Cincinnati Bengals as tight end and punter.

when they made the playoffs, in 1980, I knew that following Christmas that there's be Browns stuff in that catalog…and there was. That's when I loaded up on all my tee shirts and jackets. I got pajamas and a bath robe. It wasn't like today when you can order everything online. They only had the regional teams and the playoff teams from the previous year. So, when the Browns made the playoffs that one year, it kind of guaranteed I was getting some Browns gear for Christmas. All that stuff just wasn't available back then. Maybe you'd find a hat or a tee shirt in the store, but there wasn't a variety.

———MATT PENCEK, 35, grew up near Scranton, Pa.

I was 12 years old when I went to my first Browns game. My brother and I were real excited about going. When we got to Cleveland Municipal Stadium, I had never seen that many people in one place at one time. That was exciting. I was like a kid at Christmas time. Here, I'm going to go see my first Cleveland Browns game in person. The whole experience was just overwhelming. It was something I'll never forget. To be honest, I remember very little about the football game. I was in awe of the experience and the happening and what was going on around me. Back then, it was a whole different era. The people were different than they are today. The fans were more genuine and more real than they are today, in certain aspects and manners. It seemed like it took about three hours to get there. In reality, it didn't take that long, but just the anticipation and excitement of going to my first Browns game—that made it seem like it was taking forever to get up there.

———GEORGE KRSKA, 44, Barberton, Ohio

There's something inexplicable about how a team gets so deeply rooted in a young kid's heart. It's funny 'cause yesterday my brother said, "If it weren't for the Browns, at this point, I probably wouldn't have a need to ever go back to Cleveland, or still have any affiliation with Cleveland." As bad as they've been these years since their rebirth, it's just so ingrained that you can't not root for them. Part of it, too, is you grow up as a kid back there, and unlike the West Coast, maybe, where you've got surfing and roller-blading and other odd sports, you grow up playing driveway basketball, backyard football. You pretend to be different players. That's where it starts.

I remember my dad having 'Siperbowl' tee shirts.

———SEAN SAMUELS, 35, on growing up in Ohio

 I very much remember going to a playoff game between the Browns and Dallas in Cleveland in 1967-68. What impressed me about going to a Browns game is that you would park in the Muni Lot, a huge parking lot, for fifty cents. That price remained the same forever so it was very inexpensive. Most people parked in the same area, and there was a huge mass of people who would walk through the lot, over some grades, and go down West Third Street to the stadium.

We would frequently sit in the bleachers, which, at that time, were detached from the rest of the stadium. They weren't heated at all. What you got in the bleachers were *the* most loyal fans, the true die-hards. You couldn't access even the concession stands. Being there, and that's what's turned into the Dawg Pound, was always a different caliber of fan. They were people who were really very loyal fans.

My father was a season ticket-holder when I was a kid, and, at that point, season tickets were much more reasonable. It was something like $250 for the whole year—today, that's like one ticket for one game, depending on where you're sitting. Sports in general, especially in Cleveland, were things that were imminently affordable. At Indians games, parking was fifty cents, and you could get good seats for most Indians games for $2.00. Investment-wise it wouldn't be difficult to go to 10—15 games a year. Now, when I take my kids, it's easily $200 to $300 to take four people to a baseball game. It's a huge investment. If the kids aren't that interested in it, you feel like you're putting a lot of money out for nothing. It's unfortunate.

They have developed a long parking area pretty much going from West Sixth Street, which is on one side where the entrance to the stadium is, to East Ninth Street. That whole area now is set up for tailgating. They have huge, huge tailgating things now. When I was a kid, they didn't have tailgating.

——**STEVEN SOLOMON**, Cleveland Heights native

When I was a boy in the late 50's and early 60's, Jim Brown *was* the Cleveland Browns. We thought the team was named after him, and not its founder, Paul Brown. He was the football idol of every kid in the neighborhood. When we played football, we would imitate his every mannerism including the slow walk back to the huddle after being tackled by four or five defenders that he carried on his back for an extra six or seven yards. He was Hercules, Superman and Paul Bunyan all wrapped into one. Every time he touched the ball we thought it was going to be a touchdown. One time my brother got his autograph on a program by waiting outside of the locker room at the old Cleveland Stadium. No fee, no autograph for sale, no demands for compensation, just an autograph for a star-struck kid with a paper and a pen.

———**BOB SORCE**, Arizona Attorney General's Office

When I became the Browns' mascot, I was eight years old. They had a little Brownie, an elf, that was their insignia for a long time, and they wanted to do something different from that. My father asked Paul Brown, "Would you like my son to do something?" Paul Brown said, "Yes. That would be wonderful. Take him down to Blepp Coombs, get him an outfit, a uniform." They made a jersey for me that said, "Cleveland Browns," and put "mascot" across the top. That was in 1953, and the first game after I was mascot was against the Washington Redskins. The Browns won, and then I made it a tradition before every game to go into the locker room and walk around and shake hands with every player and wish them luck. I was introduced just like a player, "Lou Abraham, Mascot," and I took the game ball out, and I ran from the dugout, through the goalposts out to the 20-yard line. Then, they introduced Frank Gatski, the center, and I handed him the game ball and shook his hand and then went to sit on the bench with the rest of the team to watch the game. It was an incredible thrill for an eight-year old.

The thing my father became famous for was in 1946, he was delivering a message. The goal post used to set right on the pitchers' mound at one end of the stadium, which gave quite a bit of room before going into the stands. My father, instead of walking all the way around that horseshoe bend, was cutting across the field. At that time, Lou Groza happened to be attempting an extra point. The ball came flying over the goalpost and someone said, "Abe, watch out." My father, a very slight man, turned around and the ball hit him in the chest, knocked him over and bruised his ribs to the point where Leo Murphy, the Browns trainer, took him into the locker room and taped him up. My father came back out and resumed performing his duties. As he was walking through the stands, people looked at him and said, "Abe, what's the matter with you? Can't you catch a football? Give us your address. We'll send you a bushel basket for Christmas. Do you want some glue for your hands?" He was being razzed by the fans in the stands, so he took the challenge. He said, "I'll stand back there and catch the ball." He became an icon and was known as 'the man in the brown suit.' We were from very humble origin. We lived in the projects near the inner city of Cleveland. My father had this one suit, a rust brown color. That's how people started to identify him. So Abe Abraham became 'the man in the brown suit' to everybody. He stood behind the goalpost and caught all of Lou Groza's extra points and field goals. Then Sam Baker came here for a year and then, ultimately, Don Cockroft. He caught their kicks also up until he died in '82.

My father was recognized as the '#1 Fan of All Time' by the Cleveland Browns. They had a day for him—September 18, 1981, the year before he died. They honored him in downtown Cleveland, right on the corner of East 9th and Euclid Avenue. Art Modell's son, David, was there. They had a band from one of the local schools. Broadcasters and sportscasters from one of the radio stations were there. There was a proclamation from the mayor of the city of Cleveland, and from the City Council, recognizing my father. They recognized him as the #1 Fan of the Cleveland Browns and of the City of Cleveland.

——LOU ABRAHAM, 60, Cleveland

Chapter 2

The Old Man and The Wee

And Mom Makes Three

THESE SEVEN SIGNS ARE
THE TEN REASONS
SHE'S HOOKED ON THE BROWNS

LISA BROWN

Lisa Brown has been kidded by friends that the only reason she married her "starter" husband was because he was named Brown. She is single and lives in the Washington, D. C. area. She has worked for the Department of Agriculture for 27 years, including stints in San Diego and Mexico City. Lisa Brown was raised in Chadron, Ohio.

Almost before I even can remember, I was a Browns fan. My father's family came to Ohio from Spain. He and my aunts, mostly his older sister, were Browns fans way before I was born. My first Browns game was when I was four years old. Then Dad took me to as many Browns and Indians games as he could afford, which, back then was probably easier than now.

I do remember games, probably less about the actual football playing and more, especially as a child, about the sights and the smells and the sounds and how big everything seemed. Most of the times were in winter, and dad and I always took several copies of the *Plain Dealer* newspapers with us. We'd sit on several and put some copies under our feet. I remember applauding with the muffled sound of gloves and mittens. I can remember not being able to get anything at the snack stand, especially drinks, because everything was frozen.

To a little kid, that's really pretty overwhelming. Even more than that, my dad and I never missed a Browns game, whether we went in real life or whether we were watching it on TV. My mother would have to leave the house, from the time I was four, until my dad died, 10 years ago. Even if we weren't living in the same town anymore, we never missed a Browns game on TV. If we could get there, we got there somehow….if I had to fly from California, or if he flew to California to see them play there. We would call each other and spend hours on the phone while the Browns were playing, talking about the plays and what we liked and what we didn't. We both promised each other than when—*when*—the Browns went to the Super Bowl, we didn't care where, we didn't care what it cost, we were going. We used to tell my mother that. She would go, "Yeah, okay." She wasn't too concerned 'cause she *knew the Browns*. It hasn't happened yet. I promised my dad before he died that I would go if they ever got to the Super Bowl—I would definitely go.

It's funny 'cause my mother is always kidding me. She says it's too bad the Cleveland Browns weren't a man, or I would have had the most successful relationship in history because it's never faltered. It is the longest love affair of my life—the Browns.

The Browns have always, to me, been the good guys. It angers Browns fans when they do dirty things on the field. What I mean by that is—late hits, and things like that. It's like they are the 'good guys.' They pick the other team up and dust them off. They used to be one of the least penalized clubs in the league. They just all seemed to be good guys—at least historically. Maybe it's because they haven't won for 40 years. I don't know. It's amazing. And, it doesn't matter if they win or lose…you like winning…but it doesn't matter. You're still a Browns fan. People make fun of you. People laugh at you. But, it doesn't matter—you just don't care.

My dad and I went to games in Los Angeles and San Diego, when I was living out there. Then, my parents eventually moved out to the San Diego area. We would wait, every year, with bated breath, for the schedule. Of course, Oakland moved to L. A. for a while, and there was one year we got to go to three games 'cause they actually played San Diego and the Rams and the Raiders.

During the three years the team was gone, there was never any waver. There's only one football team. And, there's only one baseball team. During that hiatus, I didn't watch football at all. I spent a lot of time writing letters to **PAUL TAGLIABUE**. I never bad-mouthed Mr. Modell publicly. I didn't write to Mr. Tagliabue about how horrible Art Modell was. I just wrote to him about how much we loved the Cleveland Browns and asking him to keep our traditions—our name, our colors. It was those kinds of letters, "Please bring back the Cleveland Browns." I wrote dozens and dozens and dozens of letters. Also, I got together with other Browns fans and talked about the good old days and about the days to come. Ravens—who? Blackbirds—who? No. When the Browns left Cleveland, they were no longer the Browns.

And, we celebrated like crazy when we got our team back. When the *new* Browns came to Cleveland, they were the Browns—it was not a 'new Browns' or an expansion team. It was like we just took a three-year break, and now we were back, and just the faces changed.

I wear Browns clothes. I have Browns paraphernalia all over my house. I have Browns paraphernalia all over my office. I read any little tidbit I can find. I watch old games. I read books about Browns. When one of them dies, I cry. It doesn't matter who they are. It doesn't matter if I even remember who they were. It's amazing. Everybody knows. "Oh God, the Browns. She's nuts!" That's why it was kind of interesting for me—we're not married any more—but I'll never give up husband's name because it's Brown. Everybody kidded me that all I did was look for somebody whose last name was Brown to marry. Then it was always a joke that it was my last name—"Oh yeah, she finally became one."

Of course, we all like to sit around and commiserate about 'The Drive,' and how sad that was. Poor Ernie Byner—I wrote him a couple of letters and told him, "It'll be okay. We don't hate you. Browns fans don't do that. You made a mistake. Oh well! There's always next year." I did feel so sorry for him. That was a great tragedy for us—we were so close. My dad and I were buying our plane

> **PAUL TAGLIABUE once held the career rebounding record at Georgetown. That mark was broken by Patrick Ewing in 1985.**

tickets and hocking whatever we had to buy Super Bowl tickets 'cause we thought that year for sure we were going to be going. Deja Blue! When we have a losing season, like this year, it's, "Well, that means we're going to be picking that much further up on top of the draft."

When I was a kid, I told my dad that I was going to own the Browns. At first, I didn't know that a team could be owned, but when I found that out, I told him that one of these days I would own the Cleveland Browns. He was like, "Okay, you go." Then when I found out how expensive they were, it dawned on me that I probably couldn't afford it. That was always my big dream.

I met Lyle Alzado once, and I thought he was wonderful and was sad when he died. I loved going to watch him practice at Kent. It's funny. I like the fact that the Browns don't have cheerleaders. There's nothing fake or Hollywood about the Browns. I like the fact we have a natural grass stadium. It's good, hard, old-fashioned football...in the dirt, in the mud, in the snow, in the cold—that's what football's all about.

It's never been an individual player. It's an entity. The Cleveland Browns are a living being. It's them, and it doesn't matter who they're coached by or who they're owned by or who those 40 or 50 men in those uniforms are. It's the Browns that you love. You do love them. I haven't ever spoken to fans like Browns fans. But, how many love affairs remain through ups and downs—and mostly downs—and losing season after losing season after losing season? The Browns fans don't go away. As a Browns fan, I thought I was unique. I'm not. It's the Browns fans that are unique. There isn't a *former* Browns fan. There's no such thing. You are born and die a Browns fan. I did. I used to think I was unique—even here in D. C.—and the only reason anyone has been a Browns fan longer than me is because they're older than me.

A COOL FAN FROM HOTLANTA

SAM CHAMBERS

Sam Chambers grew up on the west side of Cleveland in Fairview Park in the '60s and early '70s. An accountant by training, he has lived in Atlanta the last 23 years where he is a reimbursement consultant for hospitals.

My memories as a Browns fan actually go back to when I was eight years old when my dad took me to my first football game ever. It was the Eastern Conference Championship game between the Browns and the Cowboys on December 21, 1968. I remember it very, very well even though it's been eons ago. We didn't have tickets to the games, but our neighbors did. Dad decided he and I would hitch a ride downtown with the neighbors and if we could find a couple of tickets at a reasonable price, then great. If not, we'd just hop on the bus and come on back home.

We were walking across the Third Street Bridge across to the stadium. He was talking to a couple of scalpers, and they wanted way too much money for the tickets. After we had talked to one of them, a fellow came over and looked at my dad and said, "Do you need a couple of tickets for you and your boy?" Dad said, "Well, yes sir, I do." He said, "Well, don't go anywhere. Stay right there." Dad watched him, and he got on a tour bus that had pulled up and parked near there. A couple of minutes later, he came out and handed my dad two tickets. Dad said, "Wow! This is great. What do I owe you?" He said, "Not a thing. A couple of our people couldn't make the trip, and they told us to go find somebody who could make good use of the tickets and give them away." The guy said, "You're going to have to sit next to my sister-in-law, who is a Cowboys fan." In retrospect, they were awful tickets, in the old stadium, in a lower level, almost all the way to the back. It was difficult to see. That old stadium had these big steel support girders in that lower level supporting the upper deck. You would always miss some of the field because there was always a pole in the way. Sure enough, we got in there, and there's this lady sitting there dressed in blue and white, cheering on her team.... Earlier, I remember very vividly coming out of a parking lot after our neighbor parked there, turning the corner and looking down that hill on Third Street going down to the stadium and seeing this sea of heads. I'd never seen so many people in one place before. I was just awe-struck by the whole thing. We get in the stadium—with 80,000 plus—watching a football game. I didn't realize it at the time, but that was a Cowboys team that had a number of future Hall-of-Famers on it: Bob Lilly, Bob Hayes, and Don Meredith. Meredith retired that off-season. The Browns won the game, and I remember very vividly seeing somebody hang a stuffed Cowboy mannequin from the upper deck—hanging in effigy toward the end of the game.

I had so much fun that after that game, my dad looked into getting season tickets the next year. It became a Sunday afternoon ritual for us from then until the time we all moved away from the area. I left in '81. My folks left in '84. We had season tickets for all those years. Our tickets were in the closed end of the stadium, in the upper deck, in the corner of the end zone. They were about half way up the upper deck. In that end of the stadium, that's where the field was farthest from the stands. The end line of the end zone ended about where pitchers' mound was on the Indians baseball field. You were a long, long way from the field in those seats. You always had to have a pair of binoculars with you because if the action was at the other end of the stadium, you wouldn't be able to see much of anything. It was that far away. We sat in front of the same guys for years. I couldn't tell you what they looked like, but if I heard their voices, I'd recognize them in a minute. They were two Polish guys. We knew they were Polish because of the food they brought with them back in the days when you could bring your own food in. They always had the best food, and they knew absolutely nothing about the game of football. They talked like they knew everything...but they didn't. It was always comical to listen to them. It was fun sitting in front of those guys all those years. I kept telling myself that one of those days I was going to turn around and look at them so I would know what they looked like, but I never did.

Teams from places like Cleveland and Pittsburgh and Chicago and Detroit—you can get all kinds of people sitting next to each other in the stadium watching a football game…and that's the only thing they ever have in common. These are people whose paths would never cross any other way, yet, for three hours on a Sunday afternoon, they're buddies. It was always fun for me to go to those games. You find people who come around you and offer to share food with you or whatever. One year, long after I had moved away, I won a contest—living in Atlanta—over Prodigy, for four tickets to a Browns game. I had plenty of frequent flier miles so I decided to make the trip and take some friends who still lived up in the area. Again, they were terrible seats in the old stadium, but there was this couple next to us who came in with this huge aluminum foil pan full of chicken wings. They were passing them up and down the row. We noticed they passed them around, and when the pan came back to them, they resealed it, and then a little later, they passed them around again. It turns out that the lady who did all the cooking—she can't stand chicken wings, but she brought them to share with everybody else. That just blew me away.

It was interesting two years ago when the Ravens played the Browns on a Sunday night in Cleveland. My folks live in the Atlanta area now. I took my dad up for a football weekend. We watched my old high school play. We went down to the Hall of Fame in Canton. I had never been in all the years I lived up there. Then we went to the Browns game that night and watched a terrible football game, unfortunately it had to be the Ravens. That's when my dad told me all the details about that first game back in 1968. There was kind of a funny thing, at one point in the second half, we were sitting underneath a catwalk that went into the press box and to some of the luxury suites that were there. Somebody up above poured a cup of hot chocolate on that woman sitting next to us wearing the Cowboy gear. Several years later, my dad and I were out someplace, and he was talking to somebody he had just met. He told them about being at a Browns game years ago and had a really nice suede leather hat. Back in the

'60s, men used to wear hats. He said, "Somebody poured hot chocolate on me at a Browns game." The guy said, "Were you sitting next to a woman dressed up in Cowboy stuff?" My dad said, "Yeah." He said, "Well, that was me. I got tired of listening to that woman cheering on her team so I dumped the hot chocolate on her." The irony of that—years later!

The attraction of being a Browns fan is that when you grow up in Cleveland, the Browns were just such a big part of the city. Frankly, the Cavs have never done anything. The Indians were awful since before I was born, except for a couple of years there in the '90s. The Browns were the ones that had won so many championships and had brought so much pride to the city. You're sitting there in the cradle of professional football—Ohio and western Pennsylvania. You connect with the team. Everybody knew what Art Modell looked like. Art did some goofy stuff and was kind of a buffoon at times, but he was 'our' buffoon. He was kind of that goofy uncle. Everybody just connected. The town would be so solidly behind the team, even if they were losing.

I can remember back in the '70s when we had season tickets. When I was growing up, we had terrible teams through most of that time. There were still 70,000 people on average every week in that stadium watching that team play...even when we were playing against Pittsburgh, who were world-beaters in the '70s. They almost always kicked our tails. It's kind of like you always support a family member because it's your family. The Browns were like that for those of us growing up there. They were family. I don't think this next generation of fans is going to grow up with that, unfortunately. The one thing that we never even considered was that the Browns would leave. They were such an integral part of the city. It's like the Yankees leaving New York. Can you imagine it being the Omaha Yankees!

Several years ago, I was able to find on eBay, a game program and an unused game ticket for that first game back in 1968. I won the auction so I've got those and a black-and-white photograph from the game.

DO SIAMESE TWINS PAY FOR ONE SEASON TICKET OR TWO??

BRADLEY GREENE

Bradley Greene is an attorney in Cleveland who had an unusual situation with his son, Jacob, when he attended a Browns game back in 2004.

I grew up here in Cleveland and can remember the first game I went to with my dad when I was nine. I got to go with him as part of my birthday present, along with a Browns coat. I'll never forget it. We had a great time. We had to park *miles* away and walk to the stadium so we wouldn't have to pay to park. We had to bundle up because it was so cold.

In 2004, my wife and I went to the home opener, and we took our five-month-old son. The reason I wanted to take him to the first game we possibly could was so that he didn't have wait until he was nine or ten years old to go to a game. I wanted to get him to that first game and make it a tradition for us. We were pretty shocked and disappointed to have to pay for him to go in. There was absolutely nothing wrong with him being at the game—it was a beautiful, sunny day. If it was freezing cold outside, there's no way we would have taken a five-month old baby. But, as long as he was going to be comfortable, and it wasn't going to be too hot or too cold, there was no reason not to take him. I wanted to start that tradition—taking him every home opener over the years. But, unless they change their policy, we won't be going for a while—until he can really appreciate it.

My wife and I had tickets for the game, and we walk up to the gate. He's in a baby carrier, literally on my chest. They say, "Where's the ticket for him?" We thought the ticket taker was joking at first but he was completely serious. We said, "He's only five-months old. He's going to sit on our lap. Why would he possibly need his own seat?" They called somebody from Ticketron and were told, "Yeah, he needs a ticket. Everybody needs a ticket." Then they brought somebody from the Browns over, and they said, "It's the NFL policy that everybody needs a ticket," which we discovered later is not true at all—it's team-by-team. But it was, and is, a Cleveland Browns policy. At least we've gotten them to acknowledge that they're going to re-evaluate and *may* change for next season. I find it hard to believe that this is the first time it's ever come up, but apparently it's the first time it ever got any press. We took him to a Cav's game and they don't charge. Most places don't if you're under two years old.

After all the publicity, the Browns organization sent our son a card that said, "Dear Jacob, We hope you're still a Browns fan. Sincerely, the Cleveland Browns." Also, they sent him sweat pants, a sweat shirt and a hooded sweatshirt. They also sent him a blanket. It was quite nice of them.

The reporter at the *Plain Dealer* who printed the story said the Browns were begging her not to run the story. They said, "Give us a week. We're going to review the policy." She said, "Are you changing your policy by tomorrow morning?" They said, "No." She said, "Well, then, my story is running tomorrow morning." It was pretty funny. Then she discovered that they had a commercial they had just come out with and it showed a bunch of babies in a nursery. They all have Cleveland Browns caps on. She said, "So you're willing to make money off of babies, and you want them to become fans as early as possible, but not doing it at the Cleveland Browns' Stadium? Is that the message you're sending?" They must have pulled the ad, because they've never run that commercial again. I thought, "Wow! We really made some changes."

Our point to them was they should either make a rule that says, "No children under a certain age," or not charge a baby a full-price seat when they can't even sit in it. After the article in the newspaper came out, the story was on every station you turned to in the morning. Then, there was a cheers and jeers section of the paper. People were saying, "Shame on the Cleveland Browns for making Jacob pay." It was really funny. But, then, some people wrote, "What morons would bring their kids to a game?" So, we got it both ways. The reporter forwarded me about 12 e-mails from other people who'd had experiences either with the Cleveland Browns or at other events. But I still would like to, and, hopefully, we will still be able to, make it a tradition. We bought tickets from a friend who has season tickets. They are really good seats and cost $65 each and then we had to pay the $37.00 for our son. With all that and $20 to park and more for food, it's an expensive day. I remembered back to when I was a kid how much I loved going with my dad. I would have liked to have been able to go more with him—there's nothing like going to a Browns game with your dad.

Kellen Winslow Sr.'s ego applied for statehood today. If approved it would be the third largest.

WHY DOES HAWAII HAVE INTERSTATE HIGHWAYS?

DAVID ZBIN

David Zbin was born in Berea, moved to Rocky River, Westlake and then to Hawaii when he was 10. After college in California, Zbin stayed on the West Coast working in broadcast television and now is a vital cog in that well-oiled Apple Computer machine.

David Zbin at age 8

My dad sold real estate in the Cleveland area and then a friend of his moved to Hawaii in 1968 and Honolulu was on the verge of a real estate boom. My dad and three of his buddies from high school actually ended up moving to Hawaii at the same time. He saw an opportunity to move to a fun, exotic place with warm weather. He took the risk, and he just loved it. He stayed there till the day he died. My mom and sister and everybody are still there. I get back there when I can.

My earliest, and favorite, memory of being a Browns fan is going to games a couple of times with my dad when I was seven or eight years old. He would take me to the games, and it's special remembering the passion he had for the team and for the game. He'd be there with his buddies, and a lot of the times, I was the only kid there. I remember sitting through freezing cold, with chattering teeth, skin-turning-blue games. At the time, I didn't know why, but they didn't seem to be bothered by the cold the way I was. My dad and his friends would be passing around the flask. They were having a great time. They were just having a little liquid fortification against the unknown!

At the time, I didn't appreciate the level of players I was watching. There were some real heroes in the game—Leroy Kelly ran the ball. I don't think I saw a Jim Brown game…I would have been too young.

Some of the guys were on that front line who blocked for Jim Brown and then Leroy Kelly—Gene Hickerson is one who comes to mind. In fact I've got pictures of myself in a #66 jersey from when I was eight years old. There was just a bond there, and you'll probably find this a pretty common thread, between many fathers and sons as they grew up.

Through the years, it was always something we had in common and shared many a time, all the way up to the day my dad died. He had been sick for five or six years, and was really sick to the point we were just trying to manage his pain and get him through day by day. We knew the time was coming, and it happened to be on a Monday night, August 14, 1995. The Browns were in the pre-season game that Monday night, and we were all gathered around him in the hospital room watching the game on the TV. We could see he was sort of slipping in and out. He was happy to have his family all around him and watching a Browns game, one more time. There were a couple of nights up to that point when he could have gone, but he was looking forward to the Browns being on Monday Night Football, and then about the third quarter, he just sort of slipped away…and the Browns won the game. It's one of those things.

I'm already deeply ensconcing the Browns into my kids—I've got three boys in high school—who have lived in California all their lives. They've been back to Cleveland one time, but, nevertheless, seeing the passion I have for the team over following them through the years, they latched onto that same thing. Growing up in the heart of 49-er country, where you've got a lot of good teams through the years, not very good right now, but they've had friends who were 49-er fans or Raider fans, and they were always the odd ducks showing up at school in Cleveland Browns tee shirts or jackets or hats. They carry the torch with me. It's a real deal. It's a real strong connection through the generations that way.

I still don't know what it is about the Browns that attracts so many fans from different places. I'm in marketing and if I knew, boy, I'd bottle it. I know for most of the people that I know who are as hard-core into the team and traditions of it, it's the lineage, the linkage, through the generations. I don't know if it's the city or the people who are from that city who have a certain, call it a character flaw, or aspect of their personality, that they cling to traditions and things to do with their family. So many are transplanted. There are huge factions in Florida. There are huge factions in California. These are Browns fans and, in a lot of ways, it's their tie back to Cleveland, back to where their family is from or where they grew up. But, again there are people who have never even been to Cleveland and somehow latch onto this team. It's probably a lot of different reasons for different people. Like with this friend of mine, Harold Manson, who grew up in Texas and has never been to Cleveland. His connection was he grew up watching Jim Brown and just was so impressed and so in awe of that level of play and that dominant of a player that when he was a kid in the '50s, and the Browns were winning championships, that was it. That was his team as a kid. It just carried through the rest of his life.

Well, for me, I grew up in the heart of it so I wouldn't know any different. I don't' know what my kids would tell you if they talked to you 20 years from now, if someone said, "You've never lived in Cleveland. How come you're such a Browns fan?" They would trace it back to me and then back to my dad and on back beyond that.

When I came to California to go to college, I followed the Browns very closely and went to every West Coast appearance. My wife and I met at the birthday party of a friend. We had hit it off real well, and she wanted to get together the next day. I told her I was sorry I couldn't because I was going to the Browns-49-ers game. She didn't understand why I couldn't change my plans…of course, she knows now.

At first, she had a sort of acceptance and tolerance of the whole Browns thing because it's really a pretty big phenomenon as far as my life goes—such an odd thing to follow at the level that I do. We have DirecTV. Now that the kids are so into it, and we sit around the TV and look forward to the games and watch them every week. Well, now my wife is right on board, too. Actually her birthday was the weekend last year of the Cowboy game in Dallas, and it was the farthest west the Browns were going to travel that year so I had made some plans to go to that game. I knew that, since it was her birthday weekend, it would be a tough sell. It got a little ugly when her mom gave her the gift of a spa getaway for that weekend, and I had to say, "You can go to that if you want, but I'm kind of hoping I can go to the Dallas game." She had to make the awkward phone call to her mom to change the plans and say, "Can you get that reservation changed? Dave's going to be in Dallas, and I'm going to go with him." So, she went with me to the Dallas game, and we had fun.

When my wife was pregnant for the first time—my son was born three weeks early—and we were totally not ready to have it. The room still needed paint and we needed to replace the carpeting. But, the newborn had a better idea so he said, "I'm three weeks early." He was born January 10, 1987, which was a Saturday afternoon before the famous 'Drive' game when Cleveland lost to Denver. I had no idea what that game was going to turn out to be but because he was born three weeks early, we didn't have a name picked out. We hadn't gotten through all those details yet. Bernie Kosar was quarterback of the Browns. I was hugely into the upcoming AFC Championship game because the Browns are 'finally' going to go to the Super Bowl. We were supposedly going to be the better team. The game was at home. I was really looking forward to it. Then, of course, all that interest got set aside while my son was born. The next morning, Sunday morning, I was getting ready to go watch the game. We still haven't got a name for our little boy. I asked my wife, "Can we name him Bernie?" ... of course, in honor of Bernie Kosar. She wanted to have nothing to do with it. She wanted our son to be named Robert after her father. I told her, "Well, that's not fair." We argued about it, and the bottom line is that I got her to agree that if the Browns won the game, we could name him Bernie. If they didn't win, we would name him Robert. Of course, he's Robert now...we came within an overtime field goal of having a son named Bernie. But, it was not meant to be...and, he might be glad about that. He laughs about it because he knows it's a true story.

I DO AND I DO FOR YOU KIDS AND THIS IS THE THANKS I GET:

We've had no family living in Cleveland for many, many years. My dad passed away, and the TV did an obit about this, in Florida. He became very, very ill from cancer right before the rebirth of the team. My sister and I knew we were going to be going back for the first game—that game against the Steelers back in 1999. I was leaving on a Saturday night flight to go to Cleveland for the Sunday game. My sister was flying in from New Mexico. That Saturday night, right at midnight, the night before the game, I got the call from the hospital that my father had passed away. He actually died the day the Browns came back to life, knowing full well that my sister and I were already going to be in Cleveland. We flew the body up. He was buried in the Browns opening-night tee shirt we bought for him the very next day….

My son is 18, and in his cognitive lifetime, he grew up watching me—he just assumed that the Indians were the greatest thing in the world—that's all he knew. The Indians are great. They're in playoffs all the time. He had no idea that there was 40 years that they were so bad they made movies about it. They had 80,000 empty seats. They were the worst team in sports. When we grew up, the Browns were the greatest team, and the Indians were terrible.

Now, he just thinks, "Why in the world are you a Browns fan? They suck." That's not that much different than anybody else. So many people, now in their 40s and 50s who have moved out of Cleveland, this was the one part of Cleveland that they were proud of, that they took with them, that was a religion.

———ROGER COHEN, lobbyist, Washington, D. C.

My father's not a hard-nosed guy. He's pretty easygoing. But, I was at college and I remember him freaking me out going, "If they make the Super Bowl, if you told me that you were going to hitchhike to San Diego, I wouldn't stop you." I remember looking at him with my mouth open, "Are you s-------- me, old man?" "No, Super Bowl's once in a lifetime." When Brian Brennan caught that touchdown pass. I'm thinking, "We're going to go to the Super Bowl." Then it was over. I showed up at college a day late. My buddy went to Xavier and I went to **Miami of Ohio**, and after the game, we just said, "Screw it." And, we got drunk that night. I remember it being my first class of the second semester. The prof said, "Mr. Karliak, you were not in my class the first day." I said, "No." He said, "I guess you're from Cleveland." I said, "Yeah." He said, "Oh, okay," and he started laughing. He was from New York, and the Giants ended up being in the Super Bowl that year.

——JOHN KARLIAK, 40, Cleveland

I took two of my kids to see the 'Drive' game. I was really lucky because another guy in the Air Force was on vacation in Ashtabula. He called me and said his brother was a season ticketholder and thinks he can get some extra tickets to the championship game, would I want to go? I told him I'd take as many tickets as he could get because I've got four boys. He was able to get me three tickets. My youngest son, who is the Cardinal fan, was 12 years old. He had a white Browns sweatshirt on, AFC Central Championship shirt. About four hours before the game, we went down to the old stadium and went to Gate 80, which is where the players came in. We were with season ticketholders so some of the players knew a lot of these people. My son was getting autographs on his sweatshirt. When Hanford Dixon showed up for the game, he got out of a big white limo, and he asked my son if he'd been able to get Frank Minnifield's autograph. My son said, "No, sir. There were too many people around Mr. Minnifield, and I wasn't able to do that." Then, Hanford Dixon asked me if my son could go in the locker room. On this shirt he has every player on the team except for Bernie Kosar and Ozzie Newsome. Ozzie was his big favorite. He wrote stories every week at school about Ozzie Newsome. I have pictures of almost all the players on the team that signed it outside, and then Hanford Dixon just took him locker to locker and had the players sign it. Of course, we still have it. But, the team loses…I blame it on the Ohio State band which played at half-time.

——DON DAVIE, 60, retired Air Force

Do you confuse Miami (Ohio) with Miami (Florida)?
MIAMI OF OHIO was a school before Florida was a state.

I grew up with football my whole life, and can remember sitting and watching games with my dad and being bored out of my mind. At some point, when I was in elementary school, I became a huge fan. When I was in high school, every Sunday we had friends of our family come over and snack and watch the game. Also, *every* Sunday we'd go to Davis Bakery and buy a Browns cake. Our theory was that the more cake we ate, the better the team would do…which never happened. Jokingly, we would 'meditate' on the washer and dryer machines. We would do, "C'mon," and we do a long hum with it. We would think things like that were going to make us win. My dad was born in Pennsylvania so he originally was a Steeler fan.…As a very young kid, I had a Steeler jacket. When I would wear this to day-care or wherever, I didn't understand when people would make comments to me about it. I didn't quite understand what they were talking about.

——HEATHER GREENE, 29, Cleveland

I'm a second-generation Browns fan. My father was a **BALLBOY** for the '48 Browns at Bowling Green, during their training camp. They worked out at Bowling Green when Paul Brown was here and Otto Graham was the quarterback. My dad was on the track team. He had been in the Navy and was able to go to school whenever he wanted to…he was a pretty good runner. It was about a mile from the locker room out to the field. After the line had run their plays, Coach Brown would say, "Go get Otto in the locker room." My dad would run back to the locker room and say, "Mr. Graham, Coach Brown wants you on the field now." Occasionally, Otto would forget his shoes, and Dad had to run to the locker room and get his shoes for him.

My dad and I used to get tickets back to the old stadium in the '60s, and we would sit in this section of all-Steeler fans because my cousin knew somebody at the box office. They would get us some free tickets, but we had to sit with three busloads of Steeler fans who had come in. They didn't even drink the beer there—they brought their own Iron City beer in with them. We'd get stuck with these seats. It always was a Saturday night game, which they did a couple

> Tampa Bay Buccaneers head coach Jon Gruden was a **BALLBOY** for the 1976 Indiana University basketball team—the last undefeated NCAA champions.

of times back in the '60s. By the third quarter, things were usually good because the Steelers would be down about 20 points, and the fans would be getting ready to clear out by the start of the fourth quarter.

——JOHN LAMB, 43, news anchor, Danbury, Connecticut

My senior year in high school, the '86 season, the two playoff games are pretty vivid memories. One was January 3, 1987, when the Browns beat the Jets in double overtime. My whole family is a big Penn State family, too. It's where I went to school. The night before, January 2, Penn State had beaten Miami to win the national championship. They were like, "Now, in less than 12 hours, the Browns are playing in a playoff game. They got down by 10 points with about five minutes to go, and it didn't look like they were going to do it. My dad was just getting ready to go out and watch my brother in a high school basketball game that night. The Browns scored a touchdown—Mack scored at just under the two-minute warning. My father was just out the door, and I yelled down to him to ask if he saw that. He said, "No. What happened?" I said, "We scored a touchdown." He came back to watch the end of the game. They ended up tying the game and sending it into overtime. Then, it ended up being a double overtime game with the Browns winning it. He missed my brother's entire game.

The next week was the Broncos game—*the drive*. When Kosar hit Brennan for that touchdown pass with about five minutes to go, I always think I jinxed it because I yelled out to my dad, "We're going to the Super Bowl." It was just one of those great moments. Then Denver got the ball at the two, and it was like, "There's no way, against our defense, that they'll be able to come back." But, they did. And, they won that one in overtime. I worked myself up into such an emotional state that I really made myself sick. I couldn't go to school the next day. All of my friends thought I was ducking out. They wanted to give me a hard time—ride me about the Browns loss. But, I seriously worked myself up so much emotionally that I got a fever, and I didn't go to school the next day, because I was legitimately sick.

——MATT PENCEK, 35, Tonkaville, Pa.

I lamented to one of my buddies—maybe it's your age at the time it's going on—but I still have never recaptured that flavor, that passion, that living and dying when the new Browns play. When I was in high school, when the Browns lost on Sunday—on Monday morning, school sucks for a teenager anyway.... But if they won, you knew you still had to go to school that day, but you also knew you could open up the sports page before you had to trudge off to school and could read about that victory that you had watched. It was the same in college. If they won, I'd call my old man, "Hey, dad, can you cut out the *Plain Dealer* sports page and send it to me?" I'd get it on Thursday, just in time before the next game was played. I loved reading it. It was just like you lived and died with it.

———JOHN KARLIAK, Cleveland area psychiatric counselor

I was a fanatic. I'm 51 now so the stories that really stick in my mind are when I moved from Cleveland to Dallas. I was still an avid Browns fan. In those days, there were no satellite dishes. Before DirecTV, local bars would subscribe to the NFL package with the bigger satellite dishes, and that's the only way you could see a Browns game. Prior to that, if the game wasn't on national TV, you didn't see it. Not only could you not see it, you couldn't even listen to it. That was the single-most thing that kicked my butt. I would move into a town and you couldn't watch, nor could you hear, the Browns games. It was horrendous.

The 1980 season was the first season after I had moved to Dallas. I didn't know what to do. So, I called my dad, and he would put the phone next to the radio. We had a bunch of Clevelanders who had all moved to Dallas, and that was our first fall without the Browns. We would get eight or nine people together. Dad would put the phone by the radio. I had my phone, there in Texas, near an amplifier. We could hear the Browns game through speakers. We'd all chip in to pay the long-distance bill to listen to the games. It was the only way we could hear the game—all pitch in four or five bucks.

Near the end of the season, the Browns needed one game to clinch. In the second-to-last game of the season, they played Minnesota. They had a six-point lead with five seconds to go in the game. Minnesota had the ball on their own 50. It was over, for all purposes. Believe it or not, they threw a "Hail Mary" pass...the guy caught it…the Browns lost. They had one more week to go and they had to win the following week. They did, and that's what got them into the '80 playoffs. To me that was my most memorable year. I listened to the whole season via radio through an amplifier in my house.

———MITCH KUTASH, Cleveland CPA and business owner

In the past, kids became fans because their dad took them to a game or they watch or listened to games with their dad. That doesn't happen anymore. It's too expensive now to go. Only the elite can afford to go. I have trouble with the economics of it. Individual sports, like skateboarding, will have more appeal to the kids. I don't know where it's going. I just keep watching the Browns. It's all been so screwed up. There's no stability. Football is screwed up. It's all so crazy. In some respects, it's brought a whole other dimension. I spend more time reading and paying attention to salaries and negotiations and arbitrations than I do the games 'cause it all happens there. Sometimes, it's interesting, sometimes it isn't.

———GENE BEECHER, 68, retired teacher

The first game my son, who was 16, ever went to was the Browns and the Jaguars a couple of years back—the beer-bottle throwing incident. That got way overblown out of proportion. The referees could have handled that a lot differently than they did. People don't realize two things—an argument went on between the referees and the coaches for almost five minutes, and nothing was said. Then, the Browns already had the ball and were running back in. The referee ran off the field. Had he explained to the fans what was going on, I don't think he would have got that reaction. There were four players from Jacksonville that were taunting the fans before that, trying to get them to throw things. It started in the Dawg Pound and just went out. They were plastic bottles. They were empty. I never felt threatened or scared at any moment. I was in a food fight back in the eighties at a concert at the Rose Bowl that was a lot scarier. My son was probably a little shocked, but he was laughing the whole time. I don't think he ever felt intimidated or scared. There were 48-seconds left in the game. There's not a lot of beer left in those bottles at that time. We covered our heads so beer wouldn't splash on us. It got blown out of proportion and the fans got a bad rap. It shouldn't have happened, and I don't condone it, but it could have been controlled, too. But, my son's first experience was certainly an interesting one.

——**KEVIN WHITE**, 43, LaPaloma, California

When I go to Ravens games, there are tons of Browns fans there. Three years ago, my son who had just turned 16 and I were in Baltimore to see the second-to-last game of the year. The Browns needed to win that game and then win again the following week against Atlanta to even have a chance of making the playoffs for the first time since the team came back. We're losing 13-7. There's about two minutes to go, and we take over on our own eight-yard line. There are 70,000 of these crazy Baltimore morons screaming. That place is loud. Next to Denver, it's as loud as it gets in the National Football League. We're sitting there, and I turned to my son, and he says to me, "You know, I think we're going to win this game." I said, "Daniel, there's not a snowball's chance in hell. We haven't moved the ball all game." We had scored the opening drive but didn't make another first down for the rest of the game. He said, "I think we're going to win this." I said, "Dan, if we win this game and make the playoffs, you can have whatever car you want." Ninety-two yards later—Tim Couch's greatest drive in the National Football League—we score, we win. The next week, you should have seen my son waiting for us to play Atlanta. We make the playoffs. The Jets beat the Packers to clinch a spot for the Browns. And...he's been driving around in a brand new Mustang ever since.

——*ROGER COHEN*, lobbyist, Washington, D. C.

At Tim Manoa's wedding, Bernie Kosar walked in. Bernie was a particular hero of my father's. I'm at Tim's wedding, and you hate to do it, but I just did it. I said, "Bernie, I'm sorry. Can I get a picture with you? I know it's a wedding, right, and I'm an obnoxious fan." He said, "Yeah, I got here a little early. I thought this was going to happen. Let's get it done." We're at the wedding, in our suits, and we take the pictures. Since I was going to give it to my dad, I thought, "Boy, I need an autograph." The only thing I could get was a cocktail napkin and a pen. Now, I've got to bother him again, right? So, I bother him again! I take another drink...and I go do it. I said, "Bernie, I'm really sorry, but I wanted to give this picture that you and I just took to my dad. I'm wondering if you would autograph this napkin for me." He said, "You're doing this for your dad?" I said, "I'm going to give it to my dad for Christmas—this picture of you and me and your autograph." He said, "That's really nice." He writes down his home address in Miami, Florida. He gives it to me and says, "Listen. Don't mess around. This is my home address so be cool with it. When you get the picture developed, send it to me, and I'll autograph it right on the picture for you, and I'll send it back to you." I said, "Wow! That's great." I did that. I put it on a plaque, and emblemized that plaque, "To my dad, Coach of a Lifetime."

He, as an old Italian man, didn't ever really say, "I love you," or show much emotion. That Christmas was the first time I ever saw a tear come to dad's eye—when I gave him that plaque—that picture of me and Bernie that said, "Coach of a Lifetime."

——RICK RIZZO, 38, Dallas, Texas

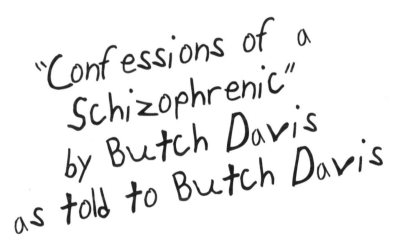

Chapter 3

Sweet Home Cleveland

Municipal Stadium:
The Land of Ahs

ACTUALLY, THERE ARE A LOT OF BUSINESSES LIKE SHOW BUSINESS

EMIL G. DAVIDSON

Emil Davidson left Cleveland in 1960, went to Paris, met his wife and moved to Los Angeles. He became a well-known television writer and filmmaker.

When I was back in Cleveland, I bought a little parking sign that said, "Parking For Browns Fans Only," which I hang on a tree in front of my house here in California every Sunday morning during the season. Also, I hang a banner from my gutter to the sidewalk at my front door—a big Cleveland Browns pennant. I just drape it in front of my house. The last game of the 2004 season, we're 3-12, we're in the pits, the team is demoralized, the organization is in a shambles from Butch Davis, and guys are coming to my house that morning…so I hung out the flag. I went into the kitchen for a minute to talk to my wife, and, as I'm doing so, I see a guy walking his dog. He stopped and stood staring at that flag. He's wearing a Chicago White Sox jacket. I went out front and said, "You know, it takes a lot of courage to fly a flag like that when a team's 3-12. Being from Chicago, you'll probably know that." He said, "No, I'm not from Chicago. My brother gave me this jacket. I was just standing there looking at that flag and thinking, 'Now, there's a guy who really loves his football team.'" And, that's right.

I have a good friend, Garren Keith, a television director who did many, many shows—*Different Strokes, Good Times* and other series. We were pages together at NBC years ago. Garren once said to me, "I always liked the Browns, and I really liked their helmets. It seemed to me their helmets said, 'We don't give a s--- about all that logo crap. We're just here to play football.'" I thought that was a wonderful compliment to the team.

When I was in college, I was a poor student, I often couldn't afford the expensive fees. I worked out a little routine with a friend of mine. One of my classmates from kindergarten through high school, a teammate all of that time, as well, and a good friend, his father was the team dentist for the Cleveland Indians. I don't know how I ever managed to not make him get me in on this deal. He always worked in the summertime, at every home game, on the Cleveland Indians ground crew. Most of the time they didn't have a hell of a lot to do except watch the game. Everybody knew the head groundskeeper of the stadium was a man named Emil Bossard.

The first game we went to, we all got bleacher seats there at Municipal Stadium, and it started pouring rain in the second half of the game. All of a sudden, we noticed that everybody was bailing out of the bleachers—literally dropping themselves from the bleachers and running to the stands in left and right field, to either side of us, so that they could be under something that was covered, and nobody attempted to stop them. There were hordes of people doing this, in plain sight.

Every Sunday home game, a friend and I would buy a bleachers seat ticket. There were open tunnels, more like runways, on either side of the bleachers heading to the field. You could drive an ambulance through there, or a truck or whatever was needed. There was always one cop guarding that entrance to the field. The cop changed all the time. We would go up to the left field bleacher side on one Sunday and ask for this Bossard kid, and tell the cop we were supposed to meet him there to get us on the field. We would say, "Have you seen him?" The cop would say, "Gee, I haven't seen him, but let me go look for him." When the cop would go look, we'd run in. There was a hill approximately 10 to 15 yards behind the end line of the end zone in back of the uprights. It was wider than the uprights. There was one little wooden bench on that hill—no back to it, just a board. It would probably seat 20 people. We managed to seat ourselves on that bench just about every home game that season. The next week, we would go to the right side of the bleachers and ask that cop if he's seen the Bossard kid that we were supposed to meet. We had these primo seats between the uprights, 15 yards, tops, from the end line, on a hill so we were elevated and had a great view. I remember very clearly seeing the Browns play the LA Rams one time. Jon Arnett, who was the star running back for the Rams, lined up for the kickoff, and he was almost sitting in my lap. He was so close to me I could hardly believe it.

But I think of the nerve of us to keep going back to that guy and to his partner with the same story every week and to have it work all season—it was a dream come true. I can't even remember who else was sitting there. In old films of the Browns, you can see that hill, and you can see that little bench. I doubt very much if you could see me if I was in one of those films.

My wife is French—you can imagine how much she cared about football when I met her in 1960 when she was 19 years old. We spent most of that year together, and it was getting kind of obvious that we might wind up spending our life together. Anyway, in the spring, I thought it was time she started learning something about the Cleveland Browns. I taught her all about the Cleveland Browns. I taught her the basic strategies of the game. I made diagrams. I did the whole thing. In the movie, *Diner*, remember the Baltimore Colts fan who gave his girlfriend a test on the Colts…I didn't give Lili a test. It was just a verbal test, and if she flunked it, I still would have married her. So, she knew a lot about the Browns before she ever came to Cleveland. When I first took her to a Browns game, she's in the stands, knowing approximately what's going on, but not really for sure. A defensive end for the Browns, by the name of Bill Glass, intercepts a lateral and runs about 70-yards for a touchdown. Of course, the fans are jumping up and down and screaming and hoping he'll make it all the way to the end zone before he gets tackled. I look next to me, and guess who's jumping up and down and screaming just as much as everybody else—my dear wife.

Kellen Winslow would give aspirin a headache.

MARRIAGES ARE MADE IN HEAVEN... SO ARE THUNDER AND LIGHTNING

MICHAEL J. FELICE

Michael Felice is originally from a Cleveland suburb 25 miles east of downtown. He is a full-time state maintenance worker and part-time bartender. He is better known as The Deacon of the Dawg Pound.

I didn't go to my first game until I was a junior in high school. We were playing the Denver Broncos. It was the first time I ever had a beer, a Mickey's Wide Mouth. We didn't get it at the game—we had it under my buddy's front seat. The game was in the old Cleveland Municipal Stadium. We were out behind 'first base.' I loved that old stadium. It was huge. It was an 80,000 seat cavernous monstrosity. When they said, "A Mistake on the Lake," they weren't kidding. It was huge. I remember the stadium was probably not even half-full. It was a cold night. I was a young kid, and it was the first time I'd ever been to an NFL game. I had been to a number of major league baseball games at the stadium when I was younger.

Now, I go to three or four games a year...but I go to *every* tailgate party—religiously. We meet at six in the morning, get into the space by 6:30, saving spots for several friends. It's all about hooking up with the same guys every week and meeting a few new people. There are people I only see during football season, and they're some of my best friends. That sounds really corny, but I know that, come football season, I'm going to see those guys.

I'm an ordained minister, licensed and authorized by the State of Ohio to solemnize marriages. One time, I performed a wedding ceremony in the Dawg Pound before the game. I actually dress in minister's garb— clothing—for all the tailgate parties. A couple from Baltimore drive in for every home game. They grew up in Pennsylvania, got engaged, moved to Baltimore for his job, and became season ticketholders. They came over and approached me. They thought it was really cool that someone dressed as a minister was down there drinking beers and partying with everybody....I'm not your typical minister, by the way... We became friends with them. Now they park next to us every week for the home games. We found out that they were engaged, and we said, "Hey, why don't we do a wedding ceremony in the Dawg Pound?" It developed, and the 'Bone Lady' got involved, and King Billy and Mike the Tail Gater, was there. It was a really neat experience to go down there and be part of the first Monday Night Football game since Cleveland came back. We made Monday Night Football. We made ESPN. My crowning glory, as a male, I was the number eight Play of the Day on ESPN SportsCenter, which made a lot of my friends jealous. They're hearing me on all the sports talk shows. We got mentioned on Paul Harvey, which my mom would have been proud of because we always listened to **Paul Harvey** when I was a kid.

They call me "The Deacon of the Dawg Pound," and I have my own football card. I have a web site and when I marry people, I raise a lot of money for charity. They're your team. You've got to support them whether or not you approve of what's going on. It's in vogue to support the winning team, but it's also in vogue to bash them. I never say anything negative about the Browns when I'm being interviewed or when I'm down at the tailgate party. I feel I'm a representative, not just of the Cleveland Browns, but I also represent Cleveland when someone from Pittsburgh comes up and starts talking to me, someone from Philadelphia, someone from Oakland, someone from Buffalo. People sometimes let their emotions get a little high, but I will never say anything bad about Cleveland.

Cleveland is a blue-collar town. If you go down to the tailgate parties, it's real blue collar. Everyone has got a common ground when it comes to the Browns. It's like the Boston Red Sox or the Chicago Cubs. You really haven't done anything in decades so everyone is rooting for you. You take your team with you. If I was going to transfer to Chicago, I'd still be a die-hard Indians fan. I purposely make it a point, when I go out of town, to always take my Indians jackets, my Browns jackets, my hats. Everyone knows where I'm from. I'm not ashamed of it. I'm proud of it.

See page 2...

MUNICIPAL STADIUM:
THE FIELD OF SCREAMS

CURTIS FRANKLIN

Curtis Franklin was employed by the Browns from 1981 until they moved to Baltimore. He was the field coordinator for game-day operations.

M any times people would come down onto the field carrying 'pocket' cameras. I would look at it and know that they didn't have a camera like the regular news people I would run into. I'd ask them, "What paper are you with?" They tell me a little local paper outside of Erie or somewhere like that. My instructions were that if I saw anything out of the ordinary, or anything that didn't belong, always challenge their credentials, get the number and our public relations director, Kevin Byrne, would check them out. Also, a lot of times, we'd get stolen credentials. The Browns would send credentials out to various media people, and some would turn up missing. I would be given the missing numbers and told to be on the lookout for them. When I'd find one, I'd call Kevin and he'd tell me just to take the credential and call CPD to escort the person out of the stadium. Many times, I was the bad guy.

A guy from NBC out of New York gave me a problem once. There was a yellow line there all around the outside of the field. TV cameramen or newspaper and magazine photographers could go up to that line, but could not go beyond it. If a guy just stepped one foot inside the line to take a good shot and stepped right back, I didn't have a problem with that. If it was NFL Films out there, or if it was a live feed, we could be lenient. But this guy would camp. I told him, "I'm a communications major myself, and I understand. If you need to step out onto the field to get a good shot, it's okay, but once you get your shot, step back." This guy stepped out on the field, and he just camped there. He would ignore me every time I asked him to take his shot and move back. I walked up and grabbed him by the back of his pants and pulled him off to the side of the field. He just went ballistic, "Don't touch me. Keep your hands off me." He ran up at me, yelling at me. We carried a radio to keep in contact with the other security people so when he approached me, I started to take that radio and was going to take the right side of his face off with it, but I caught myself. He said to one of the police officers there, "What's wrong with this guy?" He was told, "Man, the guy is doing his job. Maybe you don't know it, but he runs this field." He said, "Well, I'm going to call…." I said, "You can call whoever you want. You were in violation of league regulations. You are way past the line. If I wanted to really be a pain in the butt, I could have you taken off the field." He said, "You can't get *me* taken off the field." I looked at the cop and said, "Take him."

One Monday Night Football game, it was Halloween and the Browns were playing the Bears. Jim Belushi was on the Bears sideline. He had an improper credential, but I let that one go by 'cause his brother, John, was my idol. There was another guy, wearing a Halloween conehead mask, who wandered out of the stands down onto the Bears sideline. He had no credentials at all. I walk up to him and point back up to the stands, just giving him the benefit of a doubt. We didn't want to throw people out and wanted to be fan-friendly. This guy started doing a little shake and bake and was going to fake me out as I walked closer to him. I just reached over, tackled him, called the police, "Come get him and take him out."

Another reason why the league always stated everybody should stay behind the yellow line was because it gave the players room, if they ran out of bounds, a buffer zone and it gave people on the sidelines room to get out of the way. In the end zone of the Dawg Pound, the line went up a hill so there was really not that much room for error if something happened. This one cameraman just got plowed. He was lying there unconscious, and the fans in the Dawg Pound started throwing snowballs. I get there and I cover him to keep him from getting pelted with snowballs. Most of the people there knew me from years past so I waved at the crowd like, "Be cool, guys, be cool." I was hovering over this guy so he wouldn't get pelted until the EMS was able to get there and get him off the field.

Most of the coaches were okay, but then you had some who were not. Belichick was a pain in the butt. He was not a "people person" at all, not when he was in Cleveland. He may have mellowed since he's left the Browns. They had a TV in the locker room and in the coaches' dressing room area. At the end of the game, my responsibility was to get that TV and take it back up to the Browns office. One time, I went in to get the TV and when I walked through that door, the look on his face at me was like, "What the Sam Hill are you doing?" I opened that door and saw his look, and I just walked out and said, "I'll wait till you leave." That was one of my last responsibilities each game day was to make sure I got that TV back to the office. Once I do that, I'm able to go home. I wanted to go home. It was funny because the public relations director saw it all, and he just started laughing. I couldn't backpedal fast enough to get out of there.

On game-day operations, there was somebody assigned to the sideline of the opposing team. One time, the Steelers were in town, and I would cue the players when they were to come out on the field. The guy for Pittsburgh evidently wasn't there, and they told me to go over and cue the introduction for the players. The **P.A. ANNOUNCER** was doing the announcing, and I would tell the player when it was time for him to exit out on the field. I was standing there lining them up, and the Pittsburgh defense was coming out. Greg Lloyd, who was one of my fraternity brothers, was standing there warming up. When he was in town, I would always go over where he was to talk to him. He was there warming up and had his arms out swinging. He turned around and hit me—knocked me completely down. Of course, as soon as he hit me, the Browns fans went crazy and were raining down boos. As soon as he realized he'd hit me, he turned around and looked at me, and he said, "Oh man, let me help you up."

I usually didn't have any dealings with opposing teams unless there was an injury. When Marino broke his leg in Cleveland, that was

The public address announcer for the Houston Astros (Colt '45s) in 1962 was Dan Rather. John Forsythe, the actor, was the P.A. announcer for the Brooklyn Dodgers in 1937 and 1938.

ugly. I remember we had to walk him through the Browns locker room to get x-rays. I knew he was a done deal.

There at Muni, the football team used the same locker room as the baseball team. They would come down the tunnel ramp, and they'd go into the dugout and come out onto the field—both teams would. One game, the Browns came out of the tunnel and they would line up in the dugout. The fans on the north side of the stadium could see the Browns. As soon as they saw them, they would start cheering even though they had not finished the introductions for the visiting team—all of a sudden the crowd would just start cheering. It was like they were cheering for the last three or four guys from the visiting team going out onto the field. Art Modell didn't like that at all. He gave a memorandum to Kevin Byrne, and Kevin told me he didn't want to see one orange helmet come out of there until that last visiting player has been announced. I told him he was making my job real hard. Those guys are pumped. They're ready to get out there, and I'm trying to hold them up.

I'm looking back at the guy doing the introduction for the visiting team when Curtis Weathers came out of the tunnel. I said, "Curtis, hold up. Hold up. I was told I can't let you guys go out into that baseball dugout until the last opposing player has been introduced." At this particular game, they were introducing the special teams, and Curtis Weathers was the captain of the special teams. He takes his hand and pushes me to the side. I was fuming. Luckily, the last visiting player came out as he pushed me to the side. I had wanted to have about a three-second wait after their last guy, and then for the crowd to erupt. I was so angry. I lined them up, and he was the last one to be introduced. He'd never been introduced before so he didn't know Hanford Dixon would be the last one introduced. When they said, "Hanford," I cued him to go out there, and the place would just go berserk—80,000 people going nuts. Curtis had never been introduced before, and I'm trying to hold him to get the crescendo. I'm already angry because he pushed me out of the way, jeopardizing my job. At the end of the game, I walk into the locker room and I told him in front of everybody, "Don't you ever put your hand on me again. I have a job to do just like you do. If you don't have respect for me, at least have respect for the job I have to do. I had instructions for nobody to come out of that tunnel until that last visiting player was introduced." I read him the riot act, up one side and down the other. I don't like him to this day. I ended up working with him because at the school where I was coaching he was the community liaison for a company. He was on staff, and to this day I have very little to say to him. I just say, "How you doing?" and keep on going....

Andre Rison, from Flint, Michigan, was a bug. He was tough. He was your prima donna ball player. After one game, some of the fans were upset with him so Kevin Byrne told me to walk Andre to his car. Andre had an entourage with him. His brother had come in from Flint and he had his girlfriend with him. I got my crew and two other guys and told them we were going to walk Andre to the car and to be prepared to get physical. We got two CPD and put one in the back and one in the front, and we walked them to the car. Some guy said something. I said, "Keep walking." Andre said if this guy came near him, he was going to wreck house. The guy actually stepped up, and I pushed the guy. As I pushed him, you could see Andre and his family getting ready to do some serious damage.

It was always interesting when you had to walk Bernie to his car. The Browns did Bernie wrong when they came back. Carmen Policy and Dwight Clark and those guys were doing the "San Francisco Browns" or the "Cleveland 49ers" or something—I don't know. What they did to Bernie was just ridiculous. He didn't deserve what they did to him, as far as the way they treated him—putting him out, ostracizing him, trying to keep him far away. Again, Dwight Clark and Carmen Policy had a thing where they didn't want anybody who was involved with the old regime to have anything to do with the new stadium. The one thing Art Modell said is, "Listen, the only request I have of you is try to hire as many of the old people as you can because they're loyal. They're not loyal to me. They're loyal to the team." I was there 14 seasons under the Modell regime, and I went above and beyond, to the point of taking abuse from various players when things didn't go well. I applied for my same job with the "new" Browns, and after 14 years of experience, I didn't even get an interview. It was ridiculous. They didn't extend us a courtesy at all. How, with that attitude, was San Francisco able to be the powerhouse they were with these close-minded individuals in the power positions?

A LOT OF OLD PEOPLE LIVE IN FLORIDA...WITH THEIR PARENTS.

BRIAN NELSON

Brian Nelson, 45, of New Port Richey, Florida, has been a Browns fan since he was five. He works for FedEx and is also a scriptwriter.

My first memory of the Browns—I was sitting on my dad's lap watching the '65 title game. That did it for me. I was hooked from then on. I've been a Browns fan ever since. In Erie, where I grew up, fans are split three ways. The east side of Erie is pretty much for the Buffalo Bills. The rest of it is all divided up between the Steelers and the Browns so it's quite a rivalry. Half of my friends were Steeler fans and the other half were Browns fans, or Bills fans.

From the time I was about 12 years old, I tried to go to a game at least once or twice a year. My dad along with my best friend and his dad were also big Browns fans so the four of us would go. When I became an adult, about six of us used to all jump in a van and go up there whenever we could. We'd sit in the Dawg Pound. That was the crazy place to sit where all the nut cases were. If the game was boring, you'd always be entertained by the people around you.

Sometime in the mid-eighties, we were at a game the last week of November. It was so cold we had four layers of clothes on, and we were still freezing. There were all these guys around us without shirts on, and they were drinking Jack Daniels straight out of the bottle. One kid looked like he was a refugee from Judas Priest, the band. He had on a leather cap and the whole bit. He had a bottle of Jack Daniels, and he was sitting there drinking. He was really getting into the game at first. He was jumping up and down, and then he just started really getting stoned. It was so cold that all these people who were drinking started to drop like flies from hypothermia. There were paramedics running all over the place to get to these people, and there weren't enough paramedics to go around. This kid stood right up in front of us and just fell right in our laps. We didn't even know if he was breathing or not and didn't know what to do. There was a guy next to us who looked like the wrestler, Ivan Kolaff. He had one of those Russian hats on, had the big beard, very big with large hands. He even spoke with a Russian accent. We're freaking out. We think this guy's dead. "Ivan" comes over and puts his ear to the guy's chest. He doesn't say anything. Next thing I know he just takes his fist—his huge fist—and pounds on the kid's chest. I think he broke his rib—this poor kid just let out a yell and jumped up. We were all yelling for the paramedics to get over there. That was one bizarre day. You look at some of these people at games and you wonder how they ever got the money to buy a ticket for the game.

The old stadium was a treat. This new stadium is just beautiful but the old stadium was in pretty bad shape. You would go to the men's room, and the pipes were running across the ceiling and you could look up and see them. Every time you would flush the toilet, these pipes would leak. When you get a game in the middle of the winter, it was even cold in there. Some people would crack the window open, and the cold air would be coming in, and this water would run down onto the tile floor. People would be slipping and falling all over the place. It was total chaos.

It was common knowledge, especially if you had a Steelers jersey on, that you didn't dare wander over to the Dawg Pound. There were some pretty crazy guys there. You might have a bunch of drunks, even guys who were best friends, and they'd be arguing over what Browns player was the best, or whatever, and go at it. It was more comical than anything else.

It's not the same with the Indians fans. I like to call it *longsuffering*. I've been an Indians fan for about as long as I've been a Browns fan. They're faithful. I even keep up with their games over the Internet down here. The 1990s were very kind to us 'cause we had about a 30-year drought where it was just terrible. If you admitted that you were an Indians fan, and you went to at least three games a year, then you were definitely a fan. When they win, they really bring the people out. Even when they lose, the people come, and they love their Indians. It's just that kind of a town. Cleveland is a great town. It's gone a long time without a championship. The Indians came so close. If either one of the teams—even if the Browns got to the Super Bowl—go there, it would be like Boston was with the Red Sox. The whole town would just go crazy.

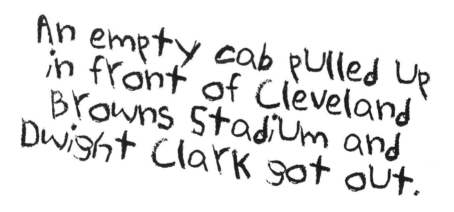

BROWNS FEVER: NO CURE

RICH SWERBINSKY

Rich Swerbinsky, 28, lives in Mentor, Ohio. He manages a mortgage portfolio for a bank and also writes for Bernie Kosar's magazine, Bernie's Insiders. *He grew up in Willowick and graduated from Eastlake High.*

I've only sat in the Pound one time in the new stadium. I was definitely not impressed. It was very different. I liked the old Pound a lot better—we'll just leave it at that. Now, it's more corporate, more family-friendly. Back in the days in the past, if you were an opposing fan, you really couldn't sit in the Pound. You could, but you were just miserable the whole game. Now, it's definitely different. The opposing fans still get razzed, but it's not as intimidating.

I can remember it being so bad that visiting fans would have to leave. Fans that would come, maybe not knowing about the Pound, and the more heated the rival, the more brutal the nature of the taunting. Some of these fans would come in, not even knowing about the Pound, just being fans of their team, possibly having bought tickets there. Maybe they were thinking they would sit in the Dawg Pound, just get the whole Cleveland experience…and then—not being able to take the abuse and the punishment—being forced to leave their seats halfway through the second quarter. It would get ugly. Back in the old Pound, people would get beer thrown at them. It was maybe not always the most politically correct…and you almost felt bad sometimes for some of the opposing fans. The Browns had such a great homefield advantage back then. It's tough. Not just here in Cleveland, but I think sports as a whole, you're not able to cheer the way you used to. I honestly blame Carmen Policy for most of that. It's worse here in Cleveland than in a lot of other new stadiums where fans have complained that the rules are too tight. My take is, "Hey, it's football." It's just eight games a year—it's not like baseball where there may be 80 home games and basketball where there's 40. Some people make those 80 home games their lives. Some of the things you see now, with people not being able to have the seating with shirts that say, "Pittsburgh Sucks," on them, or people getting chastised for standing during tight parts of a game. To me, that is just completely and utterly wrong. It's definitely a different atmosphere. Don't get me wrong—there's still nothing like going down and tailgating and the experience of a Cleveland Browns home game.

There was an attempt by the city of Cleveland to crack down on the tailgating. I've heard the same thing about the new Soldier Field. There's a line you have to balance. The Browns had some incidents with people being too drunk and doing stupid things. Some of that is going to happen when you have a football team in the Midwest, with fans as devoted and crazy. People get down at 4, 5, 6 in the morning. To a degree, some level of supervision and preventative measures is needed, but in Chicago and in Cleveland, I think it was taken a step too far. It's just really ruining the game-day experience to some extent for the vast majority of the fans that like to have a couple of beers—maybe more than a couple of beers, but are not out of control and are not a problem.

What happened in that "bottle" game is always overlooked. You hear about the "bottle" game constantly, and it was a black eye on the city of Cleveland. But, this was a Browns team, that year, if you go back to what was at stake there, the Browns team was horrible. That was our fourth year in the league—Butch's first year here. At that time, it was later in the season, and we were 7-7 so we still had a chance for a play-off spot, which this city was starving for. We played pretty well against Jacksonville, and it was a game we needed to win. It was the only time in the history of instant replay, to this day, still, that a play was reviewed after the ball had been snapped. It was on the next play. The ball was reset. The ball was snapped. Another play had begun. The officials came in and made a very questionable reversal. In any situation, in any setting, be it Cleveland, Philly, New England, New York, the reaction would have been ugly no matter where you were, given the same circumstances. Maybe it was a little worse here than it would have been at other places, probably, because Browns fans are nuts. A very large percentage of them are down there tailgating before the game. That'll be talked about forever, but a lot of people forget just a couple of the details—how big of a game it was, the fact that one call lost us the game and cost us a chance at a play-off spot. *The ball had been snapped!* That's the rule—once the ball is snapped, the previous play is in the books. It was an unfortunate situation....

About four years ago, *Bernie's Insiders* website was just starting to really get mainstream popular. It had been around as the *Greed Watch* and *The Ravens Suck Zone*, through the years the Browns were gone. Then, when they came back, it was *Browns Next Generation*. Then, Bernie got involved and it became *Bernie's Insiders*. Shortly after that, the guy who runs operations for him had a contest looking for fan contributors to write for the website. I just stumbled across it—I loved to write—I loved the Browns. I'd been writing just for fun. I'd been a Browns fan my whole life. I submitted an entry. It was an entry reviewing their draft the year that we took all linebackers. I wrote a review of the draft and the players we took and my thoughts on it. They picked four or five people from the entries, and I was one of them. All the rest of the people who won that contest are gone. They've either stopped writing or have stopped contributing to the site. For me, it was just the opposite. I started writing a column a week for the website. I got more involved with the website as a whole over the last four years. About a year ago, they asked me to start writing for the magazine, doing a Q & A with a player each month. I did that and over the last six months have gotten even more involved. Every year, I organize a draft-day party at Bunkers out in Medina, Ohio. I write about an article a week for the magazine. I've gotten a lot more involved in talking with the players. Probably once a week or two, I will interview somebody for either the website or the magazine. It's been great. It's almost been like a childhood dream come true—to really get the chance to get to know and talk to a lot of the guys on the team. I really enjoy doing it as a part-time gig.

Some of the players are more supportive than others. The fact that Bernie's name is involved definitely helps us as far as getting interviews. It's a strange situation because there was some strife between Bernie and Carmen Policy. Policy is gone so a lot of that is gone now.

At my bank workplace I manage a mortgage portfolio, and set the interest rates. About five years ago, one of our loan originators called me. He said he was doing Don Cockroft's loan. I said, "I'll give him one-eighth off his rate if he'll send me a signed picture." He sent me a real nice signed, framed picture. I've never met him, but I've heard he's a great guy.

As sports gets further and further away from fans being able to get attached to individual players, in this age of free-agency, it's almost as if Clevelanders now cheer for the uniform and not the player. That definitely was not the case with Bernie Kosar.

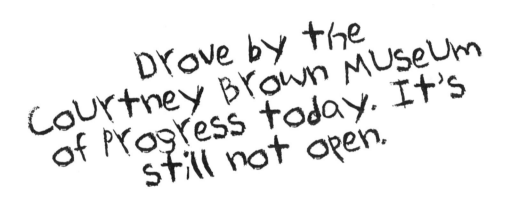

YADA, YADA, YADA

It was always interesting that in the old stadium you would occasionally find women that just could not wait in the line, and they talked their way into the line going into the men's room, "I don't need a stall, just give me a sink." You could miss an awful lot of the game going to the bathroom in the old stadium. It was the same sort of thing when we had those old, long, stainless steel troughs.

Most of these new stadiums are designed by the same architecture firm. They are all excellent places to watch a football game. You have unobstructed sight lines. They're comfortable but they're really lacking in character. There's a degree of sterility about the new places and they just don't have the character that the old places had. One of the interesting things they did in Cleveland is that the new stadium sets right on top of where the old stadium was. They said they designed it so that the 50-yard line would be at the same place.

——SAM CHAMBERS, 45, originally from Painesville

There was a "12 Days of Christmas" song about the Browns, which they probably had in every city. We used to sing that a lot...before the last Browns game, when they were going to tear down the stadium, there was one of our friends who sat by us, and we were making these great plans that we were going to take our seats with us when we left. We were trying to figure out how we were going to do it—if we could bring tools in. I thought it was just some great plan *we* had...but people tore up that stadium. They were pulling out rows of seats. I sat there thinking, "Oh my gosh, I was trying to figure out how to take my one seat." I wasn't able to get the seat out—all I got were a couple of wooden slats from the seat. There was a pay phone on the corner of the stadium, and a lot of people who drove down with us, even though they didn't sit with us, would always meet up with us at that phone booth, but we couldn't get that either.

——BESS DANEK, Sagamore Hills, Ohio

In *Pro Football Weekly*, right after Modell announced the move, Bill Wallace talked about how watching a football game, going to a game in Cleveland, is so much different than any other city. You go to the old place, and it was like going to church. You walked there in almost silence. People would huddle up, getting on the rapid transit from both directions. They were quiet, very solemn, walking down that ramp at West Third Street, and there wasn't a lot of screaming and hollering. Despite that image of the old Dawg Pound—that was just one section. To the majority of those 80,000 people, this was like a religious experience. It's totally different now. The new place is different. Fans are different. There's a whole different atmosphere. It was a real telling thing. I've been to almost every National Football League venue. Going to old Cleveland Stadium was different than going anyplace else.

The new park just doesn't engender that old kind of feeling. The team doesn't. All the fans I talk to who go back all feel the same way. As much as I hate to say it, Baltimore really has a better place than we do. It doesn't have that same kind of quiet, sterile feel. It's been hard for fans to reconnect. I'm amazed that the rebirth has gone as well as it has. I really am.

I had two great seats in the old place. I know why Art left because there were 80,000 seats of which only about 1,400 of them were any good. We had two of those 1,400. We were below the posts right about on the 45-yard line. We'd had them since 1946.

———ROGER COHEN, Washington, D. C. resident the last 16 years

The new stadium is a little more cookie-cutter, but it's a little closer. It's not what I'm used to because I'm so used to the Cleveland Municipal Stadium and Jacobs Field. But, I like the way the Dawg Pound is—they maintained the bench seating. It's kind of like its own community. When you're in the pound, you have to get along. I always sit in the Dawg Pound when I go to the games. My eyes are really bad so I have to have a radio to hear what's going on so I can kind of watch and hear the plays develop. But, there's nothing like watching them driving into the Dawg Pound to score. The fever and the frenzy that gets going there is just something you can't imagine. It's a really neat feeling.

The one memory I will always remember from going to the Browns games and sitting in the Dawg Pound is the first game after 9/11. I wanted so bad to be there for the National Anthem and just watch the players run out for the first time after 9/11. We played the Detroit Lions. I'll never forget standing there hearing the National Anthem and seeing the jets roaring over. I begged, I pleaded, and was just sacrificing my soul to my one buddy, going, "I want a ticket to this game." I'm a very patriotic person. I take pride in the country. That was my fondest memory of ever going to a football game and hearing the **NATIONAL ANTHEM** sung in a major sports venue.

———MICHAEL J. FELICE, the Minister of the Dawg Pound

I was working security at 'The Drive' game. After the game, it was like you had hit the crowd in the face with a sledge hammer. They were just stunned. I couldn't believe it. At that particular time, doing my duties, I was circling the field. When they started that drive, I was on the Denver sideline. I was going, "Oh my God, these guys are driving the ball down the field." I was coaching high school at the time. At the end of that game, I learned a lesson. When the game was coming close, prevent means 'Prevent me from wins.'' I guess that was the one thing I thought, "Marty, why did you go into a prevent? You should have been after Elway from the very first snap when that ball was on the two-yard line. You should have been after him the whole time instead of dropping everybody back and only sending four." You don't give Elway that much time to throw the ball. I was there at the end when Denver kicked the winning field goal, but I didn't really pay attention to it, and I haven't had a chance to watch it on the video to see if it was actually to the left or to the right of the upright. All I know, is when I saw the ref's hands go up, I thought, "Oh, it's a done deal. It's a done deal."

At the last game in '95, the crowd went crazy. In that time, I flashed back to all the games I had ever attended at Browns Stadium, to all the things that went on. It was just unreal. At that time, you could bring food into the game. People would bring in duffel bags, and they'd have blankets and beverages and snacks. In the early days,

> **Before Super Bowl XI, there was no NATIONAL ANTHEM. Vikki Carr sang *America The Beautiful*.**

people in the bleachers would bring in all kinds of food. They could just walk it in. The stadium was going to be torn down anyway. They had hacksaws with them. The last five minutes of the game, you'd see a guy there with a hacksaw sawing a whole section. Guys had ratchets, and they're unscrewing the bolts in the seats. They were walking out of there with everything. We were told to let them do whatever they wanted to do. But, they didn't storm the field. They didn't tear down the goalposts. Anything that wasn't tied down in those stands was gone. People even took garbage cans, anything they could for memorabilia. After everybody had left, and all the post-game interviews were over, Dino Lucarelli and I were standing there, and they shut the lights down. We just looked at the old stadium. It was empty. We just couldn't believe that was it. We thought, "Wow, this is the last time we're going to walk in or out of this stadium." It was cold, and it just had an eerie silence about it. It was indescribable.

——CURTIS FRANKLIN, Browns employee, 1981-1995

The following year, the Browns played the Bills in the playoff game. The Browns were winning, and the Bills were moving down the field. I was at the game with my stepson. I couldn't handle this. I said, "Let's go. We're leaving." He goes, "What do you mean, we're leaving?" I said, "I can't bear this. I can't take this again." We walked back to the car, got in the car, turned on the radio as we headed away from the stadium. Ronnie Harmon, a wide receiver for the Bills, was wide open in the end zone, and he dropped the pass. That was it. The Browns ended up winning. I just happened to look in my rearview mirror and see the stadium, and it was just a great feeling.

——BILL GILLAN, season ticketholder, Rochester, N. Y.

I was down at the stadium just before they tore it down. It was sad. When the Browns were in the old stadium, I didn't get to a whole lot of games. I went to a few, and I loved that stadium, as dark and dank and crappy as it was. It wasn't the building, it was the memories that came. We got to go onto the field. We went through the locker rooms. I sat in Kosar's old locker. They let us come up through the tunnel. They actually took pictures of you. They would take your camera and say, "If you want a picture coming out of the tunnel and out onto the field, just like the players did, we'll take it for you."

I went down many times as they were tearing it down, and I have a brick from the stadium. The new stadium is nice…but it's not the same. We've got awesome seats. They're opposite the Dawg Pound. But, it's not the same as the old stadium. I miss that. I've talked to a lot of people, and it just seems to be the memories from those games—the Kardiac Kids—Kosar playing. The '80s were just the best seasons for the Browns, all through those terrible games with Denver. Nobody will ever forget those.

——SUE NAUMANN, 52, Parma

The 'Drive' against Denver in the AFC Championship game in '86 is a game I will never, ever forget as long as I live. John Elway takes the Broncos 98-yards to tie the football game, and then they win it in overtime on a field goal by Rich Karlis. I can just remember that sinking feeling. You could hear a pin drop in that stadium—a pin drop. It was like your heart was just ripped out. It took a while to exit the stadium after that. The ushers had a hard time prodding us out of the stadium—not just me and my brother but the whole stadium was just sitting there in dead silence. It was like—wewerethatcloseto-gettingtotheSuperBowl—that close to getting to the Super Bowl! Our heart got ripped out and left there in the stadium. It took me quite a while to get over that. It's all that "What if?" "What if?" John Elway just broke our heart, broke our spirit.

After Modell had announced that he was moving the team, all the advertisers pulled their advertisements out of the stadium. The ring of advertising around the stadium was just black. It looked gloomy, and it was like **D-Day** or something. I shouldn't say that, in correlation with the War, I don't mean that, but it was just gloom and doom and with each passing home game, it was like, "This is gonna be it." You just felt lost for a long time.

It always comes back to—Browns fans are passionate. They're die-hard no matter what happens, through thick and thin, they're

> **The first American to jump off the boats at the <u>D-DAY</u> invasion was James Arness of "Gunsmoke" fame. At 6' 7", he was the tallest man on the first ship and the ship's captain wanted to test how deep the water was.**

always going to be there to support the team. You can always count on that, that's for sure.

———GEORGE KRSKA, 44, delivery driver

I remember the season when we lost to the Raiders in the playoffs. That was one season where it took the stadium officials a long time to figure out why there were four guys carrying a doghouse, mounted on some 2 x 4s. Like, if you had a pair of skis, and you put a doghouse in the middle of it. It took four of them to carry the doghouse into the Dawg Pound…but, only two would carry it back out. It took them halfway through the season of home games to figure out that there was a keg of beer in the inside of that doghouse. It took four people to carry it in, but it took only two to carry it back out. Of course, the keg was empty then.

———RICK RIZZO, 38, formerly of North Royalton, Ohio

 I just can't believe how different the stadium is now than it was in the past. It seems like it's so strict. The old Dawg Pound used to be so loud, and they'd let you get by with just about anything. Now, they yell at you for cussing. Some of my friends have gotten thrown out for stupid stuff like cussing. Somebody threw a plastic cup at one guy, and he just picked it up and threw it back, and he got thrown out for throwing something. The game had just started, and he got thrown out right away. They didn't even hesitate. One girl in our group has a terrible foul mouth on her. When she gets a few beers in her, she lets the 'f' bomb fly quite a bit. They came and told her that she had to watch her mouth. She said, "This is football. What the hell do you expect?" They ended up kicking her out for cussing. They told her there were kids in there, and she said, "They shouldn't be in the Dawg Pound." In the old Dawg Pound, you wouldn't see anybody bring their kids in because there was always drinking and carrying on in there.

It just doesn't have the character of the old stadium. In the old stadium, the restroom facilities for women were terrible. You'd have to walk half way around the stadium or use the Port-A-Potties. So, my friends and I would go in the guys' john all the time and nobody would say anything. It was funny. They had this little trough that went along the whole wall in the men's restroom, and then they had two stalls in there. The guys didn't care when we went in there and used their stalls. We did that a lot in the old stadium, but, of course, you wouldn't get by with anything like that now.

We can tailgate around the new stadium but they changed some things. Now you have to pour your beer into a cup—you're not allowed to sit there and hold cans anymore. If you dare step over on the sidewalk, out of the parking lot, you can get fined. I had two guys from Versailles get busted just walking to talk to somebody. They stepped out on the sidewalk with their beer in their hand. They got fined $90 apiece for open container. They couldn't believe it.

——**KAREN HOLSAPPLE**, Versailles, Ohio

As Browns fans, we really have a lot of idiots, a lot of jerks, sitting there in the Dawg Pound. One year in particular, '93, we were there. I actually didn't really care to sit in the Dawg Pound because I'm there to watch the game. It's tough to watch a game especially when you've got drunken idiots sitting behind you or near you. After a while, it just gets on your nerves. We're watching the games and these guys behind us were just so stinking drunk they couldn't even stand up, talk, walk or do anything else. There were some Steeler fans up behind them and off to their left. It kept escalating. Finally, one of the guys behind us gets up and walks a couple of steps up, and he tells this guy, "You better */(@)(@)!+ shut up or get out of here. You're not supposed to be in here anyway. This is Browns country." This Steeler fan said, "Look at the scoreboard." Next thing I know, this guy comes back down and sits down. Then he gets up, runs right up there after the Steeler fan as he was walking up the aisle to the restroom or concession stand. He tackles the guy there in the aisle. They come rolling down, and the next thing you know, there are 10-12 people involved. They come rolling down into the stands, almost came down into us. I'm like, "This is not what this should be all about."

——**GEORGE KRSKA**, Barberton, Ohio

I was born the year the Browns won the championship in 1964. After that, there were a lot of lean years when I was actually old enough to really enjoy football. I was at the game against the Oakland Raiders that we lost in '81—sat through that interception. I remember walking out of the stadium...I have never, ever heard that many people leave in just absolute stony silence. People use the expression, "You could hear a pin drop," and I literally remember walking down the ramps of old Municipal Stadium and it was just total silence.

The Browns stopped the Raiders on fourth and less than a yard. I was in the upper deck. We got the ball back, and Mike Pruitt had a swing pass off to the left, and the Browns got major yards. The guys kept getting closer and closer, and I thought, "Oh, my god, we're going to do it." I also thought of all the troubles Cockroft had, too, kicking. I wondered, "What are they going to do? Are they going to try for a field goal?" I still, to this day, didn't think the pass play was the wrong call. I just think Sipe should have thrown it into Lake Erie instead of throwing it to Mike Davis, who made the interception. I remember the stunned silence. That was my first painful memory— which should have been a precursor for things to come. I'm not one for embellishment. To this day, I'm one of the many people who, when that game is on ESPN Classic, still can't watch it.

——JOHN KARLIAK, Cleveland

When I walked into the new stadium for the first time, it was unbelievable. We were so used to wooden bleachers, substandard bathrooms, and, obviously we didn't have TV screens in the corridors or a PA system in the restroom areas. This stadium is very plush, very plush. Our seats in the Dawg Pound are in the second row so we are right on top of the field, which is pretty incredible. That's where we were in the old stadium, as well, but it's just a warmer feeling to it. We are almost dead-center at the goal posts, and we can see everything.

——CHUCK SCHUSTER, 50, Canton

The new stadium is an awesome facility. I miss the old stadium. It was just like when you played football on Friday nights in high school in the mud and the crud and the dirt…. We went to Cleveland to visit relatives and went down to the stadium site with my youngest daughter. There is an old school bus that comes in from Sandusky for every home game. It's been painted brown. In it, they put one of the original urinals from the first stadium. It's a functional urinal, believe it or not. It has a picture of Art Modell inside the urinal so you can actually take a leak on old Art there in that bus…. The early fall time of year with the pre-season games is a gorgeous time. When you get into late November and December home games, your crowd is still out there cooking the brats and the steaks. We've seen guys with tubs of lobsters. Just when you think you have something cool to eat, you'll see something new. Last year, a group of college-age guys rolled in with one of those turkey fryer cookers. They were doing three and four-pound lobsters in there and were just the envy of the whole area.

——LARRY KOPA, 57, Dayton, Ohio

I got to go games very infrequently as a kid. I remember seeing Paul Hornung play. I haven't missed a home game since '88. I have two tickets at the 40-yard line, lower deck. I have two tickets in the club seats at about the 20-yard line. The old stadium obviously wasn't as nice as the new stadium, but we had seats on the 15-yard line, upper deck. The way the old stadium was, it was a bowl. It was built in 1931. Cleveland tried to get the Olympics in 1932 but we didn't get it. You could be on the 50-yard line in the old stadium, but you were so far from the field because it was a big oval. If you were at the 15, you were far closer to the field. I'd take those seats in the old stadium any day over what I've got now. The old stadium had more character, too. Fans were more raucous. To me, you can't replace the old stadium. The new stadium is nice, but it's more sterile. There hasn't been a lot to yell about over the past five or six years, and that's part of the problem. When they're in a game, and competing for a play-off spot, I've got to believe it would be like the old place.

They've sold out every game since they've been back, but it's getting to be later every season. I have never missed a home game. I'm going to go no matter what it takes. The last game of the 2004 season, it was unbelievably bitter weather—10° and it snowed like crazy. There couldn't have been 10,000 people in that stadium, but yet I went. I couldn't get one person in my group to go with me…so I went all by myself. I braved the weather. It was just one of those things. You've got a streak going, and you're not letting anything stop it. I went, and I sat down there in the club seats. There couldn't have been two people around me, but I sat out there and watched them play San Diego. They lost 27-0. I just wasn't going to 'not go.'

My other buddies went, "You're nuts. Why would you go?" It's a home game. Okay? For as many years as I can remember, I've gone, and I'm not letting this stop me…. I was never a tailgater. I never missed a kickoff until last year. A good friend of mine died, and I had to go to his funeral…but I did leave the funeral so I could get there by the second quarter.

——MITCH KUTASH, 51, Cleveland

Municipal Stadium was both the best and the worst place to watch a ball game. When the Indians were a great team in the 1950s and late 1940s and they drew crowds of upwards of seventy thousand, there was no more wonderful place ever to watch a ball game. The place was really hopping. It was a huge, cavernous stadium. When the team started falling on hard times in the late 1950s through almost the mid-1990s, it was absolutely the worst place to watch a ball game. You'd get five or six thousand people there in a stadium that could seat over eighty thousand. There was very little crowd noise as the Indians were usually losing. You felt lonely, isolated, and quite depressed.

——DAVID NEMEC, author, baseball books

I remember being at 'The Drive' game. I was in high school at the time. I remember going with a friend, his father, and a bunch of other people. We tailgated out in the Municipal parking lot. My friend's father said that the best way to be warm at game time is to take your jackets and shirts off before the game. So, there we were in freezing cold weather, with no shirts on, just a tee shirt—that's it, playing catch football and grilling hot dogs. It was absolutely freezing, but then when we put on our jackets, we thought, "Wow. This really works." We were so stupid. I remember thinking we had that game in hand. We've got the dog bones tied around our necks, our faces painted, and each play, we'd say, "We've got to get them on this play." It was just how noisy the stadium went to absolutely how quiet it was! Walking out of the stadium after that loss, there wasn't a single person talking. I remember one guy said, "I can't believe it." Everybody looked at him like, "Yeah. No kidding. You don't need to say that."

——SEAN SAMUELS, 35, Phoenix

Chapter 4

Baltimore:
The Last Refuge of Scoundrels

HARVARD BUSINESS SCHOOL PRESS

LOYALTY RULES!

How Today's Leaders
Build Lasting Relationships

ART MODELL WILL HATE THIS BOOK!

FREDERIC REICHHELD

BAIN & COMPANY, INC.

It's Hard to Cheer With a Broken Heart

IF YOU'DA BEEN THERE,
IF YOU'DA SEEN IT,
I'LL BETCHA YOU'DA DONE THE SAME

BERNIE HAIRSTON

Bernie Hairston has lived in California since leaving Cleveland over three decades ago. He is an audio/visual projectionist as well as a performer/singer. His father worked for Art Modell.

A lot of people in Cleveland have a very negative idea about Art Modell. Because I was able to be on the 'inside,' I know a different Art Modell than everybody else knows. He was a very caring, a very loving kind of individual. He knew every employee's name, every wife or husband of the employee's name, and he knew every kid of every employee. A lot of people in organizations like that don't have a clue who's working for them or around them, but he knew every one of them.

In '62, when he bought the Browns, my father who had just started working for them, heard him mention something about moving from Lake Shore Hotel to a house. My father suggested, "Let me come and help." So my father took me, 12-years old, and my uncle, who was also 12, along with him to help Art Modell move. We have a different feel about him as an individual as compared to a lot of people in Cleveland who think he is a very bad, evil individual. He really was not like that, from my perspective. He was very caring, very loving. He thought of you as family. He thought of my father and my mother as family. After he got married, he and his wife treated us like family, all the time, and I do mean, all the time. He was a very, very fair person.

When Art's sons, David and John, first came on the scene, David, as a little kid, was a holy terror and scared the crap out of everybody. If my cousin and I happened to be there when he came, the three of us would have a great time. Years later, when John moved to LA, John, my friend, Ray Dewey, and I would all get together at either NBC or at bars and watch the Browns and keep up on our interest in music and the entertainment world.

In '87, when the Browns went to London to play Philadelphia, Art Modell told the players and the coaches they were allowed to bring their wives and girlfriends, which was kind of unusual at that time, and even more-so, they could even bring their children. When my father heard that, he asked me if I wanted to go. I said, "How soon will I have to be there?" At the time I was working for NBC Studios as a film extra. I went, and had a great time....

I remember the fun we had when we used to go to Hiram College for the Browns mini-camps. They would have a big dinner for the players and the employees. I was one of the fortunate ones to be able to be there. After the meals, the rookies would get up and sing and do little skits. It was really nice to be there to see those kind of things. Blanton Collier and his wife were just wonderful to everyone. You never saw him upset, bent out of shape, chewing out people. He was always very pleasant. Doug Dieken was like a sweetheart. He was like one of the boys on the block. He always greeted you with a great smile, even when he got his knees knocked out from underneath him, and he could hardly walk. He called my father Junebug. He would say, "Hey, Junebug, what's going on?"

Eddie Johnson was a tremendous comedian. Even Belichick, when he was not in the media's face, and when he was not really outside for all to see, was an entirely different person. He was a very warm, friendly person. I wasn't too crazy about the calls he was making as a coach, but, as a human being, he was a very interesting person.

When it was time to draft, no one in the organization wanted Greg Pruitt, but Art Modell specifically said, "I want that guy." If I remember correctly, a lot of people in Cleveland wanted to get Johnnie Rogers from Nebraska. Instead, Modell said he wanted Pruitt. That was the best thing that could have been done. It's amazing how scouts and so-called general managers are supposed to know everything, and it seems like the common guy has a better feel on what's going on.

Like everybody else, I was very upset when the Browns left. I wasn't ready to hate Modell over it because I understood what was going on behind the scenes. He was losing a lot of money. It was no longer a family business. It was more like a corporate kind of business where you had to have deep pockets. Modell would generously give money to organizations, and it was never talked about. His wife gave my mother expensive crystal for gifts at Christmas, when she could have just given a card. He gave parties for the office crew at country clubs and fancy places and serve expensive food—lobster, caviar. But, he had to make that move…for his family. We see the end results of it—they won the Super Bowl. I wish it would have been in Cleveland. Some decisions are hard, but good comes from them.

I wasn't too crazy with all the new people that came into the organization because it was too much 'San Francisco.' One of the things Art Modell emphasized was that some of the people, who were in the organization when he left, should get an opportunity to work for the new organization because of their loyalty to him, as well as their loyalty to Cleveland. None of that crew that came in from the 49ers even considered anybody from Cleveland. Everyone they had in the new organization had nothing to do with Cleveland in any way, form or fashion. That's part of the reason it fell apart.

I really enjoyed those early days with the Browns organizations, and I'm sorry it ended as it ended. I wish that the new regime at that time was able to bring in the same love, but that didn't exist.

If the phone doesn't ring, it's Art Modell.

DOWN AT THE CORNER
OF WHAT AND IF

FRED NANCE

Fred Nance is the managing partner in the Cleveland law firm, Squires Sanders. He spent 10 of his 28 years there as outside counsel to the city of Cleveland (1991-2001). He is a graduate of Harvard and the University of Michigan Law School.

I have season tickets and take clients or family to every game. If you're a male in this town, once you hit puberty, and you know what's going on, you're a Browns fan. In the old Municipal Stadium, in the men's room, they had these big troughs for urinals. One of the rites of passage in Cleveland, if you were a man, was standing next to your dad at the trough taking a leak at the Browns stadium.

In late 1993, the mayor of the city of Cleveland came to me and asked me to negotiate the renewal of the Cleveland Browns stadium lease. The lease had a 30-year term and was set to expire in 1998. Although we were starting early, the reason we were starting early was that it was clear that Art Modell felt that, while the city had taken care of the basketball team and the baseball team by building new facilities over at the complex known as Gateway, that he needed a substantially renovated facility in order to remain competitive in the league. You know how the economics work in the National Football League—the revenues that the team can derive from the stadium, primarily from luxury seating, so-called premium seating, can make the difference in the profitability of the team. The ordinary tickets are subject to revenue sharing, and are shared all over the league. There were other teams getting new facilities, and Art Modell felt that he needed the benefit of having upgraded facilities. While there was still a good deal of time left on the lease, the discussion was about, not only, renewing a lease on favorable terms, but also undertaking a substantial renovation of the old Cleveland Municipal Stadium, which had been built in 1931. It was a multiple-use facility between the Browns and the Cleveland Indians until the Indians moved out in '92. As a part of the lease negotiations, we were also talking about a major construction job.

In 1994, we came up with a $175 million renovation plan that would have been a substantial makeover for the stadium. First things first, we came up with the plan before we came up with a way to pay for it. What happened is, as we got toward the end of 1994 and early 1995, the mayor commissioned a group of business leaders, a so-called stadium task force, to look at different financing mechanisms. It became clear that, one way or the other, some type of general tax increase was necessary, a county-wide tax increase for that matter, because the residents of the city of Cleveland could not support it alone. Cleveland, at that time, was about 600,000+ people. They couldn't afford it on their own so there had to be some type of county-wide tax. Modell did not like that.

Eventually, in June of 1995, he sent a letter to Mike White. When Mike left office, he gave me that letter as a souvenir, and I have it in an étagère in my office. It's a so-called 'moratorium' letter. In the letter, Art Modell said he would like to declare a moratorium on discussions with respect to renovating the stadium, any sort of tax increase to pay for it, that he thought it would be a distraction during the course of the upcoming season. This was when the team was just beginning summer camp. He used the word 'endured.' He didn't think it was appropriate for him to endure a public debate about whether there should be tax increases to pay for this. Once that happened, needless to say, we started to get concerned. With 20-20 hindsight, perhaps we should have been even more concerned. We had no idea, and we were never able to piece together the exact time frame. We got bits and pieces in the discovery and the litigation to know that during the course of that summer he was having discussions with the folks in Maryland, the Maryland Stadium Authority, led by a guy named John Moag, who was the executive director of the Maryland Stadium Authority.... He becomes a protagonist in this down the road because—I'm jumping ahead in the time sequence—I got a call on New Years Eve, 1995 after all this crap had hit the fan. We were in this pitched battle to try to save the team and to convince the NFL we deserved to keep a team. So, he called me at home. This would have been before I took his deposition. He said, "Fred, don't make book with the NFL. If you want a team, you need to go out and get yourself a team the same way we did. I think Malcolm Glazer down in Tampa will talk to you. Here's his phone number. Why don't you give him a call?" Of course, that's something we never did. But, I, obviously, never forgot John Moag.

Back in the summer of 1995, instead of simply putting everything on ice, as the moratorium letter would have suggested, we continued to work to put some flesh on the bones of the package we were offering. By that, I mean we continued with our stadium renovation, our architectural plans. We continued to refine the financing alternatives and to finally come up with a specific type of tax. More specifically, it was a so-called 'sin' tax, which was an excise tax on the consumption of alcohol and cigarettes in Cuyahoga County to pay for the renovations that thought we were acceptable to Modell and his team based on our discussions when they were still talking to us. And, we continued to look at ways we could make the lease more economically competitive for him.

This is a vivid recollection. I recall being in the mayor's office in November of 1995, a Saturday morning, fourth of November. There was a television on in the corner but the sound was turned down. We were sitting and talking about something else, when we looked over and saw a picture of Art Modell on the screen. We turned up the sound. They had broken into the news to announce that on the following Monday, Art Modell was going to have an announcement about the future of the Cleveland Browns at Camden Yards in Baltimore. Needless to say, that took all the wind out of us. The then general counsel of the National Football League, Jay Moyer, had actually been an associate of my law firm, Squire Sanders, many years before I had gotten there. One of our partners, who knew him from back in those days, gave him a call, and we were able to set up a meeting the very next day.

It was a rainy night on that Sunday in November, 1995, and we are in Commissioner Tagliabue's office. Moyer had set the meeting up for us. The mayor, me, along with Commissioner Tagliabue and his executive vice president, Roger Goodell who ended up spearheading the NFL side of the negotiations with us. I got to know Roger very well over the course of the ensuing months. On that Sunday night, it struck me, when we were sitting there, that Paul Tagliabue was as surprised as we were at what had happened. Tagliabue and the mayor of Cleveland, Mike White, forged a relationship that night, a relationship that wasn't certain as to how things would unfold, wasn't certain as to how we would get there, but Tagliabue said to us, "We will figure out a way to be fair to Cleveland." We basically had to trust him. There were lots of different ways we could go. You better believe there was no shortage of armchair quarterbacks telling us that we ought to file an antitrust suit. We ought to try and take the franchise by eminent domain. We ought to do all sorts of things and go on the offensive.

The mayor and I went from New York to Baltimore because that Monday was when Modell was going to make his announcement in Camden Yards. I remember being there…it was pretty tough. He made the announcement, but we were not right there in the audience. We were in another room just off the area where they were doing the announcement outdoors. We watched Paris Glendening, the governor of Maryland, talk about how much fun he was having. He talked about using a secret knock on the door of the airplane to go in to meet and negotiate with Art Modell. They had to use a secret handshake to get in the door. John Moag, that chairman on the Maryland Stadium Authority, was there. They talked about the great future of the Browns in Baltimore. The Cleveland mayor, Mike White did grant some press interviews there. He said just what you would expect him to say—that this was wrong, that the people in Cleveland didn't deserve this, that we had bent over backward to give Modell whatever we could, that we had no idea this was coming, and that we were going to fight. I also remember that the mayor of Baltimore, Kurt Shmoke, an African-American, and Mayor White, who is African-American, knew each other from the League of Cities and other activities. The two of them spoke. Shmoke explained to White, "I'm sorry that this has happened, but I'd like you to try to understand that no matter how hard we tried to move our civic agenda forward, all I ever hear from people around here is 'When are we going to get another football team?'" We've got education issues. We've got poverty issues. We've got safety issues. But, all anybody wants to talk about is getting a football team. We couldn't move on as a town until we got one." We thought that was pretty interesting.

At this time, there had been no discussion about Cleveland being able to keep the name Cleveland Browns, and it was being talked as if the team would be called the Baltimore Browns. At the press conference, somebody mentioned that "Baltimore Browns sounds pretty good."

If you would ask Mike White about his priorities, he never was a big sports fan, but he was the consummate politician. He understood people. He had the ability to foresee the impact of different events. As he explained it, because he was constrained to explain it, because we also had people who reasonably said, "Why are you fighting this fight? Why are you placing so much emphasis and resources on this?" There are some economists who will tell you that the economic spin-off from having a professional football team is far outweighed by the investment that it takes, particularly as the table was tilting more in terms of the revenue that had to go to the team in order to keep a team in the '90s. We weren't the only ones…this was going on all over the country. White explained, "I'm not that big a fan. In fact, I'm not sure I would know a safety from a hat trick, but I do understand civic agendas. I understand that the perception of whether a town is a winner or a loser can have as much to do with sports as the reality of its economic vitality. We cannot afford to be an abandoned town, a town that's perceived as not being able to get it together to keep a team. To lose the team will set us back a long time and a long way, and I'm not going to let that happen."

From Baltimore, we went straight to Dallas, where an NFL owners meeting was taking place. At time, I had partners back in Cleveland who had filed a motion for a temporary restraining order based upon our lease agreement.

There is a lawyer named Jack Hollington in Cleveland, a partner at Baker and Hostetler, who had been the city's lawyer 27 years earlier when the city had negotiated the lease with Modell. He had put some language in the lease that's called 'specific performance language.' Those are magic legal words that mean 'not only do you have to pay the rent, but you also have to perform—play the game.' This meant they could not just buy out the lease, as you or I might do, if we have a condo lease, say, "I'm leaving, but here's the next two-years rent." There was a specific performance provision in the lease—the consideration for which when you have promises in a contract, they are only enforceable if there is a bargain for exchange—called consideration. The consideration for the promise to play was the benefit to the city of having the team there. There were recitals in the lease which talked about the tax revenue, talked about, beyond dollars and cents, the value to the community of having a professional football team as part of its mantle, part of its allure, the draw to others, that we are a big-league city. We were able to use that language in court.

Before we had even gotten to Dallas, some of my partners had gone into a state court here and gotten a temporary restraining order that stopped Modell from moving the team. A temporary restraining order, a TRO, is just that. It's temporary and lasts for about 10 days. After that, the court can turn a temporary restraining order into something called a preliminary injunction. The battle we fought in the courts was to obtain both a preliminary and permanent injunction to make that injunction final on the basis of the specific performance language in the lease to make them play out the balance of their three years in Cleveland Stadium.

Our thinking, our strategy, of course, was that if we won that, that would be an unacceptable scenario to the Browns and the NFL because, again, if you watched any of the films or read any of the news accounts, you'll know once Modell announced he was leaving, the remaining games that season were crazy. Those were dangerous events. The people around here went nuts. They were ripping out the seats. All of the advertisers in the stadium pulled out. There was no signage anywhere. If you can, imagine a modern stadium with no advertising anywhere in it because all of the advertisers had backed out. It was just the most eerie environment, one where there was fear for the physical safety of people, generally, in the building and, most specifically, of Art Modell and people associated with him. It was a bad scene. The notion that there would be three more years of that was something that was unacceptable to them.

We decided upon a three-prong strategy.

The first prong of our strategy was to get that injunction to get some legal leverage. We filed a second lawsuit in federal district court here, which was to go after the so-called intellectual property—that was the name, the colors, the records, the heritage, that sort of thing. We got a temporary restraining order in federal court here and did the discovery and the motion practice and eventually obtained a preliminary injunction, as well, stating that those things belonged to the City of Cleveland, not to the team. We were successful.

The second prong of our strategy was our fan support. That surpassed anything I ever could have anticipated because it wasn't just fans in Cleveland, Ohio. There were, and still are today, clubs called Browns Backers Clubs. They're all over the world, and, certainly all over the United States. Our campaign consisted of following the NFL owners around the country. During the season, they meet in different cities, not always the city where they have a team, generally a city where there's a team nearby, but they are usually in warm-weather climates. We would go to those places and try to get an audience. Everywhere we went, we were met by fans who would stage candlelight vigils, who would jam the fax machines and phone lines at the offices so they couldn't do business, who would protest, picket, march. We were greeted by them everywhere we went. They were a tremendous help. The very first thing the NFL asked us to do was to *call off the dogs*.

I remember them greeting us when we got down to Dallas. Then, there were a whole series of these meetings going on. At the same time, we're engaged in litigation. The litigation was a pitched battle. There were pretty high stakes to the two biggest law firms in Cleveland, my firm, Squire Sanders, and the Jones Day law firm. We were fighting in five different states. We had, over the course of that battle, about 39 different lawyers and legal assistants involved in one facet or another. Again, the details are something that would bore anybody other than a lawyer. Suffice it to say, this battle was fought on many fronts. There were millions and millions of dollars spent in the process. There were hundreds of thousands of hours spent fighting this battle in various forms.

At this point, it was the battle to obtain the injunction on the specific performance lease. It was the battle to obtain the injunction to keep the intellectual property. It was the battle of the presentation to the league where once the league agreed to start to talk to us…. Once we got the preliminary injunction on the lease, the NFL said, "Let's talk." Although the legal case continued, because you have to make the preliminary injunction permanent after that to get another trial, we were permitted to make presentations, first only on paper, then we were actually able to come into meetings of the NFL owners and make presentations about the viability of our offer. We had to hire economists. We hired real estate brokers. We hired university professors. We brought in our Chamber of Commerce. We brought the governor of the state of Ohio with us. We put together presentations to show that we had an economically viable, competitive package to offer, and that the stadium net revenues that Modell could derive— because at that time we were trying to stop the move—from a deal with us were superior to the deal he had in Baltimore and competitive to other deals that were in the public domain at that point, whatever information we could rely upon. We hired professional accountants. We brought in underwriters. We just had a whole panoply of experts who would go in with us to make these presentations to show them that what we were proposing was not only competitive, but superior to the alternative.

The reason we were doing all this was because, as anybody who has followed Al Davis's saga knows, the NFL has some relocation guidelines. The guidelines have criteria within them that a team must satisfy in order to get permission to move. Among those criteria was whether you had an economic reason to move…whether your old situation wasn't sustainable, and your new situation was clearly superior. We wanted to rebut that notion by showing we had a more than viable, indeed competitive and superior, economic opportunity so the move would not be warranted. That's the form. That's the criteria that we were trying to satisfy—to show the NFL that Modell did not meet their own relocation guidelines.

So it's the litigation, it's the fans raising the fury all over the country—remember the *Sports Illustrated* cover with Art Modell sucker punching. That's going to live forever. That sentiment was out there—it was nationwide. It was catchy. Cleveland sort of became the poster child for the evils of franchise free agency, which was going on in the '90s.

Let me say that when I said the mayor of Cleveland formed a relationship with Commission Tagliabue, we never sued the NFL. There were certainly people second-guessing my legal strategy. There were people offering to do the work for the city for free, who said we needed to file an antitrust suit against the NFL, needed to attack the NFL. We thought, in the long run, we would be better off nurturing a partnership with the NFL rather than attacking them. The NFL began talking to us, with individuals. I was talking with their lawyers, with their executives, and they explained to us that they had a concern because of Al Davis. When Al Davis tried to move the first time, and the NFL said, "no," he sued them in federal court in Los Angeles on the basis that their relocation guidelines violated the antitrust laws, and he won. So the NFL guy said to us, "Even if we wanted to enforce our guidelines against Modell to stop the move, we don't want to get sued again, and lose again, on an antitrust theory."

The third strategy was legislative. They asked us to accompany them to the United States Congress. We did. The mayor testified twice before the antitrust sub-committee of the Senate Judiciary Committee, chaired by Strom Thurmond, about whether there was a good policy reason to give the National Football League an exception from the antitrust laws so that they could apply their relocation guidelines to stop this sort of thing. That was a memorable experience. I was with him, and I specifically remember going in there and wondering, "Why are these guys going to care about us? How are they going to identify with us?" Orrin Hatch, of Utah, was on the committee, for instance. What I didn't know—everyone associates Orrin Hatch with Utah—was that he grew up in Pittsburgh. From the table, he said, "Pittsburgh and Cleveland have a great rivalry. I don't think this is right. This is being taken from people. We need to restore this. We need to do something about this." Strom Thurmond—how's he going to relate to an African-American mayor coming in there? He said, from the table, "I had no idea that there are hundreds and hundreds of Brown Backers in the great state of South Carolina. I know, because I've heard from every one of them so we may have to do something about this."

Senator Arlen Specter, from Pennsylvania, understood the rivalry. They never did pass the legislation, but they received us very favorably. We eventually negotiated our deal before Congress had to act. We also appeared in front of the House of Representatives. There was a representative from Cleveland named Martin Hoke, who brought this before a House committee, and we appeared and testified there on the subject of franchise free agency and what the impact on cities was of these kinds of moves.

When I say we had a legislative strategy, we also had a state strategy where we were dealing with our own state legislature to look at ways they could pass laws that might assist us in our battle, all the way down to possibly trying to take the franchise by eminent domain, which is sort of the atomic bomb we never had to drop.

While it seems like a short period of time, I can tell you it was very intense, and a lot of activity, and a lot bumps, but by February 9, 1996, we had a tentative agreement with the National Football League, a memorandum of understanding, that provided that instead of going forward with the renovation…we would build a new Cleveland Browns Stadium. The league would share in the cost, there were sliding scales depending upon what the final cost was. We eventually got $65,000,000 out of the NFL towards approximately a $300,000,000 stadium. I said that we would negotiate a definitive lease agreement with the league that would then be assigned to a new owner of the Cleveland Browns. The name and colors and heritage would remain in Cleveland. Art Modell would be allowed to go, but he would leave the Cleveland Browns behind. We would negotiate a definitive lease agreement that would have all the revenue allocations, all the details of the lease that would then be assigned, "as is," to the new owner.

When a new owner was selected, there were other definitive agreements that would implement this memorandum of understanding, something called a franchise commitment agreement, a lease agreement, and certain assignment agreements. A trust would be created to hold the actual property for the three years it would take to build the stadium before the new team would come along. That, of course, had to pass political muster back here in Cleveland. It had to be approved by the City Council. There were some naysayers on the Council who felt that we shouldn't continue with this, that we should just let the team go and concentrate on other things. That led to a big political battle here in Cleveland. Ultimately, the mayor prevailed. He got the votes. We went forward and negotiated those definitive agreements with the league's lawyers and got them wrapped up. The time frame was June, 1996, when they were finally wrapped up. We spent a lot of time following the NFL owners around, going to their meetings because that's where the people we were negotiating would be. Remember we're traveling on a city budget, staying in the Sheraton down the road from the Ritz where they're meeting and staying. We got to know the guys on the NFL teams. They would let us eat their food. We'd hang out by the pool at the Ritz waiting to be able to talk with them. Then, we'd negotiate at all sorts of strange hours because we would get the time they had available. They were doing meetings from 8:00 a.m. to 8:00 p.m. They'd squeeze us in at lunch time, or they'd say, "Meet me here at 9:30 p.m." And, we'd negotiate from 9:30 p.m. to 12:30 a.m. and come back at six—that sort of thing. It was a memorable experience, but we got it done.

The deal, as I said, called for us to build a new stadium, which began a whole new undertaking in Cleveland, but we did it. We built a $300 million stadium. I was project counsel for the deal. The city held the contract itself. We had 28 prime contractors, and we got it done. The stadium opened in 1999. There's a whole 'nother saga involving the sweepstakes to own the team and how the different groups of business people vied to be the team owners. Ultimately, Al Lerner emerged. He was the guy that the mayor of Cleveland supported. Even though, Lerner was prior partners with Modell, and had played a role in helping Art Modell make connections in Maryland, at the same time, behind the scenes, Al Lerner was always talking to the city of Cleveland telling us the kinds of things we needed to present to the NFL so that the NFL would consider doing something for us. He had sat back and watched various groups compete and ultimately decided that he didn't see a group that he thought could run the team better than he could. He emerged with Carmen Policy, Bernie Kosar and Mayor Mike White on his side, and the shouting match was just about over at that point. He paid $630 million for the franchise. He gave us even more money toward the stadium construction, poured more of his own personal money into it…and, we're back playing football.

Not once, not ever, did we consider trying to get another team to move to Cleveland. We said we would never do to others what had been done to us. We never took a single step in that direction, notwithstanding the John Moag invitation and the phone number of Malcolm Glazer to do so.

One of the real ironic things here is that Art Modell was a good corporate citizen in Cleveland. He gave a lot of money to a lot of people and a lot of his time while he was here. He was a prince of a guy. He loved to be loved. In the end, that personality trait is what got him into the most trouble because he refused to put the gun to our head by saying, "I've got to have this or I'm going." He didn't want to be looked at as taking the money out of the taxpayers' pockets when we were talking about the $175 million renovation and how to pay for it. Instead, he became even more vilified, because he crept away in the night, and never gave us a chance.

Since the Browns are a private business, I think we will never know how deep the deck was, how much trouble he was in, and his perception that the only way he could get out of that hole was to go into a new situation. Remember, PSL's—Personal Seat Licenses—were brand new back then. That was a new concept. Everyone said that was a concept that would never fly in Cleveland, Ohio. It can only fly in places where you have a brand new stadium, and, ideally, even a brand new team. Cleveland fans who had been going to football games for generations, many of whom had the same seats for generations, were not going to suddenly pay several thousand dollars apiece for the right to then buy their season tickets. Probably, part of his thinking was that the PSL revenues at a new Baltimore Stadium were going to be the infusion of cash that would float him that was just an impossibility in Cleveland. He also did not want to be the subject of debate about whether we raise everybody's taxes.

I'd heard that Paul Brown had a $30 million inheritance tax in Cincinnati, and Modell did not want his kids to be in that position. The other thing I should mention is that the timing of the announcement in Baltimore was no accident. Remember, it was the first Monday in November, so it was the day before the tax referendum in Cleveland was on the ballot, the 'sin' tax that was going to raise the taxes to come up with our $175 million. No question in my mind, that press conference was designed to sabotage that 'sin' tax because once he makes the announcement he's going to Baltimore, people would say, "What the hell. I'm not gonna tax myself. He's not even going to be here." That would then disable us from being able to say that we had the money to pay for what we were promising him. The voters in Cuyahoga County turned out and passed that tax at a level of about 76-percent in favor to stand behind it. We collected it, and we used it for the new stadium instead of for renovations to the old, and it's still in place.

The naming rights to the stadium went to the owner. That's part of what we gave up in our effort to entice them to do this deal. The owner of the team has the rights to sell the name of the stadium. It's only because Al Lerner was civic minded that he didn't sell them, and he named it the Cleveland Browns Stadium. Randy Lerner is continuing that. You know, we could be the Chiquita Banana Stadium. We put a few strings on it. It couldn't be cigarettes or alcohol, but they have the right, today, to sell it. They just haven't done it because they're civic minded. The Lerner family is a part of Cleveland.

The new stadium has a
Win Chill factor.

HOW ABOUT A SHOT OF THE TRUTH? MAKE IT A BOTTLE, I'M BUYIN' !

HARRY WRIGHT

Except for four years in the military in the mid-'60s, Harry Wright has spent all of his 60 years in Cleveland. His youth football team practiced on the same field as the Browns. He has a decidedly different, yet interesting, view of the Browns.

W e didn't get to talk to the players on the practice field, but I remember that we would stand bug-eyed as they walked past. Sometimes, if we got to practice early, the Browns team would just be coming off the field, and we would get to see them. Sometimes, some of them would say, "hello, kid." Because we knew their numbers, we knew who each one was. It was just the idea that we were on that same field. They used to let us use some of their equipment. They would leave the tackling dummy and some of the cones out there. The fact that we could play with or touch some of the equipment the Browns players had used was just unbelievable.

Growing up in Cleveland—I have to say this because it's part of the memory—growing up as a black kid in a black neighborhood and listening to my father and my uncles was that I don't think the Browns ever got the publicity or the recognition of how much they meant to, not only our black community, but to blacks throughout the country. The Browns were to football what the Dodgers were to baseball.

The Dodgers had the first black player that integrated baseball. They never talked about it in football—it's been obscured, but the Browns were the first team to have black players in the All-America Conference. What people don't understand is there were blacks throughout the country that instantaneously became Browns fans the way a lot of blacks in the South became Dodger fans. They would sit around their radios just like they did for baseball. They wanted to know about what the Cleveland Browns were doing. It was a national thing, but it

wasn't talked about back then because it wasn't considered important to the media.

I believe the first year, the only two black players in the old American
Conference were Bill Willis and Marion Motley. They were the only
two blacks in the entire league. That's one of the reason why you've
got a lot of old black men, most of them dead now, who always had a
soft spot in their hearts for the Browns because of what they stood for
at the beginning. The Browns didn't come in later on and get on the
black bandwagon, I'll always give credit to Paul Brown for not going
with the stereotype of, "Okay, I know they're going to want these players and, if they're doing it, I'm going to do." He said, "To hell with
that," and he started out with black stars. He always had black stars.

Jim Brown had a lot to do with that, too. Jim Brown was the opposite.
It had nothing to do with their character. It was the stage they were
on. They told Jackie Robinson to be quiet—to "take it," even though
he wanted to speak out. Jim Brown comes along, and now he talks
about all this stuff—the racism, the double-standard. He was the first
open voice of a black star that said, "I'm going to talk about all this
stuff—don't think I'm going to shut up." That, in a way, is the reason
why he's loved, but he's not "love-loved"….

When the Browns left town, I analyzed what went on. I've lived in
Cleveland all my life so I know how the politics here go. What people
presented to me in the paper and the media and what the politicians presented was that Art Modell was this bad, greedy guy. He just hung them
out to dry for more money. When I researched it, what I found out was
nothing was farther from the truth, and they're still hiding it today.

The truth of the matter is that they had planned to ditch the Browns and
move them off the lakefront and get them out of downtown. They
didn't care where they went—they just thought they were going to
leave downtown. They wanted that property for a convention center,
which they still haven't built today. You don't do all that building if
you're not going to build a convention center. The reason why they
haven't built one is they never envisioned what was going to happen.

When Art Modell realized they were just screwing him around and
spending money on other places, he did the one thing they didn't

think he was going to do—move the team. At the time, he was in financial ruin trying to keep that place open, and with the promise that they were going to bail him out when it came. They never did. They thought that with the hold they had on him because of his financial situation, that he would just sell the team. Well, he wasn't that type of a man. He leaves. When I realize all of this, I thought there was no reason for me to hide the truth or to give up a life-long attachment to my football team. They didn't leave on their own—they were pushed out. I decided to continue to root for the 'now' Baltimore Ravens. I never missed football once. I stuck with the Ravens.

I've never seen the Ravens play, but I bought the NFL Ticket. I did it. My son bought me a computer the year after they left, and he showed me how to go on the Internet. So, with the Internet and with the satellite dish, it was as if they never left. I could read the *Baltimore Sun* on the Internet—the same as reading the Cleveland *Plain Dealer* every day…and I could watch them play every Sunday. The only thing that changed was that the team left town, but as far as my attachment to the team, nothing really changed. In fact, it's better now than it was before. With the old Browns, if the game wasn't sold out, you didn't get to see the game.

The front office that we once had here—the front office everyone hated and thought wasn't that good—we ran out of town and called bad names. Belichick and part of the front office—the scouting and personnel guys— ended up in New England. The other side of that, Modell and Ozzie Newsome, ended up in Baltimore. Guess what—between those two groups, they won four Super Bowls. How ironic is that? Plus, Kirk Ferentz goes to Iowa and Nick Saban to LSU.

When you're on a bad cycle, whatever can go wrong will go wrong. It's not bad luck—it's that you miss your opportunities. It's like the guy who plays the same lotto number every day. He forgets to play it one day, and it comes up. Well, you can't blame Lady Luck. You're not likely to ever get it back again because you missed your one opportunity. Don't blame Lady Luck.

I understand now that since they inadvertently ran them out of town and didn't want them back, they tried to lure Ozzie Newsome back here to run the organization. Well, hindsight is 20-20, not to realize how good some of those people were and not to have given them a chance. The other thing was that for some reason when Art Modell bought the Browns in '62, two years later, he fired Paul Brown because he didn't think the team was progressing the way they should be. People here never forgave him for that even though the Browns put out very good teams over the course of the next 10 years. Even though it turned out to be the right move, because the Browns won a championship two years after they fired him, that still didn't please the most fans.

There is a revision of history here of what was the 'good' Browns and what was the 'bad' Browns. If anything is related to Art Modell, it wasn't that "good," but I was here. There was no Browns Backers before Art Modell got here. It grew to be the largest group of any group in the National Football League, but, for some reason, they won't equate that to what Art Modell did. To this day, many people have their own slanted view of the Cleveland Browns. You've got to get people who know what they're doing, whether they have any attachment with the Cleveland Browns or not. People want to bring Bernie Kosar back for the front office, and bring Jim Brown back to do this and that. Aw, come on. You can't. It's gone. Great memories, but you can't keep reliving it.

I was a Browns fan right up until 1995. The irony of it is, people keep saying to me, "How could you change your allegiance?" Well, I didn't change—you guys changed. The current Browns are nothing but an expansion team. I kept telling them, "Look, the National Football League did this to appease you guys because you guys wanted to go home again." For them to say to leave the name, the colors and the history, there is no history with this team! You can't attach the history of the Cleveland Browns to an expansion team which happens to have the colors and have the name, but that's it. The history followed them to Baltimore.

LOYALTY OUTSIDE THE WALLET

FRED REICHHELD

Fred Reichheld was raised a rabid Browns fan in Parma. After graduating Harvard in the early '70s, Fred became one of America's premier business writers and speakers, focusing on loyalty. His next book, Good Profits, Bad Profits, *is due out next year. He resides with his wife, Karen, in Wellesley, Massachusetts and summers in his incredibly beautiful home in Falmouth on Cape Cod.*

W hen I went to Harvard College, I figured that no one would care about the Browns. It was astonishing the number of Browns fans I bumped into, not just from Ohio, but classmates whose families lived all over North America. The Browns are something more than a sports team. There's something about a basic set of principles that that team stood for—hard work, not flashy overpaid stars, but it was teamwork, the highest standards of excellence and a lot of people connected to those basic ideas.

My first book, *The Loyalty Effect*, was with Harvard Business School Press and eventually became a *Business Week* best seller, It focused on this idea that I got from the Cleveland Browns, among other places, that loyalty is fundamentally important to a good life and to financial success. That argument was so radical and counter-intuitive to most people in this day and age that they almost started putting my book in the fiction section in bookstores.

When I was on my promotional tours to promote the loyalty effect, I recognized that there was a special opportunity in Cleveland and northeastern Ohio. Very shortly before the book came out, Art Modell announced that he was moving the Browns to Baltimore, which was just a crushing blow. There was something ethically and morally wrong, and I couldn't put my finger on it. It was incredible how many people, not just in the United States, but around the world that this really touched a raw nerve for them. There was something wrong.

When I came back to give my tours, I told my publisher we ought to have a special little label designed for the cover of the book, an orange one with brown print. It would say, "Art Modell will hate this book." We put it on all the books that went to Cleveland and, sure enough, sales were enormous. People would come to bookstores and ask me to sign the book while they told me some story about the Browns.

Everybody is loyal to something. Loyalty has fallen out of favor these days. What I'm convinced of is that it continues to make sense—my guess is that the Browns made enormously bad decisions economically by giving up or weakening that bond of loyalty that was so strong between the fans and the community and the team itself.

Leaders have a responsibility, ultimately, to embody the values that they believe in, that they are loyal to. Loyalty isn't so much to an individual or even to a team logo, it's to a set of ideas or principles that are worthy of self-sacrifice. Tom Brady left millions on the table on his recently signed contract—that is self-sacrifice. Loyalty is all about putting principles and relationships ahead of your own short-term selfish interests. It's that basic idea that some things are worth sacrifice that creates greatness, not just in sports, but throughout society, and including business. Most senior executives have forgotten that. There are a lot of executives who say, like most of those other quarterbacks in the NFL, "Hey, the market is peaking. The market says I should make a ton of money even if that demotivates the team, I deserve it." Well, that's what happened with most teams. Somehow, Brady and a number of the other players on the New England Patriots have seen that there is definitely more to life than maximizing your short-term compensation. Loyalty is about treating people right and making them want to invest in a relationship which is the basis of growth and real success.

Values and ideals are what people get really excited about. Those are the things that are worth sacrifice. The people on the teams that embody those grab that power. The Celtics, the Browns, the Green Bay Packers—they all stood for something really important, not just to the game. They stood for vital ideals and loyalty to those ideals made as much sense as it does in the Armed Forces. It's treating people right.

No team ever has had more loyal fans than the Cleveland Browns. That makes me proud to be a Cleveland native.

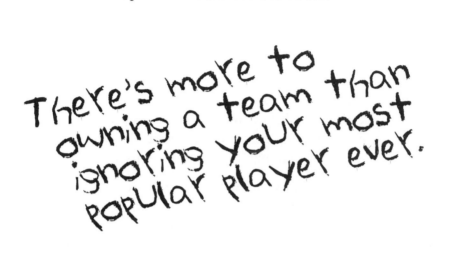

There's more to owning a team than ignoring your most popular player ever.

Flush twice— it's a long way to Baltimore!

UPON FURTHER REVIEW:

I'm not an Art Modell basher. The guy did an awful lot for the league. The entire time he owned the team, they put a good product on the field. In his defense, I really think the thing that put him over the edge was the Robbie family, who owned the **DOLPHINS.** When Joe Robbie died, his family had to sell that team because they couldn't afford the taxes. There are merits of truth in that. He had a big impact on the league. He had a lot to do with television contracts. He had a lot to do with the progressive rule changes. I don't have any faults with Art. He did what he felt was in the best interests of his family. I don't think he showed a lot of class, but, the fact of the matter is, he's gone, and we have a new team…and that's fine.

——**DON DAVIE**, San Antonio, Marshall High Graduate

There are those who say Modell was not treated well by the politicians in Cleveland, and that's why he did it. The only good thing I can tell you about Modell is that a friend of mine is the son of a former PR guy for the Browns. When Modell did what he did, this guy was about to retire. Modell doubled his pension money so this friend of mine has always had high regard for Modell.

——**MARSHALL BASKIN**, Los Angeles

Art Modell was such a part of the city. He feels that he can't go back to the city for risk of his life. It's hard to picture how someone who put 35 years of their life into something, be such a big part of that, can walk away from it. If you look at what he was before, his ties to the city are kind of amazing. There's a whole wing to the Heart Center in the Cleveland Clinic where you walk in and see a huge mural of him because he was such a big donor.

——**STEVEN SOLOMON**, 45, Fairfax, Virginia

The guy spearheading the opposition of Art Modell going into the Hall is Tony Grossi, the Browns beat writer for the *Cleveland Plain*

> **The undefeated 1972 DOLPHINs (17-0) beat only two teams with records over .500. They were actually three-point underdogs to the Redskins in Super Bowl VII.**

Dealer. He's the one, as the stories go anyway, that each year when Modell has been put on the list, he gets to lobby as the media representative for Cleveland. He gets to lobby against Modell's induction into the Hall. It'll probably go through once they don't have to deal with the issue of Art getting up on the podium in Canton—just a stone's throw away from Cleveland. It was interesting when all this happened, Modell was actually saying to the media that he feels bad that he can't go back to Cleveland and watch his team play when they go back to play the Browns. Some of my friends in Atlanta just don't understand that. I say to them—at the time the Smith family still owned the Falcons—"Well, do you know what Rankin Smith looks like?" They say, "Well…no…I don't." I say, "Well, that's the thing. Everybody in Cleveland knows what Art Modell looks like." There are only a couple of airports where he could fly in, Cleveland Hopkins and Burke Lakefront. There are people at each airport who would know that was Art Modell. Trust me, inside of an hour, it would be all over the local radio stations that Modell is in town. Some nut would bring a gun to the stadium and try to shoot him. There's no doubt. There are no metal detectors at the gates. There are people who are just that passionate and, unfortunately, that misguided that they would take it out like that.

In 1995, the rumors hit. They had been erratically flying for a year or more, but nobody took any of them seriously, they just thought people were making stuff up. The rumors really hit on a Friday, and we had a game in Cleveland on Sunday. We were sitting there with about 40 or 50 Browns fans. A big shot from **NBC** was there covering the game. If I remember right, his son worked for Modell so he had some inside information. There, before the game, they asked him, "What's the deal?" He said, "It's a done deal. The Browns are moving to Baltimore after this season." I remember just sitting there in complete shock at what I was hearing. I thought, "It just

> **NBC** Sports President Dick Ebersol, recently paid **$50,000** at a charity auction to have Carly Simon tell him the name of the subject person in her song, "You're So Vain." Only Simon, Ebersol and that person know the identity, rumored to be Warren Beatty, James Taylor or Mick Jagger.

can't be." That following Monday, Modell made the announcement there in Baltimore. I will always remember him standing up there saying, "You know it all comes down to a simple proposition—I had no choice." The reality is that the guy was such a terrible businessman. He controlled both sides of his stadium lease. That's the irony of this whole thing—him saying he couldn't make any money in that stadium. But, the way the transaction was set up, the city of Cleveland leased that stadium to something called Cleveland Stadium Corporation which was Art Modell. The Cleveland Stadium Corporation then had a lease with the Browns and the Indians. The Browns always got preferential treatment in everything. Cleveland Stadium Corp. leased it for next to nothing from the city, and the Browns paid a ton in rent to Cleveland Stadium Corp., and they still didn't fix the stadium up. There's some of the larceny that's going on all over the country with sports teams trying to get cities to build multimillion dollar stadiums. As much as I like the new stadium, it certainly lacks some of the character that the old place had. I was there for the first game back in '99. I remember walking in and thinking, "This is too nice. This isn't supposed to be in Cleveland. We're supposed to have that *old place.*"

A book has been published recently about how the new Browns were set up to fail when they returned to the league. Apparently, there were some owners who were saying, "Hey, the Browns franchise is worth a half-a-billion dollars." They were going to sell that team to whoever ponied up the most money. They didn't really care who would make the best owner.

There was an NFL owners meeting in Atlanta, and they bused several loads of people from Cleveland down to Atlanta to picket outside the hotel where the owners were staying and to have a big rally presenting these huge petitions that had been signed all over the Cleveland area. We got a lot of the Browns fans from the Atlanta area to show up. They also bused a bunch of people down, including John Thompson—or, Big Dawg, as he is known—the guy you always see on TV, the huge guy that sits out in the Dawg Pound. He's a nice guy, and I had a chance to talk to him for a few minutes. He's actually a computer supply salesman. People get on him and say he's such a publicity-seeking, glory-hound. I said, "No, how many 450-pound guys do you meet?" He's easy for the cameras to spot, and that's how he ends up on TV all the time. I got to meet him and met the mayor and thanked them. I said, "I don't live in Cleveland anymore, but even when I lived up there, I wasn't in the city limits so I couldn't have voted for you, but I appreciate what you are doing." He grinned when I said, "And, that's coming from a **REPUBLICAN**—to a liberal Democrat." We had a nice rally and had a party afterwards at our Browns bar. I got to sit down and have a beer and eat chicken wings with Greg Pruitt, who was one of my all-time favorite Browns players. It was a very emotional time for all of us. Our team was gone, and we didn't know whether we were going to get a team back, at that point, or not. But, we weren't going to go down without a fight.

We have people who were organized over the Internet, which was not nearly as big as it is now and not as many people had access to it. Fax drives would be organized where we would send faxes to all the other NFL team offices. Several of the teams ended up changing their fax numbers. We tried to tell Browns fans to do it at night so we're not tying up their fax line during the day. "Set your fax machine to send it at night." I sent out hundreds from home, long-distance calls all over the country letting them know that we didn't want a relocated team in Cleveland. We wanted a new team. We wanted an expansion team even though, at this point, we would have thought we'd have a better team by now. We wanted our own team, our own identity. We didn't want to get our team back at somebody else's expense.

There were a couple of teams at the time who were squawking about relocating. There was talk about Tampa Bay before the Glazers bought them. I remember hearing something about Atlanta considering relocating, but I don't think that ever really went anywhere. That was just the Rankin Smith's way to extort money out of the city of Atlanta. I heard a little bit about the **Vikings**. It was a difficult time. I did not watch a single NFL game in the three years that the Browns

> **Richard Nixon gave the eulogy at Woody Hayes' funeral….
> Joe Namath was the only athlete on President Nixon's
> famous "enemies list."**

> **The Minnesota Vikings have not been in the Super Bowl
> since the Lou and Bud Grant era.**

didn't play—'96 through '98. I'm more of a Browns fan than I am an NFL fan so if the Browns aren't playing, I usually don't watch. These days, if it's a game that would affect our division or if we happen to be in a playoff hunt, I'll watch that, but other than that, I don't watch NFL games at all unless my team is playing.

——SAM CHAMBERS, co-director of Atlanta Browns Backers

The only time my son ever saw me cry was the day after the announcement the team was moving. Kevin Byrne, the vice-president, is a very close friend. We talk weekly all year long. He said right before the '95 season, "We've got problems with the city on the stadium." I said, "Oh, Kevin, bull----, everything will get squared away." He just kind of blew it off, and I blew it off. I forgot all about it.

I can tell you when I know Art made the decision to move. It was that season, 1995, we had a Monday night game with the Bills. I flew back to go to the game. The next day was the first Indians play-off game in 40 years. **Monday Night Football** was born in Cleveland in 1970—first game ever. When you had a Monday Night Football game in Cleveland, it was *the event* of the decade. The city shut down. It was unbelievable. I got off the airplane, and I did not see one mention of the Browns. I picked up the *Plain Dealer* at the newsstand at the airport. I had to turn to page 16D to find that there was even a Monday Night Football game. The Indians were the front page, and there was a special supplement. I turned on the radio in the car—it was all Indians, Indians, Indians. I'm thinking, "Art Modell has been this team's landlord for the last 30 years, and now when he gets his chance to shine on Monday Night Football, he is second class. He's second banana in his own town." I'm thinking this is when Art said, probably to David, "I'm gone." I'm convinced. When everybody hated Art, I loved Art. I was his biggest defender. I thought he just cared too much, tried too much.

> John Lennon's death was first reported to the nation by Howard Cosell on **MONDAY NIGHT FOOTBALL**...In 1999, Monday Night Football became the longest-running prime-time entertainment series ever, breaking a tie with Walt Disney at 29 years...Even when Monday Night Football ratings hit an all-time low, it still ranks in the top five during prime time for the entire year.

Of course, I joined in the bandwagon. I was very active here in Washington trying to get as much activity as we could to get the team reborn. I did everything I could, spent the better part of a year working towards it. I've now forgiven Art, certainly. But, I don't think I'll ever forgive David. I don't think I could handle that. That was the hardest thing. The two worst sights were seeing, and I'm a huge Democrat, Democrat Governor Glendening gloating up there with Modell with the 'Baltimore Browns' banner the day of their first press conference. That sickened me so much. And then seeing David on the Today Show the day after they won the Super Bowl. Those were the two worst days. Since then, everything else is fine.

———ROGER COHEN, 53, season-ticketholder, Washington, D. C.

I was suspicious of Modell from the first day. Here's this New Yorker coming to town—why did he buy the Cleveland Browns? One of the reasons he did was he thought he was buying the "New York Yankees of football." That's what he said to somebody at the time. Really, if you make a lot of money at business, and he hadn't made all that much money, he managed to come up with 200,000 or 300,000 dollars of his own—I'm not even sure it was his own—and then he got investors and financed all the rest. I was suspicious of him from the get-go. Really, if a guy makes a lot of money, is very, very prominent in business, you don't know what he looks like, you don't go to him for quotations unless you're from Business Week. He doesn't get his picture in the paper all the time. He isn't getting quoted on TV all the time. I felt very strongly that that was a large part of Modell's motivation. He wanted to be very visible. He wanted to flex his muscle. He wanted to buy celebrity…and he did. He also ruined a terrific franchise.

In fairness to him, he did a lot of good things for the city while he was there over thirty years, and in a single moment, he dashed all of that for money. He is totally persona non grata in Cleveland, I'll guarantee you. That's a shame. It turns out, by the way, that he wasn't such a shrewd businessman. How do you get in the hole owning the Cleveland Browns that filled their stadium every week? How do you come out of that losing money? In that era, the players weren't even demanding the million dollar salaries. He gets bailed out by the deal in Baltimore. What happens after two or three years—he's in a money squeeze again, and he has to sell out. We all just wish he would have sold at the time he moved them. We're still trying to recover from that. We're building a team from scratch. It's got the same name. It's got the same uniforms. We pull for them the same, but they haven't attained anything even vaguely resembling the old Cleveland Browns yet. I certainly hope they do.

——**EMIL DAVIDSON**, 68, Los Angeles

At the Green Bay game, Art Modell announced, prematurely, that the team was leaving. We had told him that if was going to announce that, announce it at the last game 'cause the fans are going to lose their minds. But, he wanted to go ahead and announce it then. I guess he was getting pressure from the media or somebody because the public relations director, Kevin Byrne, kept asking him not to announce it. But, he went ahead and announced it on a Saturday, and we played Green Bay the next day. After he made the announcement, we all had a briefing because we figured it was going to be squirrelly out there.

I doubled up the crew and contacted our courtesy squad to help in watching our players come on the field and go off the field. And, we had to monitor the crowd—in case somebody tried to throw something, we wanted to be able to identify him and get him out of the stadium. I told the men, "The bleacher people are not going to come out. The Dawg Pound people are not going to come out. These people respect the game." One thing I could say about the Dawg Pound is that they were fans—true fans. They wouldn't do anything to take away from the demeanor of the game. If anyone was going to come out, they would do it at the last game.

I felt the problem would be at the home plate end of the stadium where the end zone is. At that time, the Browns and Indians played in the same stadium. The pitchers mound was in that part of the field. By that time in the season, they had removed the pitchers mound. I didn't feel like they would come from the sides because the fence was so high that we would be able to spot them before they made it onto the field. Sure enough, at the end of the third quarter, going into the fourth quarter, the fans started coming out of the stands. I was watching my crew do their job. As people would come out, they were able to catch them just before they got out on the field.

——**CURTIS FRANKLIN**, 1995 Field Coordinator, Game Day Ops

You live and die with the Browns. I still can't believe they left the city. That was just bizarre. I had just moved back and got the season tickets again, and I heard all these rumblings that Modell was going to sell the team, and he was going to move it. I said, "If I know anything, I know the Browns would NEVER move." Not this team—with the backing that it has and its fans! Then I was at work, and somebody came in and said they heard it on the radio. I still thought that was ridiculous that "there was no way…. No, the Browns can't leave Cleveland." Then I ran out to my car and turned on the radio. I sat there when I heard them say it, and I just started crying. I could not believe it. Nobody could ever have written that script.

The team is so tied to the city. This is a blue-collar town. Football has always been popular here. The character of the team seemed to fit the town. There was nothing flashy. The team was pretty much built on running backs and just grinding it out, and a tough defense that really meshed with the city. That's why the new team really hasn't caught on yet. A lot of it is because of the way, when the new team came back, they didn't embrace the old. They wanted to create their own identity, but they made a big mistake. That's such a shame because there's a huge backing, especially with Bernie Kosar. That guy could run for governor, and he'd probably get elected. To shut him out was so silly. He could have done a lot to help that transition.

To me, everything has changed. The new stadium is really nice, but it doesn't have the character of the old one. There was something about it. It was a little rough and tumble, but it was more conducive to the Browns fans. Not that they were that rowdy. People really exaggerate what happens down there. It just was different. It's because the team, too, doesn't have the same excitement as the old team did. That move really took a lot out of the team—even just watching is not the same. We lost a lot when they left. It's starting to come back a little bit.

———JO ANN MATOUSEK, conference manager, Cleveland

We'd heard leaks in the press that the team might be leaving Cleveland, but, to a man, I think we all sat there and went, "No way. I don't know where this information is coming from, but there's just no way the Browns will ever leave Cleveland." Until it actually happened, I think everybody was in denial. I can't think of one person who bought into it and said, "Yeah, it's going to happen, for sure." The local TV stations here came to my house right after the move was announced because they knew I was a huge Browns fan. They asked me to get four or five fans out of our group and have them at my house so they could interview us. One of our guys that we call Top Dawg did break down right on the camera. He couldn't help himself. He just couldn't even bring himself to talk to them. He was never ashamed of it—it just came out. That's how much people love this team. There was no way I would have followed the team after they moved to Baltimore. To this day, they're my most despised team in football. They took Pittsburgh's place. They took Dallas's place. They took Denver's place.

—DAN JARVIS, Albuquerque, New Mexico

I'd like to go on record that Art Modell can rot and die in hell. If there ever would be the travesty in justice that he would somehow be inducted into the Hall of Fame, I will be one of the thousands who will go down to Canton and block the doors. He took the money in this good, great city for many, many years when there was an inferior product on the field, i.e. the Forest Gregg, Nick Skorich days of the '70s. We *still* sold out that stadium. We lived and died with them, and we filled his coffers. Through his own mismanagement…. And, he got jealous when the Indians got the sweetheart deal to open up Gateway, which became Jacobs Field. He could have got in on the ground floor. It was his own fault. For him, with all of his subterfuge and all that other crap that he pulled in the deal on the tarmac of the airport. It was just the most despicable act of betrayal. I said on the Jim Rome show, national talk radio, that he and his ------- son can rot in hell. He lost all credibility and integrity with this city. I just find him a despicable person. Any good that he did in helping Rozelle in the early years getting the TV contract and all that he might have done, to me, was totally obliterated by his duplicitous actions. He's a disingenuous, contemptible human being. Anything that comes out of his mouth, to me, holds absolutely no water.

When the Ravens won the Super Bowl, there were still remnants of the players who were here. I remember calling Jim Rome the day after the Super Bowl. I said, "Scoreboard! You won. We, as Clevelanders, can't take that away from you. Having said that, when we win, we'll do it right. We'll do it with players we are proud of, not people who are under investigation as being accomplices of double murder or whatever. We'll have a coach we can be proud of. We'll have an owner that we can be proud of. So, when we finally, finally hoist that **Lombardi** Trophy in Public Square or in front of the new Browns Stadium, we will shed tears of joy, relief, and will truly embrace this team as our own."

———<u>JOHN KARLIAK</u>, Cleveland

When I was in Indianapolis, I remember verbatim where I was and exactly what was happening. I was heading from Indianapolis to Richmond, Indiana on business. I was just about to get to Richmond, and there was a news flash that came on the talk radio station I was listening to—they were preparing to go "live" to Governor Glendening, Maryland's governor. I was driving, and he was announcing that the Cleveland Browns were leaving Cleveland. I was driving in my car and listening to the first announcement. They used the words, "Baltimore Browns." I pulled off…here I am, a 38-year-old male hearing them say, "Cleveland Browns, now Baltimore Browns. Governor Glendening to speak momentarily. We're cutting live."

I got off at the first exit I reached, pulled into a Burger King parking lot, and put the car in park. I just sat there listening to this on AM radio. I couldn't even drive. I was like, "Wait a minute. What?" I just sat there in Richmond, **Indiana** and cried…like a little baby…I couldn't believe it.

After that, all is good. The interesting thing is that when I was in Indianapolis, living there, during the hiatus, one of my accounts was actually the Indianapolis Colts. We did the telecommunications for the Irsays residence and also the Indianapolis Colts practice facility. A friend of mine was an athletic trainer, so I started rooting for the Colts a

> Vince **LOMBARDI** never said, "Winning isn't everything, it's the only thing." That line was originally said by John Wayne in the 1953 movie, *Trouble Along The Way*. Lombardi said, "Winning isn't everything, but trying to win is!"

> By winning percentage, Indiana ranks 12th in all-time Big Ten football standings behind the University of Chicago.

little bit, since I had no one else to root for. But, it never really was the same. I didn't *have* to watch the Colts on Sunday. Not only that, I didn't read about anything in the NFL. *It didn't matter.* Who cares what Pittsburgh did? What Houston did? It didn't matter. It was funny. It was like the hockey lockout. I like the Dallas Stars, and I enjoy going to some hockey games, but they were gone, so I didn't look for anything. It was a very similar situation with the time when the Browns left.

————RICK RIZZO, biotechnic executive

During the three years the Browns were away, I just gave up on football—my house was never so clean. It was a terrible time. No nothing. I would look at a score now and then, but didn't feel a thing. I just waited. It was rough. It was very hard. So many people just could not believe that it would ever happen. I know the Steelers are our rival, but I like Steeler fans—they're good fans. They're dedicated to their team like we are. When Modell made the move, there were only two teams that said, "No, this is wrong. You shouldn't do this." It was the Pittsburgh Steelers and the Buffalo Bills. That's why there's always a special bond between them. When the Browns weren't there, Buffalo invited a lot of the Browns Backers up to their games, and I know a lot of people who went during that time. There's a Steeler Backer club here in Tennessee, too, but it's not as big as ours. They contacted us and expressed condolences It was like a loss in the family. Usually they don't call us too much, but at that time, they did. It was a sense of loss for them, also.

And, we have a team here, the Titans, and we Browns fans *lost* one of our own—he became Titanized! This was terrible. I remember when I found out about it. Someone said, "Norm's become a Titan fan." I said, "No. He can't do that." I wanted to call in people and have an intervention, or something. He said he just couldn't wait, and we were devastated. But, he was the only one we lost.

The rest of us just waited 'cause we knew when Art left, he left the colors there, he left the traditions, the records, the team name. We just hung in there until they came back. That's a lot about our loyalty. What I like about the Browns, too, is the sense of tradition. They are a very traditional team. They have the same helmets. Everybody says they're ugly, but I think they're beautiful. They don't have flashy uniforms. When you go to the games, you don't have the **dancing girl cheerleaders**. It's football. It's traditional football. When we see other Browns fans, we have that sense of tradition and that loyalty, 'cause we all hung in there. That's why it's family. That's why we're who we are. That's why there's so many of us.

——MARILISSA SALYER, Nashville

When we heard that the team had been moved, there was absolute disbelief. We played the **Chargers** that year in San Diego, and a bunch of us went down as a group. There was a picture of me in the newspapers holding a sign that said, "Dear Santa, Art was bad." I was shocked and had a lot of anger. I also was privy to some of the inside information and knew why Art was taking the team and what was really going on. There was a lot of greed, money-wise. To me, that's all it'll ever be—it was all for the money. None of the Browns fans that I know of became Ravens fans. I do battle with some people out here who were Rams fans and still want to be Rams fans. I just don't see it. I don't see how, after Georgia Frontiere took their team away from here, I could never be a Rams fan. And, I can never be a Ravens fan.

The year before the Browns left—I hadn't been back in a year or so—I really just took my time to look around there in the old stadium. I didn't know why I did it, but I'm really glad I took that little part of extra time at the end of the game.

——KEVIN WHITE, 43, California resident 25 years

The Dawg Pound has changed a lot. It was really cool that the bleachers were where the blue-collar people sat. There was an awful lot of spirit out there. You could almost break your hand getting high-fived, after we'd score, by somebody you've never seen in your life. The

> When the Dallas Cowboys **CHEERLEADERS** started in 1972, each earned $15 per game—the same amount they receive today.

> The **CHARGERS** were originally the Los Angeles Chargers in 1960, the first year of the AFL. They were owned by Barron Hilton of the Hilton Hotel chain. Hilton owned the Carte Blanche credit card company and named the team Chargers to promote the credit card.

tradition just got on 'almost' steroids there when it got to the Dawg Pound. Now, for the Dawg Pound, they're charging $75 a ticket and a thousand bucks for the privilege of buying them. I don't see the same spiritedness there used to be. I just don't think that people who make that kind of money and can afford these games will make fools out of themselves like we did.

During the three years they were gone, I couldn't go with another team. For all the years, I've been a fan, the only teams I would pull for was the Cleveland Browns and whoever was playing Pittsburgh. There, for a three-year period of time—and please don't tell any of my friends—I actually was pulling for the Ravens because they were the old Browns. I was really happy to see them win the Super Bowl. Actually, I wanted it to be a 20-20 tie with one second left to go in the game, and wanted to have to kick a field goal that would land on the crossbar and Modell have a stroke, not knowing whether it went over or not. If you don't hate Modell, you can't really be a Browns fan. That guy paid three or four million bucks for a team that's now worth three hundred million, and how can he complain about not being well compensated? Cleveland was a fool for not building a stadium for him. That old stadium was a depression-era project—it had to be almost 70 years old. It was probably okay for baseball, but it wasn't built for football. If you really wanted to see a football game, the place to go was the Akron Rubber Bowl. It would only seat about 30,000. I saw an exhibition game there once, and it was almost like Arena Football—it was that tight....As far as I'm concerned, the Cleveland Browns have had the best sports announcers of all time. Before Gib Shanley, we had Bill McColgan, who was tremendous. Shanley was the best. My favorite line of all time was, "Pitch to Brown. He's got a convoy out in front of him."

——BOB TRACY, 58, Washington, D. C.

During 1948 to the present, when my father was alive, we always went to Browns games. My father got season tickets in 1953. In 1962, Art Modell came to Cleveland and became a very close friend of my father's. My father actually made no-interest loans to Modell. Through that, my father got season tickets right on the 50-yard line, first row.

Modell would come to our house for dinner…. I found a promissory note for a $15,000 personal loan in my father's office one day. Art Modell even ended up dating some of my girlfriends. He was quite a playboy. He and my father were men about town. My mother died when I was a freshman at University of Miami so by this time, my father was a swinging bachelor.

Art Modell never, never knew much about the game of football. He had the idea, and he was driven, and he knew what he was doing—did very well with the television contracts. He had his hands on everything. He ended up firing the *legendary* Paul Brown. He fired him when the Cleveland newspapers were on a strike. Paul Brown *never* forgave Art Modell. He got a good payoff, and then Blanton Collier did win a world championship.

Art got a lot of money when he went to Baltimore, but he mismanaged it. I don't know if it affected his personal worth so much, but that's what happened with the Browns in Cleveland. Then, he got in the same kind of mess in Baltimore, even with all that money and the new stadium. He ended up selling to Steven Bisciotti. Modell's son, David, had been some kind of a vice-president in charge of, maybe, towels and jock straps. They spent thousands of dollars monthly on cigars. Bisciotti owns the Ravens, and David Modell is now out of that organization.

—————ROBERT BRENNER, 66, Shaker Heights, "Hurricane Bob"

Butch Davis was seriously injured today while changing positions.

Chapter 5

Today We Ride

On the Road Again

WASHINGTON: FIRST IN WAR FIRST IN PEACE LAST IN THE NFL EAST

SCOTT BROWN

Scott Brown grew up in Painesville, northeast of Cleveland. He is vice-president of a Washington, D. C. international organization serving Jewish college students around the world.

My family had season tickets for the Browns games. Early on, we sat on about the 25-yard line behind one of the famous poles in the old Cleveland Browns Stadium. Then later on, my family had upper deck seats on the 45-yard line. These were passed on to us by a friend who passed away—we just lucked out there.

When the Browns played Pittsburgh in the playoff game a couple of years ago, I was in Israel helping to lead a group of students. My youngest daughter was home watching the game 'cause she was real interested in it, too. Also, we had a deal where I would call her and get updates. I was at a huge, huge mega-event with thousands of students from around the world. I could hardly hear my own voice. I remember running into the bathroom with my international cell phone during halftime to call her. She said, "Daddy, daddy, it's unbelievable. We have this many interceptions, and Danielson or whatever his name was has thrown so many touchdowns. You wouldn't believe it. We're winning by— whatever the score was." My first thought was how cute it was that I'm in Israel and my 10-year old daughter is telling me the Browns score. Then, I had to think to tell her, "Honey, as a Browns fan, I've got to tell you—don't get too excited." There I was sitting in Jerusalem telling her this, "We've got a long way to go. It's early in the game." I was trying to give her some perspective.

After hearing that they were up, I was really interested in hearing the score again. I'm walking around at this big event, knowing it had to be toward the latter part of the game. I see this guy, among thousands of people from all over the world, wearing a Cleveland Browns hat at the phone booth. It was so noisy you could hardly hear anything. I go over. Sure enough, there we are during this playoff game…he is on the phone with his father, who is watching the game on TV, and is telling him the play-by-play. I figured that I was going to latch onto this guy. I stood there next to him, when I probably should have been working, for about 45 minutes. He would say to me, "They're on the 30." It was just the funniest scene. There we were amongst all these people—two Cleveland Browns fans who found one another. He was telling me what was going on, and it wasn't sounding good. But, then I had to go back with our students and get on our bus. I knew he was going to continue to be there and would hear about the game so I gave him my cellular number. He called me a half hour later, as we're driving down the road in Jerusalem, to give me the bad news that they had lost. I wasn't surprised. I knew when I saw him there that it was not going to be a good thing. There was something that said to me, "Ideally, this should be a really cool thing that this guy and I would find each other in the middle of this throng." But, I felt there was something 'not good' about this, and I couldn't explain why.…

In the Dawg Pound these days, there's a thing, "Drink the **juice**. Drink the juice." What it is, these guys a couple of rows up who are always drunk have yellow, hot pepper pickle juice. They pass it around. My brother-in-law, who is a **New England Patriots** fan, was sitting there in the Dawg Pound with me when the Patriots were playing in Cleveland. After they called him an ---hole and pointed to him and did all the things they usually do, he felt obligated to *be a man* and drink the juice. They passed him up the juice, all the while yelling, "Drink the juice. Drink the juice." He drank it and was sick for a week afterward.

> **O. J. Simpson's cousin is Ernie Banks. Their grandfathers were twin brothers.**

> **The New England Patriots played a regular season home game in Birmingham, Alabama in September, 1968.**

ROOTIN' FOR THE BROWNS WAS LIKE FLYIN' TWA FOR THE FOOD

ROGER COHEN

After graduating Beachwood School, in 1970, Robert Cohen earned a degree from Northwestern and returned to Cleveland to work for a large public relations firm. He lived in Chicago, St. Louis and Los Angeles, and has resided the last 16 years in Washington, D. C. where he is the vice-president of the Aircraft Owners and Pilots Association.

I never lost my love for the Browns. After St. Louis, I moved to California in 1979. Interestingly enough, the gentleman who I hired to replace me at TWA when I left St. Louis was Kevin Byrne who had just been fired by the then **St. Louis football Cardinals**, and who later became vice-president of public relations of the Browns and then the Ravens.

In California, I normally would watch the games all by myself and had never watched with a girl. That Monday night game in 1979—the Browns against Dallas—I actually watched with a date. The Browns blew them out so I said, "That's the girl for me." We've been married now for 23 years and have two boys.

Through all of that, there is not a day in my life that, at some point during the day—usually more than one—before I was married— before I had kids—before I had a job—before I had anything, that I didn't think about the Browns…sometimes for significant portions of the day. I still maintain season tickets. My license plates say "CLE FANS"….

> In the 1970s, a St. Louis football Cardinals fan bought an ad in the St. Louis Post-Dispatch offering to sell the "Official Cardinals Playbook" with "all five plays illustrated, including the squib punt."

Cleveland hated Mike White, the former mayor. I do politics for a living. Every movement, no matter what it is, has to have an individual, at least as a figurehead. The rebirth of the Browns—I'm going to give Mike White all the credit in the world for being that person. The *Washington Post* in March of '96, actually had a story that the league had come up with a solution that was the best solution, which would have been the perfect solution, which was just keep the Browns in Cleveland, get a new owner in Cleveland, and give Art the expansion team in Baltimore. It made perfect sense. But, Art wouldn't go for it....

Those three years without the Browns were the best of my life. A lot of people really enjoy Browns Sundays. I don't enjoy it. I don't like Sundays at all. It's gut-wrenching. I'm never happy. I'm never satisfied except on those rare occasions after a win. I don't eat. I don't drink. I'm a different individual. It's not something like, "Oh, I can't wait for the game to start." I can. That's why I loved those Sundays. The best year was the year right before we came back, which was '98. We knew we had the team coming...I played golf every Sunday... relaxed...watched football when I wanted to. It was a totally different experience....

Back in the mid-eighties, when I was living in Los Angeles, I was the guest of the Raiders, flew on the team plane back to Cleveland but, obviously, I was rooting for the Browns. I flew with their team on the team airplane with their sponsors and boosters. The treatment that those fans and the Raiders got from the then-Cleveland fans in the old place was the worst thing I'd ever seen. That was the worst I'd ever seen. It always embarrassed me....

I was in St. Louis for the one great year of the St. Louis football Cardinals. St. Louis is one of the greatest baseball cities in the world, a terrific hockey town, **SOCCER** town—no one in St. Louis gave a s---- about the football Cardinals. The Baltimore fans really had their hearts wrenched out when their team moved. When the Oilers moved, no one cared. When the Rams left LA, no one cared. And, those who

> **More U.S. kids today play soccer than any other organized sport, including youth football. Perhaps, the reason so many kids play soccer is so they don't have to watch it.**

were Los Angeles **Rams** fans are dead now. I knew them. I knew them when they were in the Coliseum, when they were in Anaheim. I was there for those great Ram teams of Eric Dickerson and John Robinson. No one really cared when they left. I'm telling you right now that the day when the heavens part and the Browns are in a Super Bowl, the ticket will have a value beyond comprehension. If people thought the Red Sox World Series tickets were something, you try getting a Cleveland Browns Super Bowl ticket. People from, literally, all over the world will be clamoring for that ticket. From Condoleezza Rice to Henry Aaron to people in the most far-reaching outposts of this world, that will be the hardest ticket....

The first thing we did when we moved to Washington in '88 was buy a huge dish...pre-DirecTV. I said, "I don't care what kind of house we have, but we've got to have a dish because I'm not going to miss the Browns games." I can understand why people don't get together to watch now, but it's great if you're out of town. When I travel and will be gone over a Sunday, I always look on the web and find a Browns Backers group and where they're meeting so I won't miss the game.

I didn't miss a game from the time I was five-years old till I went away to college. My first night at Northwestern University was the first Monday Night Football game ever. I can remember being sick one year in the title game year, '64. I was at home sick. I remember that was the game when Walter Beach made about three interceptions. He usually stunk. He was a defensive back. It was his greatest game as a pro. When I went away to school, it was hard to keep up. When I moved to St. Louis, in those mid-seventies years, those were tough years. Those were terrible teams—terrible, terrible, terrible teams. It was pre-satellite TV, and I still tried to follow them as best I could. I would go to places and try to hook up on a radio or do this or do that. Then, I was in LA for the miracle Sipe year. Kevin Byrne, my front-office friend, was at our wedding in 1981—actually the first screening of the Browns highlight film was at my rehearsal dinner. Kevin brought the editor's cut, and we stopped the rehearsal dinner—

> **The Rams, who began as the Cleveland Rams, were named for the Fordham University team.**

that was our entertainment at the rehearsal dinner—a hand-delivered Browns highlight film from the '80 season, the miracle season....

I still have yet to be at a "new" Browns home game that we've won. I cannot even remember the last game the Browns won, that I saw, in Cleveland. I'm going to take a wild guess that it might have been in 1974! That's 30 years. Just a regular-season home game...I cannot remember one since then. I could not handle going to the last game at old Municipal Stadium. I was too emotional. When that was happening, I never thought it was going to be the end. I just could never picture life without the Cleveland Browns. I never did believe that was going to be it. I really didn't. I always thought something would happen—they would come back.

I feel guilty if I miss a play—I really do. I watch every play. My wife, Janet, says, "You care more than the players do." Oh, a whole lot more than the players do! I lived without the Browns for three years, but I don't know how I would have lived if I knew they hadn't come back...or if we had the Cleveland 'something or others.' It wouldn't be the same. I get up in the morning, and the first thing I do—check the *Plain Dealer* online. I'm checking *Bernie's Insiders* the last thing before bed. I think about it at night. I think about it driving to work. I think about it at work. Am I obsessed with it? Yeah! Am I going to admit it? Yes. Will I ever give it up? No.

HE LIVES IN PHOENIX—"THE VALLEY OF THE SUN"...IN SUMMER, THEY SHOULD CALL PHOENIX "THE SURFACE OF THE SUN!"

JOE KULLMAN

Joe Kullman graduated Kent State in the early seventies and headed west where he became hooked on Phoenix. He has been a reporter and editor for the East Valley Tribune *the last 25 years.*

When I was 10 years old, I got into sports and became both an Indians and a Browns fan. This left me with some my most vivid childhood images—going to my first baseball game, going to my first football game—the Browns winning the championship in '64—it's like yesterday. I can remember the game, and remember reading about it, and everybody being ecstatic. That whole atmosphere around that championship is really a vivid memory for me. I was a kid in the Jim Brown era. That was a special time, a special thing.

In the 90s when the Indians had a really good team, I flew over to stay with a friend in Southern California to see the Indians play a three-game series in Anaheim. I went to the Saturday and Sunday games. As I was getting ready to go to the Saturday game, I put on an Indian shirt. My friend, who was not from Ohio and was not particularly an Indians fan, goes, "Well, aren't you concerned you're going to be wearing that shirt in enemy territory?" I said, "Don't worry. The Indians have a lot of fans all over the place, and there will be some there, so I won't be alone." I got to the game and I swear—I'm not exaggerating—that it seemed like as many as half the people in the stands were Indians fans. Even the Angels fans couldn't believe it. There were people with Indians caps and hats and rooting for the Indians all over the stadium—*in Anaheim*. It stunned me even though

I knew the Indians had fans in southern California and some would be there, I was just surprised at how many.

That has been a similar thing with the Browns, too. When they play the San Diego Chargers, there will be a lot of Browns fans there. The reach is just surprising. It's nice when you're living in a place that has a winning team 'cause it makes it a little less boring. The one thing I can tell you is the first time after the Cardinals came from St. Louis to Arizona, they played the Browns here. It was during Kosar's time. Again, the same thing, I knew there'd be a lot of Browns fans. We were standing in line behind a guy and his wife wearing Cardinal jerseys and caps. The guy looks at me and goes, "This isn't a Browns home game is it?" That's exactly what he said. It's amazing and funny.

I'm not what you call a major, big football fan. I'm a football fan—I watch games—I keep tabs on it—I follow the Browns. But…when the Browns are in the playoffs, I turn into a BIG football fan. It's something beyond football, in a way. It's one of those things that you don't know quite explains how it got that way. I remember being at the house of a relative-in-law's family in a small rural town in the middle of the state of Ohio, closer to Columbus than to Cleveland. His mother was a typical **rural Ohio** woman, living there in their farmhouse. We were visiting there on a Sunday afternoon, and the Browns game was on. She's a quiet woman, for the most part. The Browns are driving for a touchdown. The halfback has the ball, and he's running toward the end zone. She's jumping out of her chair, yelling, "Get in that end zone. Get in that end zone!" It completely changed her personality from what you would think it would be—an otherwise quiet, country woman to a rabid football fan.

There are seven kids in my family, and you watch a game with my mother, and she's just out of her seat always. We always joke that she's coaching from the sidelines all the time. She turns into this crazy woman during a game. One time, when we were back there

> **NFL footballs are made in Ada, Ohio. Each team uses one thousand per year. The balls are made from cowhide, not pigskin. The balls used by kickers are different and are marked with a "K".**

visiting, we went to a Hall-of-Fame game with the Browns playing the Bears. We're there early. In that stadium in Canton, you're closer to the field and the players than when you're in Browns Stadium. We're in the stands and the Browns are warming up. Bernie Kosar is out there on the field, and my mother spots him. She goes, "There he is. There he is." She's shaking me because she's so excited to see him in person. It would be like someone else seeing the Queen of England. It's just those little things that inspire that rabid fandom.

I recall going to a game in late December, several years ago, against the 49ers. It was a freezing cold day. The wind was blowing in off the lake. It was so unbearably cold. It was icy, and the players are having a hard time holding onto the ball. The Browns won 7-0. It was like nobody could move. But, the stadium was pretty packed, and the people were braving the cold. It was one of those days where a casual fan, or even a regular fan, would say, "You know, it's too cold out there…." That day, a lot of people were drinking from paper bags to stay warm—getting their antifreeze. A little nip to ward off the evil spirits and chill of a late afternoon. The fans were packed in, people were still out there going nuts, even though they were practically fighting frostbite.

I was watching a playoff game between the **Indianapolis Colts** and the Denver Broncos. Even though, it's years later and nobody on the Broncos now was on the Broncos back in the '80s when they were playing the Browns in the championship games, it's still like, "Good. Denver lost."

I don't have a lot of big dramatic memories, just a lot of little ones, and it connects me to all the memories I have of growing up in Cleveland and being a kid in that area. People have discussions about, "Whose uniforms do you like?" I have the theory about why the Browns have the best uniform; although, other people say, "Brown and Orange? What's that?" I always think, "Okay, if you think about brown and orange and you take brown paint and orange paint, and you combine it, it's gold. It turns to gold." The other thing is from a kind of

> **Tony Dungy, INDIANAPOLIS COLTS coach, is the last NFL player to throw and make an interception in the same NFL game. He was a defensive back and a backup quarterback for the Steelers.**

poetic, aesthetic point of view, when you think of football—and I associate football with these crisp autumn days and with the Indian summers back in Ohio with the leaves changing to reddish-gold-brown-yellow, and you take that orange, brown, white, the colors of Cleveland—you imagine that in the color mix, and it brings back that aesthetic fall. It just goes with the leaves and the color and the hue of autumn. ...so I say the Browns have the best uniforms for football. Football is not summer. It's winter...but it's really fall...traditional fall.

After the Red Sox won the World Series, there were a lot of articles and conversations about people who were die-hard Red Sox fans and how it goes down to the families, that peoples' wish for their lives was to see the Red Sox win a World Series. I thought, "The Browns fans are just as intense. There may be fewer of them because there are more people in New England, but the Browns fans are the same." You look at the Browns and Indians, and you can rationalize and say, "The players are just players. It's a business. They may or may not have any links to Cleveland." So, it's like, "Why should I care if they win a championship?" I really care for the fans more than I feel for the players. I care for the fans I remember, as a kid, who were avid Indians and Browns fans, and in all their lives, they still haven't seen a championship.

Coach Butch Davis— Oxymoron or just moron?

DON'T EVER SIT BEHIND THE POPE AT THE MOVIES... IF HE'S WEARIN' THAT HAT!

MITCH KUTASH

Mitch Kutash, 51, owns The Improv and The Funny Bone Comedy Clubs in the greater Cleveland area.

In the Bernie Kosar days, I went to an opening game in New Orleans. I have Kosar shirts and shirts for other players, but I also have one with my name on it. So, for the first *and* the last time, I wore that shirt. It was the day after the Pope had been in New Orleans. The whole place was wearing pope hats. It was their home-opener, first game of the season, and everybody was pumped. I sat in the upper deck, midway up. The whole time they were barraging me, yelling my last name. It got to the point where I couldn't take it anymore. New Orleans won the game, and I had an absolutely miserable time. Since then, I have never worn a Browns jersey to another away game.

When we go into a city, there's always a comedy club owner there who can get us a ticket, and we usually have nice seats. In Indianapolis, we had seats in the loge—the owner's loge. I don't think my partner had any clue where we were. We were there watching TV before the game, and they were making comments, mostly unfavorable, about the owner of the Indianapolis Colts. My guy's sitting there agreeing with them. Who are we sitting in front of, but the owner of the Colts? We were kicked out of that loge quicker than you could snap your fingers. We were gone!

I'll never forget when they announced the team was actually moving. What was unusual is—I own comedy clubs, right—they announced it in November of '95, and in January of '96, I got a call from a fellow from

Baltimore. He wants me to come to Baltimore and look at doing a club in the Inner Harbor. I had to literally tell the guy, "Listen. You stole my Browns. I have no interest in even coming to your town." I wouldn't go.

But when the Browns had first announced they were going to move, I thought, "What the hell? It's a $60 Southwest round trip flight if you book it far enough in advance. I'll just go to Baltimore." It would be the same as getting up in the morning and driving downtown to a Browns game. How much further would it be to drive to the airport and go to the game. So, I was committed to doing that. I was going to see them in Baltimore. Then, practicality hit in, and I lost interest in doing that. But, early on, my thought was to just go. It's only eight home games a year. I never did do it though. Anger hit in, and I decided it was a bad idea.

Except for ten years, I've lived my whole live in Cleveland. There's no question in my mind, it is the most avid sports community in the country, bar none. I lived in Dallas in the middle of Cowboy heaven. I lived in Miami. A Browns fan—even an Indians fan—is just a more dedicated, more fanatical human being than anybody I've ever seen. I'm sure Pittsburgh is the same way. It's the blue-collar mentality. Even in Cleveland, you weren't as crazy an Indian fan as you were a Browns fan. When the Indians went to the World Series, and they became competitive, it got us crazy As soon as the Indians became the 'old Indians' again, now we're still drawing 18—19,000 a game. It was always a Browns town, even though the Indians were there a lot longer. The Cavaliers are now drawing big, too. Cleveland will support a winner like nobody else. But they support the Browns—win or lose. That's the only team they'll support both ways. The Cavs and the Indians, if they're not winning, well….

I travel the world. Almost every week, I'm someplace else. I can never understand how a person can be raised a Cowboys fan, or a **Giants** fan, or a Bears fan and move somewhere else and, all of a

> **More NFL games have been played in the Meadowlands than any other stadium. Until 2003, Wrigley Field held the record even though Wrigley had not hosted an NFL game since 1971.**

sudden, become a fan of that town. Some people can do it, but I just don't understand it. Even Giants and Yankees fans are always there. They stay.

I'm always looking at the other comedy clubs and their schedules. I see the grand opening of this new Funny Bones in Pittsburgh. I see who's playing there in late September—Drew Carey! I'm sitting there going, "How the hell did those clowns get Drew Carey to come to their club?" He would *never* do a comedy club. If he came to Cleveland, he'd do the Gund Arena, which seats 20,000 people. He's never gonna do my club in Cleveland, which seats 350 people. It just isn't going to happen. So, I get on the phone and talk to one of the guys who does our bookings and ask, "How the hell do my ex-partners in Pittsburgh get Drew Carey? I just can't believe they did it." Then, it hits me like a brick! Drew is in Pittsburgh for what—the Browns weekend. The weekend he's at that club, the Browns are playing in Pittsburgh. It was the first regular-season game in the new Heinz Field for the Steelers. They got Drew to come to Pittsburgh and perform at their club…it had to be with the understanding that he was going to see the Browns while he was there. And, he went. That was the only comedy club I have seen this guy do, outside of Los Angeles, in the last ten years. That's how they did it! They had to have used the lure—come to Pittsburgh and see the Browns.

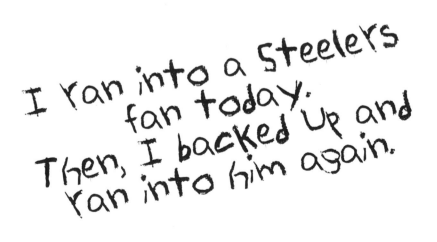

I ran into a Steelers fan today. Then, I backed up and ran into him again.

IT WAS A FOOLPROOF PLAN, AND THESE WERE THE FOOLS THAT PROVED IT!

JOHN LAMB

John Lamb is the news director at WLAD in Danbury, Connecticut. Lamb, 43, was born in Shaker Heights and has lived in The Nutmeg State the last 35 years.

When I moved to Connecticut, there were four of us Browns fans that got together. We went down to Bobby Valentine's, a great sports bar in Stamford, Connecticut owned by the baseball manager, to see if they could turn on the game on the satellite dish. For a couple of weeks, there was just that group of four or five us there. An article in the local paper mentioned that we had met at Bobby V's, and that article got reprinted in the *Plain Dealer*. The next week, we had 65-70 people there to watch the game. The next week after that, it was 85 people. It got to the point where you had to get into the bar at noon in order to get a seat so you could see the game. They put us in the big room, and, all of a sudden, it was the big Browns bar of the area, as opposed to just three or four guys wanting to see the game, which is all we were really looking to do at the beginning. We just kind of stumbled onto this giant Browns fan base.

Most of these fans were people who had transferred from Ohio. But, we also had a group of people who just were Cleveland fans. What happened around here in the '60s was the Giants games would be blacked out, so they put the Browns game on TV every week. There was this whole mass of people who, every week, got to see either Jim Brown or Leroy Kelly…and they just became Browns fans.

It's funny because you can always tell who they are—they're the ones who are the fans of the Browns, but not so much the Indians and the

Cavaliers. And, you'll find somebody who's a Browns fan but who is worried about the **Yankee** score. Then you know…that's one of *those* guys! They became a Browns fan in the '60s and just stuck with them because they saw them every week. Probably two-thirds of the people have some ties to northeast Ohio. But, there is that 'funny' third.

The funny thing was that when we started in '88, these people got together at bars, and the NFL started trying to crack down on them. They had this thing where they started sending out letters to club owners that were showing the Browns games on the satellite dish, basically pirating the signal. These letters told them, "You better not pirate these signals anymore, or we might get an injunction against your bar."

We found another place to go. We went to another club, and they just didn't tell anybody about it this time around so the NFL wouldn't get a handle on these. There was a whole lawsuit about this because the Browns fans are asking, "Why don't you want us to watch the games?" The reason the NFL gives is that they think that by blacking out these games, they're helping the local team. This is absurd, of course. No Browns fan is going to go to Giants Stadium and sit in the stadium because the Browns aren't on TV. It just made no sense.

What ended up happening, after the bars were sued, a group of bars in Southern California sued the NFL, and other bars around the country joined in the suit. Anheuser Busch came out with a big announcement before the '89 season that said, "We don't think the NFL should crack down on these bars. We've got people drinking beer at 10:00 in the morning out in Los Angeles. Why don't you guys just back off?" The next thing you know, they're building new satellites and selling everybody DirecTV.

Now we don't get 100 people at Bobby V's anymore because 75 percent of the people we used to have either have a satellite dish or know somebody who's got one. Furthermore, every bar has one now. It's

> **The YANKEES' pinstriped uniforms were designed by owner Colonel Jacob Ruppert to make Babe Ruth look skinnier.**

not like you have to drive 25 miles to get to a bar that's got the Browns game. All you need is five people who want to watch it, and they turn it on. We have a central location where we get together but it's not like the way it was in the days before everybody had their own satellite dish when we would have the place packed and not be able to find a seat. On top of it, the Browns were good in those days....

During the three years without the Browns, I just stopped watching football. Unfortunately, everything is really different now than it used to be. When the Browns went out after the '95 year, there were all these great quarterbacks in the league, guys like Marino and Elway and Aikman and **Montana** and **Young**. All these guys were still in the game. You come back, and it's a bunch of players named Byron Leftwich, Joe Schmoe. So, I didn't know any of these guys since I didn't watch football for three years.

I did not really think, when the whole thing started, that we were going to get the Browns back. No city had ever gotten their team back, with their records and their colors. Since it had never happened, I said, "Well, why is it going to happen now?" I didn't think there was a chance. I did support all the Browns efforts, and I sent out all the petitions and responded to all the e-mails I got. I still sent it out to everybody, it's just that I wasn't particularly optimistic. After the first 6—9 months, you could see that the movement was gaining some headway. It was like, "Oh, wow, this is pretty good." The Browns Backers were a renegade organization, and, at one point, a secret, "Don't tell anybody." We'd ask, "Who was the draft pick last year? Oh, you know, okay, you can get in the door." We were doing stuff like that, keeping our club a secret. When the lawsuit was settled with the stadium that allowed the original Browns to move and that brought in

Joe **MONTANA** did not start until the fourth game of his junior year at Notre Dame....Montana was awestruck by Huey Lewis and once sang backup with his band.

In the 1983 Holiday Bowl, Brigham Young University quarterback Steve **YOUNG** caught the winning touchdown pass in a 21-17 victory over Missouri.

another Browns team to Cleveland with the same colors, same record, the Browns Backers remained a party to the settlement.

We became an official thing, all of a sudden. Now, they treat us really nicely. They send us hats, and press clips and things to pass out to people about the Browns Backers. They have an actual Browns Backers coordinator who's in Cleveland who contacts us by e-mail all the time. We get four or five mail notices a year from them to tell us how to keep it together and sign up for this or special offer on that. It's kind of cool. But, no, I didn't watch any football at all during those three years. I turned off. I don't think I even went to a Super Bowl party. I found other things to do with my Sundays. Can you imagine?

I know that they are an 'expansion team,' but they're a *bad* expansion team. They've made a million blunders. Everybody can tell that they've been making a lot of mistakes. Yeah, they are an expansion team, but they also were kind of snake-bit. They got a lot of injuries. They had a lot of the wrong people in the front office, and on the field, so what can you do? That's the way it always is. We always grumble about the Browns. If they were any good, we'd still find the one flaw and point it out. We wish we could have had one extra full-back—even when we were 12-4 in '86. We wish Kellen Winslow didn't ride motorcycles.

Vandals did $400 damage to Municipal Stadium. They blew it up.

With the Browns not being in the playoffs, I definitely have teams I hope *don't* make it. I don't like the Jets. Definitely don't like the Steelers. Don't like the **Patriots**. So, Go Colts! The Steeler thing just kills you because Ben Roethlisberger's an Ohio guy. The Browns, in another inept move, needed a quarterback, and yet they passed on this guy. He's from Finlay *and* went to Miami of Ohio. He was right in front of their face for seven years. They just let him go right by—he goes right to the biggest rival…and kills us. That's just enough to drive you up the wall. The Steelers get Big Ben, and we get Easy Rider.

We're all Ohio fans, too, and we're like, "We like the kid. We like Roethlisberger." We hate the Steelers, and we're p------- that they got him, but we can't even hate him because he's a nice kid, and he's from Ohio. That even p----- you off more because you can't hate him. If he was from Pennsylvania, then we could just out and out hate him. Then, it would be okay, "I hope you die!" But, now you can't say that. He's an Ohio kid.

> As a result of a public contest in 1960, <u>PATRIOTS</u> was selected as the team name. Many years later, when considering a name change, the owner decided on the Bay State Patriots. That name was never adopted over concern about Bay State being abbreviated in headlines. Management decided on the New England Patriots.

> In the history of the <u>PATRIOTS</u>, they have played home games at Harvard Stadium, Boston University Field, Fenway Park, Boston College and, in 1971, they made their debut at Schaefer Stadium in Foxboro. Schaefer was the one stadium to have when you're having more than one.

BEER:
MORE THAN A BREAKFAST DRINK

RANDY MULLINS

Randy Mullins of Troy, Ohio lives 60 miles north of Cincinnati and more than 200 miles south of Cleveland. The only Browns games that he has missed were while he was serving with the Marines in Beirut, Lebanon.

My father was a Browns fan, and he liked the Lakers and **Notre Dame**, the Celtics and the Cincinnati Reds. So, now, if you could see our house, you would understand that small legacy of my father. Our entire house is decorated in Cincinnati Reds, Notre Dame, Lakers, Celtics, and Cleveland Browns memorabilia. The whole house—it looks like a sports bar. In one room, we have a big-screen television and we have people over to watch the games. We are wall-to-wall Cleveland Browns fans. We actually painted the room like a Browns helmet. The sides of the walls are orange. The front is dark brown with a white stripe. The ceiling is white. It looks like the Browns helmet.

In '91-'92, I was working for a telemarketing outfit, and I was on the road in Lafayette, Indiana. I was staying at a Ramada Inn that had a Damon's Restaurant inside it. The Browns were playing the Pittsburgh Steelers in a playoff game. It started snowing. Everyone was gathering at my friend, Mike's Ohio house for the game, and my brother was coming from Kentucky to watch with us. I got off work

> The Oakland A's colors are green and gold because their late owner, Charles O. Finley, grew up in La Porte, Indiana and loved Notre Dame...when he bought the Kansas City A's, he changed their uniforms to the Notre Dame colors.... The Green Bay Packers also adopted Notre Dame colors because Curly Lambeau played at Notre Dame.

Friday and went to the Ramada Inn with my boss and a couple of people from work, and we had a few drinks. I decided I wasn't going to go back to Ohio that evening. I thought it wasn't a good idea—it was snowing like crazy, and they're warning people that it was a winter weather storm and advising people to stay off the roads.

It's about 7:00 on a Friday night, and the game is Saturday afternoon at 1:00. We started doing shots of tequila, and we did probably half a dozen shots and were also drinking beer. Then we started drinking Jack and Cokes. They all left. I'm sitting at the bar by myself. Finally, at midnight, I went upstairs to my room. I was drunk—there's no doubt, I was completely drunk. I was lying in my bed, and the phone rang. It was my older brother who had driven all the way from Kentucky. He was calling me from a hotel in Troy where I was supposed to have met him. He called my room there in Indiana and said, "Where are you?" I said, "Oh man, I got hammered. I have just drank for the last six hours down here at this bar. There's no way I'm going to make it, and I don't think I'll be able to make it tomorrow because they're calling for 12-13 inches of snow. It's awful here." He said, "Oh, you wuss. It's awful in Kentucky. It's awful in Ohio. It ain't no different in Ohio or Kentucky than it is in Indiana. You loser. You closet Bengal fan."

So, as stupid as that sounds, that's all it took. I got my clothes on. I jumped in the car, and I drove to the gas station. This gas station was a block from my hotel…it took me 10 minutes to get there, and I'm the only car on the road. There ain't nobody on the road. I go in the gas station. They're getting ready to close up. I said, "I need some coffee." I got a 20-ounce cup of coffee and a 16-ounce cup of coffee. She told me, "I don't know what you're doing, but you're not allowed to be on the road." Of course, I'm drunk, and I'm trying to decipher what she's saying, and she says, "They've just announced it, and you can get arrested. If you're not an emergency vehicle, you can be arrested if you're driving tonight. The roads are undriveable."

Well, I got on the highway. Lafayette to Troy is probably an hour and 30 minutes or maybe an hour and 45 minutes. I left there at 12:30 a.m. It's almost indescribable. I did not see another car or truck on the highway. It was like driving through a swarm of bees the entire time.

I could see nothing. There were no vehicles on the road. I was going about 25 miles an hour.

I freaked my brother out. I went to his motel's office and had the guy call his room and tell him he had a visitor—at 6:30 in the morning. That's how long it took me to get there—six hours. That's how bad it was snowing. He opened that door and he couldn't believe it. I walked in with a 12-pack of Bud Light. I said, "Now, Wuss, let's start drinking, boy." I drove six hours in that blizzard to watch the Browns play the Steelers. To top the story off, to make it laughable, we went over to Mike's house, the game started…and I passed out. I passed out sitting up in a kitchen chair, just sitting there in front of the TV with my head hanging down. I slept during the whole game. I missed the whole game.

It could have been worse—a lot worse. It must have ben my first day with that new brain.

Kellen Winslow:
The promise of a
lover, the performance
of a husband.

TWO BROTHERS ARE STEELER FANS... THERE MUST HAVE BEEN A MIX-UP AT THE HOSPITAL

PATRICK NIEDER

When Patrick Nieder was raised in Erie, Pennsylvania, he never dreamed that someday he would become president of the Northern California Browns Backers Club... while living in Jacksonville, Florida. He is a letter carrier for the Postal Service.

In Erie where I grew up, we had some Bills fan and a ton of Pittsburgh fans—each city, including Cleveland, is about 100 miles from Erie. It's mostly Cleveland and Pittsburgh fans. Buffalo, when they had their run four years in a row, we'd see a bunch of Buffalo fans. It's a good area to be in. I actually have two brothers who are Steeler fans. I can see how my younger brother is a Steeler fan 'cause they were good when he was growing up, but my older brother—I'm trying to figure that one out. I know they were bad in the '70s, but when they started winning them all, that must have been when my older brother became a Steeler fan. I've just stuck with the Browns through thick and thin, hoping that one of these days before I move on to the next life, they'll win it again.

When I was a kid, the Browns were *the* team with Jim Brown, Leroy Kelly, Frank Ryan, Paul Warfield and the gang. I've been a Browns fan all my life. The last time the Browns won the title, I was nine years old. Next month, I'll be 50 years old so I'm still waiting for them to win another title.

When I was a kid, we were all playing electric football, it was always the Browns against the Packers. In the early 60s, it seems like it was always the Browns and the Packers. During high school, the Browns weren't all that good.... In '85, the Browns got Bernie, and satellite

TV started coming on strong, and the Browns started to become good. We could go to the sports bars that had the satellite and watch the games, and we really got into it and started traveling around to the games. Whenever they played in San Diego, Oakland, or **Seattle**, we were flying there to see them. That's another part of running the club is helping people to get tickets and flights to different cities, and trying to hook up with other Browns Backers clubs at these games.

I started the Northern California Browns Backers back in 1994 in the Sacramento, California area. We started out with about 60 members, and we're currently up to 597 members. Things are good. I just transferred to Florida in October and nowadays with the Internet, I can still run everything in the club and stay in connection with the other officers in California.

In 2000, the Browns played in Oakland. We took 365 Browns fans to the game. There were Raider fans sitting around us, and they were telling us that some of their fans are so bad, these Raider fans won't even bring their kids to the games. I guess it's like anywhere—the biggest percentage of the people are going to be decent, but then you're going to have your small group or handful or whatever where it seems like some of those people there don't even know who's on their team, they don't care what the score is, they're just there to get in arguments and fights.

A couple of our members got to the stadium and paid to park and pulled their cars in, but the parking lot was full so they had us go down the highway about a mile, and then they shuttled us back on a bus. Of course, you get on the bus, and everybody on the bus is a Raider fan. Here I am, all decked out in my Browns jersey, Browns hat, orange high-top Converse All-Star sneakers. I took one look at all those Raider fans on the bus and said, "Hey, is this the Browns bus?" It was before the game so nobody was drunk yet. Luckily for us, one of the members of our gang was able to park in a close parking lot, and they

> **During the SEATTLE Mariners first year in 1977, they measured the distance to the fences in fathoms. A fathom is 6 feet. For instance, where a park may have a sign that denotes 360 feet, the Kingdome would have the number 60....**

gave us a ride back to our vehicle so we didn't have to ride on the shuttle bus after the game, which we lost. That would have been ugly....

The year the Browns played Jacksonville in Cleveland—the bottle-throwing incident—a sportswriter wrote an article in the *Sacramento Bee* comparing the Browns fans with the Taliban. When I saw that, I was like, "Okay, here we go." I e-mailed all the Browns Backers presidents and all our members this guy's e-mail address, along with the article, and they just bombarded him. When he got back to me, I said, "What about opposing teams fans going into Oakland?" He said, "We don't throw bottles at them." I was like, "What about this? What about that?" He just kept on sidestepping it. Then, finally, with all these e-mails that we were hitting him with, he e-mailed me back and said, "Okay, uncle, uncle. I give. I give. It's great how you are all behind your team, and I hope some day you guys will like one of the articles I write." That shows how well coordinated the Browns Backers Clubs are.

I've gone to games to Oakland, Arizona, San Diego, Houston, Seattle and Cleveland, but, being from Erie, Pennsylvania, I've never been to a Browns-Steelers game in Pittsburgh. In these other cities, you'd hear stupid comments, but you just keep on walking so there's no big confrontation, but Oakland it's different. That last game we all went to, this one Raider fan, when he came up to his seats in the upper deck, he looks and sees all these Browns fans sitting there. Right from the get-go, every word out of his mouth was 'f-this, f-that!' On and on and on. By halftime, the police had him down on the ground with his jersey half ripped off, had put the handcuffs on him and were walking him away. All 350 of us Browns fans stood up and started barking. It was great!

The thing is they're not just that way with the Browns fans. It's every opposing team. If they see anyone with an opposing team's jersey on, it's like, "Hey, you. You're an idiot!" It's just seems like they're trying to get into a fight. It's pretty sad. If God doesn't destroy Oakland Raiders fans, he owes Sodom and Gomorrah an apology....

Since the Browns came back, I've gone back home every year. I actually have season tickets in the new stadium, in the opposite end zone from the Dawg Pound, since '99. Until last year, I lived in California for 25 years. For the last five of those years, I had the season tickets. I wait for the schedule to come out and see when they have back-to-back games at home. I go home for a few games, and then I sell the rest of the tickets to members in our club or relatives. I've never been stuck with a ticket. That's pretty incredible.

I used to laugh at the Raider and 49er fans out in California. The Raiders never get to watch any of their home games on TV because they never sell out. They were in the Super Bowl a couple of years ago, and in the playoffs, and they still weren't selling out games. I say to them, "Look at Cleveland. They've sold out every game since they've been back in '99...they've gone to the playoffs once since they've been back."

I argue with fans from other cities when they say, "Oh, the Browns have never been to the Super Bowl." I say, "So what? What does that mean? Before the Super Bowl, football players weren't football players—Jim Brown, **Y. A. Tittle**, Bart and all these guys? The Browns won a lot of professional titles." When I hear that stuff from other fans, especially the Buffalo fans, I say, "I'd rather be 0-0 than 0-4." For a while there, we could say the same to Denver fans 'cause they're always giving us a bad time since they whupped us. Then, they finally won a couple.

Y. A. TITTLE was the first NFL player on the cover of **Sports Illustrated...December, 1954. The Y. A. stands for Yelverton Abraham.**

THIS GUY'S FROM PITTSBURGH. NOT THAT THERE'S ANYTHING WRONG WITH THAT!

KENNY RODA

While growing up a die-hard Steelers fan in Pitts-burgh, Kenny Roda never dreamed his life would revolve around the Cleveland Browns and their fans. Roda came to Cleveland in 1982 to play bas-ketball at Baldwin-Wallace and never went home. He became Sports Director of the BW student sta-tion and interned at the Dolans' cable station. When the Dolans bought WKNR, Cleveland's All-Sports Station, he moved there where he hosts an extremely popular afternoon show.

I've been here in Cleveland since '82. Everybody tells me I'll eventually become a Browns fan. The one thing I'll say is that the Browns fans are very similar to Steeler fans. It's a passion. Once you're a Steeler fan, you're always a Steeler fan. Once you're a Browns fan, you'll always be a Browns fan. I haven't changed when it comes to head-to-head.

When the Steelers play the Browns, on my radio show, for those two weeks, and everybody knows this, I root for the Steelers. It makes for great conversation. It makes for the two best weeks of the NFL season because it's just back and forth. "You suck." "Go back to Pittsburgh." We have a blast with it. But…if the Steelers are out of the playoffs, I root for the Browns—for a couple of reasons. Number one, I've got friends here my age—I'm 41 born in '64 the last time the Browns won a championship—who are Browns fans, but they don't remember the Browns winning a championship because they were a baby. They've never experienced what it's like to have a team go to the Super Bowl and win a Super Bowl. As a kid, I experienced that four times in six years. I want my buddies to experience what I experienced. Four Super Bowl championships, two Stanley Cups, two World Series—as a sports fan, that's the ultimate. In '79 Pittsburgh won the Super Bowl and the World Series. You get to stick out your chest. Your team's the best. As a sports fan, that is the ultimate. That's the best feeling. You can brag, and you can be proud of your city and your team. When the victory happens, there are grown men hugging each other and crying and celebrating like they've never done it before so, as a Steelers fan, I root for the Steelers first, but I can honestly say, if the Steelers are out of it, I root for the Browns and want them to win so these passionate fans in Cleveland who are very similar to the ones in Pittsburgh will know what it's like to celebrate a championship. I also have some friends who have played for the Browns or who are currently on the Browns, and I want them to do well. I want them to have the opportunity to be in a championship game and win. Some people don't think you can be a Steeler and a Browns fan at the same time, I think you can. I'm pulling for the Browns and hoping that my buddies will celebrate a Super Bowl championship or if it's the Indians or if it's the Cavaliers, just some championship in the city of Cleveland. These are the best sports fans in the country. I'll put Cleveland's fans up there with anybody.

Ohioans get to participate in the two best rivalries in sports. Browns-Steelers twice a year plus, Ohio State-Michigan. That gives you three separate weeks of some of the best fans you can find anywhere leading up to the best game in college football and the best two games in the NFL every year. That's something I think is very special to Ohio sports/football fans.

Growing up, I felt the Browns were the rivals. You hated the Browns. You wanted to beat the Browns. I think if you ask any Browns fan, "If you only won two games out of the year, you'd want it to be Pittsburgh." It's very similar in Pittsburgh. If you were going to have a lousy team, and you were going to only win two games that year, you wanted it to be the Browns—or at least you wanted to beat them at home. You don't want to lose to them at home. If you talk to Steeler fans, they'll tell you the same thing.

When I was in college, I'd see my friends and they'd always say, "You're still a Steeler fan, right?" "Yeah. Absolutely." I think some of my buddies find it interesting that I admit it on the air on WKNR. I say, "Hey, I'm a Steeler fan." We talk about it during the week. I think a lot of people wonder how a guy from Pittsburgh has made it in radio in Cleveland, especially when admitting he's a Steeler fan. It actually works out in a great way for me. It gives the fan the opportunity to rant and rave and yell and scream and moan…at a Steeler fan on the radio, which is something you normally wouldn't get. You normally would get the homer side of it where it would be all positive Browns stuff, "Go Browns." Here, it's just the exact opposite. For that week, they can call up and gripe and moan and yell at me so it's therapy, for Browns fans. It makes for a lot of fun for me. I get some buddies of mine to call up from Pittsburgh just to make sure that I haven't converted fully, 100-percent. They stir it up and it makes for a great two weeks during the NFL season.

I still take a beating because I supported Couch and thought that if this guy wasn't lying on his back 50 times a year and wasn't shell-shocked because of the offensive line that he might still be the quarterback here, but other people disagree because he was the #1 pick, and he was supposed to be the savior. I also took a beating for tearing Butch Davis to pieces. I was one of the big anti-Butch guys. I called him *Frankenbutch* because he was the monster that Carmen Policy created—gave him total power, and he ruined the organization. Now that Butch has gone, other players that I'm now getting to talk to outside of the locker room now can speak freely about how bad it was with Butch Davis. They now say to me, "Hey, you were right. You were hitting a home run. You hit the nail on the head. It was that bad in the locker room, but we just couldn't say it." I could tell Butch was a phony from the get-go. What backed it up was I went to cover the Fiesta Bowl when the Buckeyes beat Miami. I had my suspicions about Butch then, and the sportswriters from Miami told me, "A lot of people are going to think this guy's the greatest coach in the world. You're going to find out that he'll tell you one thing one day, and he'll lie to your face, and you'll find out he changes his story . He's just a flat-out liar. He has the biggest ego of anybody you'll ever meet." My suspicions were right and they hit the nail on the head, as well.

I've been here on the radio since '92, and I hear the same thing from some fans— telling me to go home and that Pittsburgh sucks. It's just the same thing over and over. I know how passionate the Browns fans are. I'm waiting for something new. I want to hear something different. I'm waiting to honor that Browns fan who comes up with something that's original now…not just the same things. I'm waiting for that special caller that comes up with something that catches me by surprise and maybe leaves me speechless. I haven't gotten that yet.

I truly enjoy living and working in Cleveland and sparring with the wonderful, knowledgeable, and passionate Browns fans…but don't tell them I said that.

If squandering assets were a crime, Modell would have been in jail years ago.

'TIS BETTER TO TRAVEL WELL THAN TO ARRIVE FIRST

It's more than football. It's something that connects you with your father and growing up. It's a very emotional thing—following the Cleveland Browns. Lots of people could care less about professional football teams, but, for better or worse, I have suffered along with them—cheered with them—and I look forward to every fall, hoping that, "maybe this is going to be the year where they actually go to a Super Bowl." There's always next year. I plan to live at least until the Browns go to a Super Bowl! It may take 30 years, but whatever. It's going to be great when we see Browns' yesterdays tomorrow.

Living in all those other cities, I never became a fan of any other professional team. I'm actually a bigger Cleveland Indians fan than a Browns fan, and, even the Cavaliers, with this miracle of Lebron James that they got. I have never been a Bears fan. I have never been a 49er fan. I've never been a Dodgers fan. I've never been a **Cincinnati Bengals** fan. I have always been a Cleveland Browns fan. Sometimes I would get ridiculed for it in these various cities, but I never even *thought* of backing another team. That was my team.

A lot of people I know become fans of the teams where they live. I have, for better or worse, never been able, or desirous, of doing that. I've always followed the Browns. I have emotional highs and emotional lows, but, to me, that's better than not caring. The "Drive" and the famous "Fumble" happened. My wife had to take the kids and leave the house 'cause I was unlivable for three or four hours.

The worst people in the history of the world were Adolph Hitler, **Michael Jordan**, and John Elway!
——MARSHALL BASKIN, Los Angeles resident since 1976

> The Bengals, owned by the Paul Brown family, were named after the Massillon (Ohio) High School Tigers, whom Brown coached before he became head coach of Ohio State and the Cleveland Browns.

> **MICHAEL JORDAN** was given his first set of golf clubs by fellow University of North Carolina classmate, Davis Love, Davis Love, Davis Love....The Roman Guy.

Even though I've been gone from Cleveland for 23 years now, I've always followed the team. When I went to school at the University of South Florida in Tampa, the city of Clearwater adopted the Browns as their 'adopted home team' since the Buccaneers were so bad, so at least I could get news about the Browns by reading the Clearwater newspaper. On the days before the Internet and before NFL Sunday Ticket, unless the Browns happened to be on national TV, I never got to see them play.

The Browns never played in Tampa while I was there, but they played a couple of times in Atlanta during the time the Falcons were awful. There would be at least as many Browns fans in the stands as there were Falcon fans. It used to be that the joke around Atlanta was that "Somebody parked their car with two Falcon tickets on the dashboard and while they were gone, somebody broke in and left four more."

——SAM CHAMBERS, 45, Atlanta

I went to Perth, Australia in 1983 to film the **GLOBETROTTERS** there. I was in my hotel room in Melbourne on a Saturday morning when I received a phone call from the shippers of that film. They told me they had misplaced the film. I was there in the room, middle of the day on Saturday, waiting on this phone call back from the shippers. Out of sheer lack of anything to do, I turned on the television set, and they're showing a replay of the highlights of the previous week's Cleveland Browns game. I could not believe it. Here I am in Melbourne, Australia, in 1983, on a Saturday, turn on my TV in my hotel room, and there's the Browns! That was a huge treat.

Then in '93, my wife worked for Mattel. They sent her to London on assignment. Because she was French, we had gone together to Paris and stopped back in London together. We got in touch with a couple we know. She is an American, he is Japanese. We went out and did whatever we had to do for the afternoon while my wife was working at Mattel's office. We got back to the hotel at about five in the afternoon, and there was this urgent message to call the wife. I did so, and she said, "Quick, turn on your television set—they're

> In 1972, Bill Cosby signed a lifetime contract with the **GLOBETROTTERS** for one dollar per year. In 1986, the Globetrotters gave him a nickel raise. Cosby made several appearances with the team and is an honorary member of the Basketball Hall of Fame.

about to show the highlights of last week's game against the 49ers." The Browns had beat the 49ers that week, and they had no business doing it. But, there I was in London, again in my hotel room, and who comes on the television? It was British television doing a program on the rabid Browns fans and showing the game in the process.

——EMIL DAVIDSON, 68, Los Angeles

I'm a season ticket holder from Cincinnati. Thirteen of us travel 500 miles every home week. Every game is memorable for us because we all caravan up there. We also always pick an away game to go to. Twenty of us all flew together down to Dallas last year for the game. We just made Texas Stadium like a mini-Dawg Pound. We have a pretty big tailgate every week in Cleveland so we just had a spin-off of that. We got there really early, and it was very hot—100°—so we found a small tree just outside the stadium that was putting some shade down. Before we knew it, we probably had 100 people there tailgating with us. It was great because the Dallas fans were like, "Wow, look at these guys." All of us had our Browns gear on. We had a good time. The Dallas fans were pretty much in awe of us. They don't have anything close to that. They treated us real well. There was no disrespect. People generally have respect for us because we travel so far, and we were so into it. We're there to support our team not to show disrespect to any other fans.

We always pick a cool place to go every year. The year before that, we went to Kansas City. My biggest memory from Kansas City would be that we actually took our seat out of Arrowhead Stadium. It just was by chance that we were in the second-to-last row. The guy in front of us—his seat came off. He was a season ticket holder and he commented that the seats always come off. Before we knew it, the back of one of our seats came off, so we just kind of escorted that out of Arrowhead as well. The Kansas City fans treated us nice. The stadium is not as loud as what everybody says that it is. They don't even open their tailgate lots until 9:00 in the morning for a 12:00 o'clock game. That was kind of weak for us.

——JOEY McGREGOR, 37, Cincinnati

Oakland is a horror story. I'll never go back there. It was absolutely awful out there. When we go to away games, we usually go from Friday to Monday, and we wear our Browns clothes all weekend long. Normally, people are nice to you. They're like, "Oh, it's cool that you came here to see your team." But, out in Oakland, they would as soon have killed you as looked at you because you had a Browns shirt on. It was awful. All the horror stories they tell about it is true. We had three buses from our hotel that pulled in there, and those fans were taking trash out of trash cans and throwing them at our buses. I was afraid to walk into the stadium. The fans there kept coming over and picking fights with everybody.

The best place, by far, to watch a game is New Orleans. I've been there twice, and they're like 'southern hospitality,' all over the place. Before the game on Friday and Saturday, the natives are just so friendly. In 2001, Michigan and Ohio State played on Saturday, and they had big parties for us. The bars and even the casino opened the back room and rented two big-screen TVs and let us go in there and watch the game. They're really nice down there.

——KAREN HOLSAPPLE, Versailles, Ohio

A long time ago, I was an NBC page. So, as a former page, I knew the ins and outs of NBC very well. NBC, at that time, had nothing in the way of security. Nothing. Anybody could walk in there at any time, go just about any place. In '95, the Indians were playing the Boston Red Sox, and we couldn't get it on television, so we went over to NBC. There was security already by then, but we talked our way in and found ourselves in the only place we could see the game, Switching Central, where we should not have been, where all of those buttons affected everything seen all over the country. Somebody finally discovered us sitting there, and they just about died. Before that, I would come in on Sunday mornings.

I would always call the sports department the day before to make sure a Browns game was coming through Switching Central. Many times, a Browns game that was played up the coast would be televised back to Cleveland. It would come through Switching Central, but it would not be on in LA. I saw many, many, many games that way over the years, standing in the hallway looking through a glass at a monitor that was probably 12 to 20 inches—looking at it from 10 or 15 feet away. They got to know me well enough there, that they would offer to pipe it in to a viewing room which was right next door.

I just walked six steps, turned left, and I'm in this little screening room with a big monitor—where there are six or eight seats.

One day I went in there, must have been the '84 season, and as I entered the room—to my horror—there were two guys sitting there. It was the Pittsburgh game. I'm not sure how they got in—I can't remember their stories. One of them was a fellow named Greg Pierce and the other was Mark Breyer. The moment I saw them, I thought to myself, "Holy Cow, I hope they're not Pittsburgh fans." They looked up at me—and they later told me, "The first thing they thought was, 'I hope he's not a Pittsburgh fan.'"

——**EMIL DAVIDSON**, Filmmaker, Los Angeles

Road trips are great. At the away games, their fans are all different. At Dallas, I was disappointed because their fans were kind of laid back. They weren't into it as much as I thought they would be. There's no way it was as rowdy as a Cleveland game, or as loud, or as intense, or as emotional. I can't explain why, but I was disappointed in that. It was a very close game, the game where Eric Turner tackled their tight end on about the half-yard line to end the game so it was an exciting game down to the end. Browns fans made more noise than the Cowboy fans.... The Denver fans were brutal. Through the whole game, they just talked smack in a way that was still in good taste, but they were relentless. We were just two Browns fans in the middle of a Denver crowd. They were very vocal about their team. They got on us.... San Diego is real laid back. It was your 'Southern California' attitude game, nice day, everybody just having a hot dog and a beer and then caught a football game.... Phoenix was almost like a home game. It seemed like half the crowd or more is for the other team, which I thought was kind of odd. But, that's how it is every game.

——**DAN JARVIS,** New Mexico Browns fan

In '88, we went to a game in Pittsburgh. There's no love lost between us. You pretty much don't say much when you're in enemy territory. Some people are ridiculous in that they go and just get stupid silly drunk. I can't understand that. If you're going to pay good money for a ticket to go to a football game, I would think you'd want to be sober to watch the game. There was a group of five of us, and we were walking into Three Rivers Stadium. We were getting harassed and harassed and harassed. I was biting my tongue. Finally, I just said, "You know what? I can't take this anymore." I went over and confronted these Steelers fans and said, "What's you guys' problem here?" A Steeler fan said, "You're Browns fans. You don't belong here." I said, "I have every right to be here just as much as you do. Just because I'm a Browns fan and you're a Steelers fan doesn't mean we can't get along." A guy came up and said, "We hate the Browns, and you hate us, but you're right." He put his hand out and shook my hand and gave me a big hug. He said, "Hey, come over here. Bring your group over here. Why don't you eat with us?" I said, "Do you realize how much of a taboo this is—for us to do this?" He goes, "Yeah, but what the heck? You only live once, unless you're Shirley MacLaine." We sat there and acted like we were best friends in the world. Afterwards we went our separate way.

———GEORGE KRSKA, Barberton, Ohio

There is nothing like the Raiders. I can just go on and on. Three or four years ago, we took a group of 18 Browns fans—all were my friends and relatives. I bought pretty good seats down in the lower section in the middle of the field. I knew, of course, that we'd get accosted, and it would be pretty ugly. But, I just had no idea the extent things would go to. We got to the parking lot around nine in the morning, expecting to tailgate. We had two vehicles. We were all decked out in our Browns colors. Every spot that we would pull into, these Raider fans would actually block them—they'd stand arm-to-arm blocking these spots until we had to go somewhere else. We knew we were not welcome there. Finally, after circling the whole stadium parking lot, one of the security guards came up to us and said, "I've just got to warn you. I'm not going to be able to protect you guys in here. I don't know if you want to be here dressed like that, but I don't want the responsibility." He was basically encouraging us not to park in the parking lot dressed in Browns gear. Although we had already paid to get into the lot, we decided to drive out and park somewhere nearby on the street. As we were driving out, with our 'tail between our legs,' my brother-in-law was in front of me and was talking on the phone because he was getting a little nervous. So, to egg him on a little bit, I took a giant Browns flag and hoisted it out the window of the car. Well, it began raining beer bottles and cans. It was as if you gave the flag to 'open fire.' People just started pelting us with garbage.

We park about a mile away near a train track and had our own little tailgate party there. Actually, I ended up meeting some other Browns fans who were there who saw us and thought it would be a safe haven…safety in numbers kind of thing, so they joined up with us. We received all kind of verbal abuse on the way in to the stadium and throughout the game. We had some kids with us—at the time my kids were 10 to 14 years old—and they just got an earful. In hindsight, I probably shouldn't have subjected them to that, but it's all part of the lore. They enjoyed it since we all got out of there alive, but the pinnacle of the whole story was that we were sitting down on about the 30th row off the field, and to get up to the restrooms and the concession stand, we had to go under a tunnel. Overlooking that tunnel up above are the luxury boxes for the Raider fans. Every time we would make a trip up the stairs to go out to that tunnel, the people in the luxury boxes would lean out the window and spit on us. That's just the ultimate in crudeness or crassness—to actually spit on somebody, but that was our experience at the Raiders.

———DAVID ZBIN, San Jose, California

I would never, ever just go to see a Ravens game. I took my 10-year old daughter to the Browns-Ravens game the year when Jamal Lewis had a couple hundred yards running and set an NFL record. That was a disaster to watch. I was at a Browns-Ravens game when Couch threw a winning touchdown in the last 30 seconds. I almost got in a fight with these guys who happened to be sitting near me because they were totally obnoxious Ravens idiots. The guy kissed me twice during the game when good plays would happen. Finally, I had enough! Because of the Art Modell thing and the taking the team thing, I have nothing but contempt for the Ravens. Baltimore fans are really intense. I guess it depends where you sit. If you're in the cheaper seats, you get crazier fans. They're rough. I don't know how they compare to our Dawg Pound, but they're rough.

When I'm at Browns games, and see Pittsburgh fans—while it's rough and there's a lot of action and fights—there's a level of respect. We've been at this for a long time. We're like Joe Frazier and Muhammad Ali—there's just some respect.

———SCOTT BROWN, 48, Fairfax, Virginia

Oakland is the worst place for a visiting team's fans to go. They thrive on this 'bad boy' image. They like to fight and beat up on each other. I'm not the least bit interested in that. I can tell you this, my wife, my associate producer and another friend went to an LA Raiders—Browns pre-season game. We were in a parking lot across the street from the Coliseum in a little private parking lot that probably parked 20 cars. We were very much pinned in. There was wall-to-wall traffic, and a parking lot in front of us on the street. Cars were getting out of that lot, one at a time, every few minutes… maybe, if you were lucky and pushy enough. We're locked into this position in the lot. All of a sudden, a fight starts to my left in the parking lot between two Browns fans and three Raiders guys, one of whom is wielding a piece of wood. They outnumber the guys three to two, and this other guy's trying to use a piece of wood. I opened my car door and screamed, "Stop it. Cut that crap out." The guy with the wood raced over to my car. Of course, I closed the door very quickly and locked it. My wife is sitting next to me. My associate producer is not a fighter. The guy comes over to my window and starts clubbing my drivers' side window with that piece of wood, fortunately not doing any harm, but it wasn't for lack of effort. Then, they moved off. Then the two Browns guys showed up there, and one of them had his right hand inside the left side of his jacket. I heard him say to his friend, "I've got a gun." If these guys had come back, and if that gun fight had started there, I was in a position where we could not move. Fortunately, that did not happen. But, I want no part of the Raiders and their fans. I always root against the Raiders. This type of behavior is something to be proud of? This is something to boast about? Nazi Germany was boastful about being merciless and brutal. I'm sorry, but I've got nothing for the Raiders. Nothing for the Raiders. It's like being in Beirut…"I'm going to a Raiders game. Cover me."

——**EMIL DAVIDSON**, Los Angeles

The Steelers fans got banned from the bar that we are at in Stamford because they lost a playoff game a couple of years ago and their fans broke some stuff and kicked out the door. The Browns didn't do anything like that…we just lost the game, and got in our car and drove home. Yankee fans are real difficult. I go to Yankee Stadium to see the Indians every year. Until the Indians got good right around the mid-nineties, nobody ever said anything to me. I would go to every game, every year, for 25 years. But, as soon as the Indians got good, and they looked like they were a threat to the Yankees, that's when we started catching flak from the Yankee fans. That's when they started flicking popcorn at me and stuff like that—giving me a hassle.

———**JOHN LAMB**, Connecticut resident, Shaker Heights native

More Pittsburgh fans tailgate here before the game than fans from any other team. The Pittsburgh fans are actually really, really good to deal with. We get our Cleveland fans who are young, they got the tickets from somebody else, they're morons, and they're drunk. A bunch of the people from our tailgate party always go to Buffalo for the game. There will be a big Browns contingency there when we play. Our people follow their team. It's going to be nasty weather, but these guys were all drooling for the chance to go to Buffalo right now. In Buffalo, when we lost our team, they actually had Browns Appreciation Day. They set aside a bunch of tickets for Browns fans to go watch a game. And, the Steelers were probably one of the more supportive NFL teams after we lost our team. They wanted the rivalry to come back. All those towns are just blue-collar towns, hard-working people. I lived with a Steeler fan—my twin brother is a Steelers fan. It's horrible on football weekends. The Steelers—that's all I get to hear—all weekend long. If I don't go to the tailgate party, I'm working at the bar on Sunday afternoons. We'll be watching the game and all I see is him and his Steeler buddies coming into the bar just razzing me all afternoon. I hope an unclean yak sits on their beers.

———**MICHAEL J. FELICE**, 37, Mentor, Ohio

Occasionally we'd have problems when Cincinnati came to town. The rivalry with Pittsburgh is still big, but it's toned down a little bit. The Cleveland fans are caught in the middle. They don't know who to hate more—Pittsburgh or Baltimore. The rivalry is still there with Pittsburgh but it doesn't have the magnitude it had before the Browns left town. And, the Dawg Pound is nothing like it used to be. It's a corporate Dawg Pound now. Most of the seats are bought by corporations. What's really funny, I notice that a lot of the fans who are in the Dawg Pound are not really from Cleveland, they're from surrounding towns south of Cleveland and north of Columbus. Very seldom will you find someone there now who is actually from Cleveland. It's funny because they don't really know the old history of the Browns.

————**CURTIS FRANKLIN,** ex-game day Ops

Some of my cohorts are a little nervous about going up to Oakland because their fans are nuts. All the stories you hear are true. One time, I saw a Raider fan almost kill a Pittsburgh fan, who almost asked for it, but still it didn't call for such a reaction. Other times, I've seen them actually urinate in cups and throw it over onto opposing fans. That's not football. Maybe they invented the Original Whizzanator. It's all right to be for your team, but opposing fans have the right to be for their team, and there should be a respect issue involved in there, too. We're all human beings, regardless. That's missing in sports today, it seems. Now, down at San Diego…they're too laid back. That's why I wouldn't be surprised if they eventually wound up here in LA.

————**BERNIE HAIRSTON**, Studio City, California

 Oakland is a bad place to go. I would never send an enemy there. When we were there, the Browns were winning 14-0. I walked out to get a beer and smoke a cigarette and watch the game on a big screen in the lobby. A guy there told me that I had guts wearing head-to-toe Browns clothes in there. I said, "Well, look, I like my team like you like yours." He said, "You know, we've killed a person out here, a Pittsburgh fan actually, for being in the parking lot carrying a sign that said, "Oakland Sucked." I said, "Well, that's something to be proud of. And, everybody said Cleveland is bad…I guess we ain't nothing." Some other older man was standing out there. He was real nice and said, "I wouldn't worry about it." I said, "I'm not." They had so many security guards right in front of all the Browns fans. It was odd—I'd never seen that before— so many cops like that standing just right in front of our section. We saw a few fights. They just all looked like gang-related. It was awful. I've never seen anything like it. My friend was so scared that she wouldn't even get out of her seat to go down. It was just unreal. As soon as our bus pulled in, full of Browns fan, and we had older people on our bus, and those people were ready to jump them—just

'cause they had Browns clothes on! I went, "Come on. It's not even a rivalry!" The day before the game, we went to San Francisco. We were wearing Browns clothes all weekend, and the people were telling us, "I wouldn't wear that stuff." I went, "Well, that's all I brought. I have nothing else." People were telling us not to go out by ourselves wearing our Browns clothes 'cause we might get jumped. I thought, "This is crazy."

——SHARON FREEMAN, 34, Russia, Ohio

The slogan of the Baltimore Browns Backers Fan Club is "Behind Enemy Lines" and their tee shirt shows a Dawg-Pound dog holding a dead raven in its jaws. I moved here before the Browns moved here to become the Baltimore Ravens, or as we call them 'the Ratbirds.' I lived through that debacle. In fact, I attended the press conference when Paul Tagliabue waved the contract, signed on Al Lerner's plane, that Art Modell had signed to move the team here. I walked away in disgust as Paris Glendening, the then governor of Maryland, crowed about bringing a team to Baltimore. That's not to say that Baltimore doesn't deserve a team—Baltimore does. It's a great football town. But, nobody deserves the Browns besides Cleveland.

At that press conference, they were still being talked about as the Baltimore Browns. I do tee shirts on the side—silk screens and glass etching and things like that. I had a supplier who just went crazy with 'Baltimore Browns' **MERCHANDISE**. When Modell said, "Oh, we're not going to call it the Browns," he unloaded a whole bunch of stuff. I have a beautiful Baltimore Browns sweatshirt I got for $5…a piece of Browns memorabilia of a name change that thankfully didn't hold. The various sports stores around here were just unloading Baltimore Browns stuff like crazy.

——STEVE EMERICK, Canton, now living in Baltimore

Women buy 70% of all NFL merchandise and 44 percent of all major league baseball merchandise.

The difference between Kellen Winslow and government bonds? Government bonds mature.

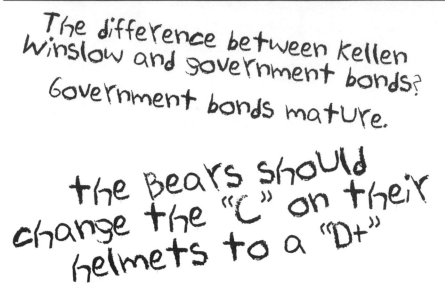

the Bears should change the "C" on their helmets to a "D+"

Butch Davis isn't smart enough to know he's dumb.

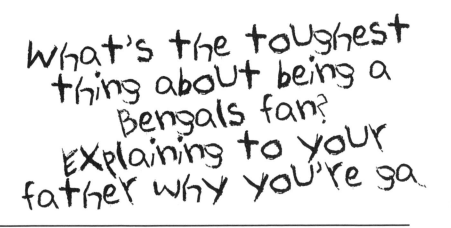

What's the toughest thing about being a Bengals fan? Explaining to your father why you're ga

Chapter 6

Put Me In Coach

It Was A Ball!

WIT HAPPENS

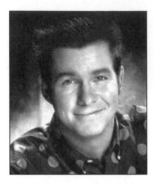

CHUCK BOOMS

For over three years, Euclid High grad, Chuck Booms was the #1 headliner in the country for The Improv Comedy Clubs. He was the co-host of Kiley and Booms on Fox Sports Radio for 26 months, the #1-rated afternoon radio show in the country, A Booms secret: When he wants to break up with a girlfriend, he tells them he's going to name his first child "Sonic."

I've been a Browns fan since I was a kid. I have plenty of opinions, but, as you will note throughout this, my opinions are actually facts. They're just ones people have denied and don't want to talk about.

Presently, I'm a political commentator. I'm a paid contributor to the Fox New Channel. I've done *Fox and Friends*. I've done *Larry King Live* and a ton of *Politically Incorrect* with Bill Maher, who is a good friend. Actually Jerry Springer and I have done many TV shows together. He's a liberal from conservative Cincinnati, and I'm a conservative from liberal Cleveland. We said the 2004 election would come down to Ohio. We were right so we were on multiple shows together and called ourselves, "The Buckeye Boys."

I'm convinced that if I were the owner of a team, I would say to a coach—if I was hiring Romeo Crennel, I would say, in his contract, "If you ever play any game not to lose, you're fired immediately after that game," so that none of us ever have to sit through that. You know and I know when they're doing it. You can see it plainer than day—just setting on the ball and afraid to do this, afraid to do that, afraid to blitz. That was shaped by Shottenheimer. The Broncos got the ball on the two-yard line, and they've got to go 98-yards. This genius, Shottenheimer, takes Chip Banks and puts him on the bench— the fastest linebacker in the AFC, and, still, to this day, the biggest shoulder pads ever issued to a linebacker. You've got Elway where he can only go so far—he can only go ten yards back. You've got him penned in. Marty, the dip---- goes into a prevent.

Guys like this should not be allowed to coach, in my opinion. Those players work out, lift weights, condition their bodies, take the hits— do so much at the behest of an idiot like him. Then you get into the big game, and that's why Marty will never win a big game. He's just not going to. If Marty took over the Browns right now, he'd be perfect, as long as it said in his contract, "You realize that when we get to be 12-5, or 12-4 or 10-6, you're done. We're going to bring in another guy to take us to the next level and win a Super Bowl." 'cause he cannot do it....

I could take you step-by-step of what happened to the Browns, where, how—I've done it for everybody in this town. Some get angry. Some huff and puff. But the facts speak for themselves, and I have facts on my side. These other people speak from nonsensical, emotional platforms of disinformation. They have no idea what they're talking about. I call those the "**Tim Couch** haters." They don't like Tim Couch. You go, "Why?" "He stinks." The last time he was the starter for the Browns in 2002, he was an NFL best 6-2 on the road, with no line, no running backs and receivers that were sketchy, at best. *And—he stinks*? Okay. The facts don't say that.

The facts say that in 2002 he was 6-2 on the road. He won seven of his last 10. When we were 7-7, and the Ravens were 7-7 at Baltimore—the loser is out of the playoffs—Davis has p----- away the time-out. We had the ball on the 10-yard line. Couch took us 90 yards to take them out of the playoffs, keep our hopes alive. Phil Savage, who is now the general manager, when asked, "Would you take a look at Tim Couch going into next year?" he said, "Absolutely." Somebody said, "Why?" He said, "Because I've never gotten that drive out of my head. Any kid that could do that with that calm and

> **TIM COUCH** was the leading scorer in Kentucky high school basketball his junior year. When he was in the eighth grade, he averaged 16 points a game with the Hyden varsity.

that control against arguably the best, or one of the best defenses in the country—at their place—obviously can play football." He also has eleven or twelve fourth-quarter comebacks. Everybody says, "The true measure of an NFL quarterback is what can he do when the chips are on the line, there are no time-outs, everything's against you, the ball's in your hands. You can either win the game for your team or lose it." Couch had a terrible team around him, and 12 times, he's won it. To put that in contrast, let's take Dante Culpepper, who the media all seem to have a love affair with. The Lions blew a playoff game to the Vikings last year when that idiot missed the extra point. The Vikings held on to win. They gave Culpepper credit for a fourth-quarter comeback. You know what number that was for him— five! You would argue with me that Culpepper's got a little bit better weapons than Tim.

Ron Wolf was brought here and, before Butch Davis treated him like garbage and embarrassed him, he was reviewing players at the behest of Carmen Policy. When he reviewed the quarterbacks, he said, "I don't know why the coach continues to say there's a problem here." He reviewed Tim in all aspects of his game—everything—you know how thorough he is, and he gave Couch a "B." He gave Kelly Holcomb a "C," meaning Holcomb is a very adequate backup. If you need a guy for a game or two, he's your guy, obviously not a starter. He gave Couch a "B" and that was off of everything he had accomplished up till then. He even said, "You put together an offensive line and give him some time to throw," which he had never had time to throw, "look out."

Davis chose not to spend any time with Ron Wolf or to even speak to him at all. He just made as if that never had happened. In late 2002, Couch got hurt and Holcomb had to pick it up in the Steeler game. But you don't then go into the next year and take the kid's job away from him. Nobody would do that. No coach has ever done that. Butch Davis did it. He said he had a gut feeling. That's a lie.

SOMETIMES, GOD JUST HANDS YOU ONE.

DON COCKROFT

Don Cockroft was an all-stater at Fountain-Ft. Carson High School on the eastern slope of the Rockies near Colorado Springs. He was a surprise third-round pick of the Browns in 1967 out of tiny Adams State College. He never returned to his beloved Colorado, now residing in Canton.

Being a small town farm boy, going to a small high school and small college, moving from Colorado to Cleveland was a definite culture shock. On my first trip there, we arrived at night, and it was kind of like, "Holy Cow! What am I doing?"

When I was a senior in college, I led the nation and had a 48+ yard punting average. A lot of teams had shown interest and contacted me—but not the Cleveland Browns. It was the night before the draft when I got a phone call from their general manager. He introduced himself and indicated that the Browns were considering drafting me fairly high the following day and wanted to know if I'd play ball for the Cleveland Browns. That was the first year of the common draft, which meant that only one team could draft you. Of course, I wasn't going to say "no," but I remember, as soon as we hung up the phone, going to find an atlas to see where in the world Ohio was, let alone Cleveland. I remember so clearly saying, "Man, that's a long ways from Colorado."

I started and finished my career in Cleveland. My rookie season I did hyperextend my knee and wasn't kicking well, and they put me on injured reserve. After a couple of weeks, I said, "Look, I'm ready to kick." Back then, if you went on injured reserve, you were out for four weeks. They sent me down to what was then called the Akron Vulcans. I was going to kick for them but the team folded before I ever got in a game. My first year I actually spent on the taxi squad, but I had 13 active years with the Browns. People ask me, "When did you retire?" I say, "I never retired. I was fired." I say, "**Jim Brown's** the only player I know of in Cleveland Browns history who retired. The rest of us were fired."

Going clear back to college days at Adams State, I punted four years. Somebody told me the other day that I still have the highest career punting average in college football, 45+ yards. When I led the nation my senior year, there were people starting to talk to me about pro football, I had an immediate question in my mind. I was a Baptist and prior to that I was brought up in a denomination where it was black and white—the bible. Certainly, their interpretation was that Sunday is the Lord's Day, and you should rest on Sunday. It's not a day to play. It's not a day to certainly go out and play football. I always questioned that because we were farmers and those cows needed to be milked on Sunday, too. The fact was that I had a very serious question that I needed answered, and that was: Can I play pro football on Sunday and still be a Christian? That denomination actually taught that you could lose your salvation. That's a frightening thing. I asked my mom and dad, "What do you think?" Of course, they wanted me to play pro ball if I had a chance. They said, "Pray about it, son." I go to the pastor, and, he said "Just pray about it."

A couple of things happened that made me feel God was opening doors. One day at college, before I was drafted, the radio was on. All of a sudden, I heard this gentleman speaking on the radio. It was a very strong Christian testimony. The radio guy said, "Well, ladies and gentlemen, you just heard from Bill Glass, All-Pro defensive end of the Cleveland Browns." I didn't know anything about the Browns at that time, but, man, it was like—wait a minute! "Sounds like a really strong Christian to me, and he's playing football; he's an All-Pro." That was a revelation.

I wasn't drafted yet but I was picked to play in the North-South Shrine Game in Miami. The coach that year, and this is kind of neat, too, was Eddie Crowder, from Colorado University. Being in Colorado and having had a great career and certainly a great year, Eddie Crowder called our coach and said, "Hey, we want this Cockroft kid

JIM BROWN was selected in the 1957 NBA draft by the Syracuse Nationals.

to be our kicker for the North team in the North-South Shrine Game." There were 48 in our senior class in high school, 1500 students at Adams State, and all of a sudden I'm being invited to participate in a nationally televised game. It was awe-inspiring. I went down to Miami to be the punter for the North team in that game.

Well, we get back to the altitude thing—I'm telling you for the first 10 days in Miami, I couldn't punt the ball 30 yards. It didn't go in the air. It didn't go anywhere! I remember that there were national headlines, "North All-Star Punter, Cockroft, Finds it Difficult to Kick at Sea Level." I had people sending me papers from everywhere. I was really, really struggling. I went into that game thinking that if I didn't do very well, maybe God is trying to show me something. As it turned out, I averaged 46-yards a punt. I was nominated for the Most Valuable Player. We won the game. I kicked a couple of pretty good field goals. After the game, my roommate said, "Let's go celebrate." I said, "Man, I'm just gonna hang around. God answered a prayer for me tonight." He looked at me like I was weird.

I worked very, very hard at trying to be the best—whether I was quarterback or defensive back or kicker. Although I worked very hard at it, I also knew that God gave me a talent and the ability to be able to do that. I felt, when I went with the Browns that if I made it, particularly with my denominational belief and background, that God would want me to use that to honor His name and to share His love with whomever would listen. That's the premise I went into pro football with.

I was supposed to kick in the All-Star Game when the College All-Stars played the World Champion Green Bay Packers. I didn't even get in the game. We didn't get close enough for a field goal. **Steve Spurrier** was on that team, and he punted. But, when I got to the Browns, thank goodness Bill Glass was here—a strong Christian man. I could lean on him, and we could share together with some other players. That first year I was on the taxi squad. I was in a car accident and messed up my back. Now, I'm really wondering…. I know God is not the author of confusion, but of peace. I get here, and

> **Steve Spurrier was the only quarterback to go 0-14 in one NFL season—with the '76 Buccaneers.**

I know that we can all be a testimony for God, and we should be, wherever we are at, and no matter how successful we are. But, I also know that if you're a pro football player, and people want to hear what you have to say, you've got to be successful. Fortunately, I'd signed a two-year contract. I watched Mr. Groza kick for his 21st year, in my heart, knowing I could kick it further than he did—didn't know if I could kick it any straighter. Gary Collins was our punter, and I knew I could do that. But, I had to watch that first year.

Came back my second year and things weren't going very well. To me, this was my life, and it's the most important thing I can share with anybody, even today. I knew I could kick, but things weren't going well. A gentleman came by my dorm room at Hiram College after a practice. He was big enough to fill up the door. It was Monte Clark, offensive tackle for the Browns. He walked by the door and looked in, and he came back. I guess he could see that I was down. He looked at me and said, "Don, do you believe the Bible?" He didn't even let me answer. He said, "Read Proverbs 3:5-6." And, he walked down the hall. I picked up my Bible and read, "Trust in the Lord with all your heart, lean not unto your own understanding, but in all your ways acknowledge Him, and He will direct your path." I'm telling you that I read that four or five times. I got up, locked my door, and got on my knees. I said, "Lord, help me trust you more." That's all I prayed. Call it a miracle. I don't call it a miracle. I think that's how God works. If we trust him, quit worrying about this, that and failure, we'll have a peace in our heart, and we can do what we're supposed to do. I will share, and I do, and I believe today that if Monte Clark hadn't taken 15 seconds out of his life to ask me a question and tell me to read that, I seriously wonder if I'd have ever made it into pro football. It wasn't that I couldn't kick, I just was too worried about failure.

So, in 1968, I came back to the Browns, and that's where Monte Clark came into the picture. I made the Browns, through prayer and, again, never discount hard work and God-given talent, and had a phenomenal rookie season. After the 1971 season, when I'd had a lousy year, the Browns had drafted a kid to replace me. I came back in 1972, and I really had a peace because whatever happens is going to happen. I want to do what God wants me to do. Billy Graham had a crusade that fall. They called me and said, "Would you share your testimony at a **Billy Graham Crusade** at the Stadium?" You know what I thought? I said, "My career is over, but what a tremendous way to leave Cleveland. To be able to stand in front of 40,000 people and tell them Christ is the most important thing in your life. God has really orchestrated this pretty well. I'm done with football, but what a way to leave." Well, I wasn't done.

That year was when my success really began. As a kicker in pro football, you're either the hero or the goat. Right after I retired, there was a quiz on the radio, "Cockroft had 17 opportunities to win games with kicks in his career. How many did he miss?" The answer was, "None." Some of those were probably **extra points** at the last seconds but many of them were field goals.

I could have kicked longer, but I thank the good Lord for being able to do something that most kids only can dream of. God gave me the opportunity to share with thousands of people. I was talking to some kids the other day at a school, and I can honestly say that I never loafed one time in junior high, high school, college and in the pros. My talk was "Unseen Dreams." In other words, what you do today, you may not see the results. But, what you do today, someday will become a reality. I was trying to share with them that you can't loaf—you don't loaf—you give it a hundred percent. I'm just thankful that I walked away from it knowing that, "Hey, I gave the Browns a hundred percent." I am grateful for the Cleveland Browns, the Browns fans and the opportunity I was provided in Cleveland.

> The first event ever held at Texas Stadium when it was opened in 1971 was a **BILLY GRAHAM CRUSADE** with Roger Staubach as the guest speaker.

> John Madden lost his long-time partner after SuperBowl XXXVI when Pat Summerall retired. Pat Summerall's real first name is George. He is called Pat because when he was a kicker with the New York Giants football team, the newspapers would print: "P.A.T.-Summerall." P.A.T. stood for "Point After Touchdown." Summerall played minor league baseball against Mickey Mantle.

NOSTALGIA'S NOT WHAT IT USED TO BE

ED GOLDSTEIN

Some people refer to Ed Goldstein as the Browns #1 fan even though he never attended a game at Municipal Stadium. He has lived in California since 1945. His uncle, Herman Goldstein, was a well-known sports-writer for the Cleveland News.

The Browns, back in the old All-America Conference, first started coming out here to play the Los Angeles Dons. They would play the 49ers the following week up in San Francisco because San Francisco was also in the All-America Conference. They would stay at the old Green Hotel in Pasadena, normally late in August. I would go out and stay with my uncle at the hotel, and watch them practice. The old players like Otto Graham, **Marion Motley**, Dante Lavelli, and all the old Hall-of-Famers—I was friendly with all of them. That was my first true love affair—the Browns back in '46. From '46 until '55, I never had a problem at all because they were in the championship game every year.

In the late '50s, I was about 18 years old. The Green Hotel was a retirement hotel back then. If you were young, you had to be a football player to stay there. I would get a lot of autographs there. These guys didn't make much money then. I, as a teenager, was buying the players Cokes in the Coke machine in the lobby of the Green Hotel.

> **MARION MOTLEY**, Alan Page and Dan Dierdorf are all Canton natives and are enshrined in the Pro Football Hall of Fame in their hometown. Page worked on a construction crew that built the Hall while Dierdorf and his father attended the groundbreaking ceremony.

The '55 championship game was played here in Los Angeles. It was Otto Graham's last game, and the Browns won 38-14. I walked off the field with Otto Graham's arm around my shoulder. I was 15-years old at the time, and it was probably the highlight of my life. The Browns won seven out of the 10. Things fell on a dry spell, then Jim Brown came along.

If you go to the Hall of Fame in Canton, they have four Browns jerseys there, Otto Graham, Lou Groza, Jim Brown and later they put in Ozzie Newsome. If you look at Otto Graham's jersey, from back in the early years, the numbers these guys wore were anything they wanted. Otto Graham was 60. Lavelli was 56. Motley was 76. Then in '51, the NFL changed it where they used a numbering system.

Quarterbacks had to be from 1-20. Running backs and linebackers, etc., were 20s, 30s and 40s. Centers were 50s; guards were 60s; tackles were 70s, etc. So, in the '51 season, the players had to switch numbers. If you look at Otto Graham's jersey, you will see the number 14 on the jersey, and the background shows '60' where they took off the old number. My son looked at it and said, "They didn't buy new jerseys?" I said, "They couldn't afford new jerseys back in those days."

I still consider Otto Graham the greatest quarterback of all time—I don't care what anybody says. Anyone who can take his team to a championship game 10 straight years and win seven of them… nobody is ever going to touch a record like that. He was the highest-paid player at the time. He made $35,000 a year. Jim Brown, when he retired, was the highest-paid player, and he made $75,000. Now this s--- Randy Moss pretends he's mooning people and he gets fined $10,000, and he says, "That's like somebody losing fifty cents." It's appalling. At least, as a kid, I had a chance to root for a team and players. Today, kids only get to root for a uniform. One day you're rooting for a guy, and the next day you hate his guts. It's a shame. Kids today don't have real heroes anymore. The ones they do have disappoint them. The country is long on celebrities, short on heroes.

Otto Graham was the consummate hero. He never smoked. He never drank. The day he passed, just last year, I cried as much then as if I'd lost my own brother. I used to correspond with him. He had Alzheimer's in the later years. He signed many things for me, hats, jerseys, footballs with his name on them. After his death, I sent a donation, and his wife wrote me a beautiful letter back thanking me and thanking me for corresponding with Otto in his later years.

I really miss the old Browns. What Art Modell did to the team—in a way, I really can't blame him. When Joe Robbie, the owner of the Miami Dolphins, passed away, there was not enough money to pay the inheritance tax so his kids had to sell the team. The whole reason for Art moving the team was to put the money away so his no-good son, David, could have the money to pay the taxes when he died. As it turned out, he ran through the money and lost the team anyway.

Art did more for the NFL than a lot of people. He was the one who first initiated the television package, and they owe him a lot. He was the one who instigated the merger of the AFL-NFL. There are questions as to whether or not he should be in the Hall of Fame. I know a lot of Cleveland fans are very bitter. I'm bitter that he moved the team, but if Al Davis is in the Hall of Fame, Jack the Ripper should be in the Hall of Fame. Al Davis would sell his mother's grave for $50,000. He's a whore. The two biggest whores in football are him and Georgia Frontiere, of the Rams, who some people feel had her husband killed to get the team…Carroll Rosenbloom.

It's ironic that the Browns moved to Baltimore and became the Ravens. You know where the Orioles came from? They came from St. Louis. They were the St. Louis Browns. So, two Browns teams, both moved to Baltimore, and both became two birds.…

The Browns used to always wear white, and there was a reason for that—it was the intimidation factor. A guy looks bigger in white than he does in other colors. That was one of Paul Brown's ideas. Also, then, they wore shoulder pads which were about three inches too large for their shoulders so they'd look like behemoths coming out onto the field to intimidate the other players. They even wore white helmets at first, and the first thing to change was the helmets to go from white to orange.

IT'S NOT HOW BIG YOU ARE, IT'S HOW GOOD YOU ARE!

GREGORY PRUITT

For nine seasons, Greg Pruitt thrilled Browns fans with dazzling runs. The native Texan loved Cleveland so much that he now lives there permanently. The Browns chose Pruitt with the first pick of the second round of the 1973 draft.

In high school, I can recall watching the Cleveland Browns and Jim Brown, and then would go outside and try to re-enact things I saw. One Sunday, Jim Brown ran a sweep to the right, got to the sideline, and he turned back upfield and five guys hit him. He broke the tackle of thesc five guys and went on to gain big yards. There was a guy by the name of Charles Law, a friend who tried to re-enact that move later that day when we played outside. Charles Law ran the ball to the right. He slowed down to try to re-enact what he had seen on TV. Three or four of us hit him…and we broke both his legs, one of his arms and bruised his sternum. I saw Jim years later and told him that I knew one guy who didn't like him—his name was Charles Law.

I was runner-up for the **Heisman Trophy** at Oklahoma. The question mark was my size. When I was a senior, our coach, Chuck Fairbanks, got the head coaching job at New England, where he had three first-round picks. I was pretty confident that the question mark of size—who knew that better than the coach I had just played for— would not matter. I felt I was probably going to play for New England

> **What Heisman Trophy winner has made the most money? The 1959 winner, Billy Cannon of LSU, was arrested for counterfeiting in the early '80s and spent almost three years in jail. Technically, he is the only Heisman Trophy winner to ever "make" money.**

so, I went out and planned a celebration party. I had access to the draft information as it came in. After the first round, I wasn't drafted, and I didn't know really what to think. I went out to play golf, and that's where they found me. I was on the golf course playing by myself. They told me I had just gotten drafted by the Browns. I was happy to go anywhere after the first round passed by.

Coach Fairbanks took Sam Cunningham, John Hannah from Alabama and another lineman. I was upset with Coach Fairbanks that he hadn't drafted me. Our Browns played him one year when, if the Patriots won, they would have clinched a spot in the playoffs. We'd only won three games so it was pretty much written in the books that they were going to win. I was leading the league in kick-off returns, and they were going to kick the ball away from me. We studied the film and saw that they had a soccer-style kicker. We noticed he was putting the ball on one hash mark when he was trying to kick one way, and on the other if he was trying to kick the opposite way. So we lined up single file. Wherever he placed the ball, we would go to the side where we thought he was going to kick the ball. I was always the right returner so when we lined up, he set the ball up to go left, so I went left. Then he called time out. He went to the sideline, and you could see by Fairbanks' hand expressions and his body language that he was not happy with the time out. The kicker came back out and he line-drived the ball to me. I ran it back 88-yards for a touchdown. That put them into a situation they really hadn't planned on. We went on to upset them, and they ended up in such a tailspin that they went from clinching a spot in the playoffs to not even making the playoffs at all. It was sweet....

One day, I was watching Super Stars on ABC and I said to myself, "I can do some of those things just as good as some of those guys." So, I called my agent and asked him to look into my being on that program. He called me back a day or so later and told me to write a letter to ABC to let them know I was interested and to see if it was possible for me to participate. We were going to hold the letter until I played a real good game. The next game was against New England when I was MVP on a Monday Night game. After the game, I went straight to the main post office and mailed my letter.

About five days later, I got invited. I went to the Super Stars. I was talking to Earl Campbell, who was there, and asked him what he had put in his letter. I didn't even know then that he was laughing at me. He said, "Well, I didn't put anything." He waited until all the guys, Lyle Alzado, Walter Payton, Tony Dorsett, Joe Theismann, Lynn Swann got together and he told them, "Greg Pruitt wrote a letter asking to come here." That made me mad...I went on to win the Super Stars. It was a pretty good competition. I told them afterward, "Maybe you'all should have written a letter."...

Head coach, Forrest Gregg, was so tough in practices that he would make you do these up-downs—about 100 before practice. He would walk and just talk, "I promise you're going to be tough. I promise you're going to be in shape." Browns players, when he turned his back, would stop to rest. They were so spent they couldn't go any farther. One evening, at our regular meeting, we got ready to watch film. He turned the projector on, and it looked like somebody's homemade film. He'd had somebody in the stands filming the practices so they caught all the guys who were stopping when he wasn't looking.

I was traded to the Raiders for a conditional draft choice. When I went to the Raiders, the first person I met was Al Davis. I sat down and talked with him and Al knew everything about me—high school, through college, through the NFL. He told me that he had traded for me for a provisional draft pick so not to expect to play very much that first season because he would give the Browns the lowest pick possible. It was for the third-round pick...and the next year I went to the Pro Bowl.

I retired before the 1985 season. I really never left Cleveland. I had a home in Cleveland which I kept. While I was with the Raiders, I rented a place in California. I had played here nine years and knew I wouldn't play another nine. I really liked Cleveland better than I liked L. A. I have a construction business here and work with realtors and with different cities on pre-sell violations. Like if you sell your house, or if you buy one, the city comes out and inspects your house and lists all the violations. Then, the buyer can either accept it with those violations at a reduced price, or he can request that the violations be corrected. Either way, whether it be for the buyer or for the seller, I correct those....

I was upset when the Browns left Cleveland. I really didn't think it would happen. I've got a lot of friends, and they just assume that I've got insight into what's going on. I told them, "Aw, this won't happen. This is about a stadium. All owners threaten to move in order to help get the stadium. He'll never leave. He'll probably get his stadium." I was real upset.

I played with the Cleveland Browns. I played with the Raiders. I've talked with guys from other teams, and I don't think there are greater fans than the Cleveland Browns fans. In 1996, I went with the fans to present petitions at the owners' meeting in Atlanta. They presented over 2,000,000 petitions. I qualify myself by saying I was with the Browns when they went to Baltimore. I was with the Raiders as they went to LA. I'm from Houston and the Oilers went to Tennessee. If you look at what happened with those last two, those fans really just let it happen. When I think of the result of what the Browns fans did, they created a situation where it was much tougher. The owners had to pay something to the city they left, and it is much more difficult these days to just get up and move.

What we were fighting for was tradition and history. We were part of that, and we didn't want that to go. Browns fans are the best fans of any sports team anywhere in the world.

Name the Raiders coach...
win valuable prizes

DEC. 4, 1995 · $2.95 (CAN. $3.95)

Sports Illustrated

Battle for the Browns
Art Modell sucker-punched Cleveland, but the city is fighting back

SPORTS ILLUSTRATED

OCTOBER 8, 1956

a Time Inc. weekly publicati

25 CENTS
$7.50 A YEAR

COACH BROWN
AND
QUARTERBACK RATTERMAN

CAN THEY KEEP
THE CLEVELAND BROWNS ON TOP?

Sports Illustrated

AUGUST 26, 1985 $1.95

BANKING ON BERNIE

eveland Pins
s Hopes On
ernie Kosar's
illion-Dollar Arm

0 10094

724454

34

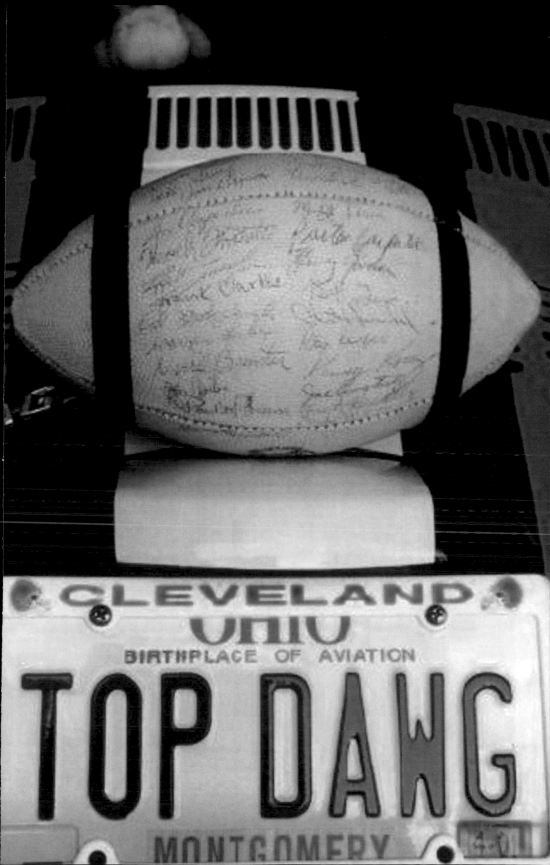

Somewhere in Mexico there might be a pickup truck missing its upholstery.

Browns fan, David Zbin, put a Browns helmet decal on Jim Morrison's tombstone in Paris in the middle of the night when The Doors were closed. (See story on page 259)

The famous Browns "helmet car" created by die-hard Browns fan, Larry Kopa. (See story on page 226)

CHEVY CHASE ONCE HOSTED THE OSCARS... HENDRIX ONCE OPENED FOR THE MONKEES... THE BROWNS ONCE FIVE-PEATED. THERE ARE SOME THINGS YOU JUST CAN'T MAKE UP.

MARC SHACK

Marc Shack lives in Painesville where he is a quality engineer and a real estate agent. He has been a Browns fan for over 50 years.

Some of my fondest memories are away from the game itself. In the early years, when I was real little, we used to take the bus to the rapid transit and then take the rapid transit down to the Terminal Tower. We'd get a piece of pizza in there, and then we'd walk over to the stadium and wait in line to get into the bleachers. We used to have to pay a dollar to get into the bleachers, but it was not a reserved seat. You just waited in line with everybody else. So, Sunday morning was waiting in line with a lot of other people to get into the bleachers, which today they call the 'Dawg Pound.' It wasn't called the Dawg Pound then.

When we sat in the bleachers, even back then, it was kind of a crazy crowd. They couldn't wait to get in there and get their beer going and rooting hard. It was a wild thing. In those days, they used to kick the ball into the seats, and everybody would fight over the ball so one of the prime spots to get was right behind the goalposts. I remember watching Lou Groza kicking the ball into the air and everybody trying to get it. That was fun. Then, the cops would come and take it. I understood it was just a rumor that they would then donate those footballs to a youth football league in Cleveland.

Many years back, my sister was a bookkeeper for the Browns, and as a Brown employee, she got two tickets. She used to go herself. Then when she passed away, Mr. Modell gave us her tickets for that year, 1974, and we started buying them after that. I was raising a family and really couldn't afford the tickets at that time. In 1980, I took them over from my parents. They had actually been in my parents' names. I've had them ever since. When the Browns left and then came back, they honored the old ticketholders. We got first choice of the PSLs, and first choice of seats. I got to write down what kind of seat I wanted and what price range and wound up with pretty decent seats. But, I have to tell you, I miss the old stadium. The new stadium is nice, but there was just something about that old stadium that was great. Now, I'm a little upset with the seats I have, but it's not an easy thing to change them. Since my sister worked for the Browns, during those years, I would go up to the office. I actually met Art Modell and Chuck Heaton, the sports writer at that time for the *Plain Dealer*, who had an office up there, and a couple of the players who would come in and out....

Years ago, my dad was tending bar part time in a bar in Eastlake. Bob Gain, who was a former Cleveland Brown, was a regular in the bar. He invited my dad to bring his family over for a day-after-Christmas dinner. My dad accepted so the day after Christmas, my mom, my dad and myself headed out to Eastlake to visit Bob Gain and his wife…who were *not* prepared for us to be there. It was one of those in-the-bar kind of conversations. All of a sudden, we showed up, and they did everything they could to make us comfortable. My mom was definitely not comfortable. Bob Gain showed me his trophy. He was the Most Valuable Player in the College All-Star game. The trophy was bigger than me. I was probably 12 years old at the time.

Bob Gain handed me a gift on the way out the door, saying, "Don't open it till later." We left kind of fast. We didn't really have dinner with them. I got home, opened the package, and it was a football signed by all the Browns—Paul Brown, Jim Brown…. It was an old-style football, which was white and had the rubber bladder in it and eventually it all dried out. There was no way to preserve it. It's all dried out and pretty bad, but I still have that ball. I can still go back and look at the names and remember those guys.

MEMORIES, LIKE HEROES, NEVER GROW OLD

It was great to meet Bernie Kosar when we were in New Orleans for a game. I hollered over to him, "Hey, thanks for the party last night." As part of our package deal, he had been at the same party we had gone to the night before. He came walking over to us, asking if we'd had a good time, and, "Are you guys getting ready to go to the tailgate party?" So, we got to walk down Bourbon Street with him, and talk to  him. He had on his Dallas Cowboy Super Bowl ring, and he offered it to me for me to check it out. He went up to do a radio interview with Brian Brennan, and just left me with his ring. I bet I had it for 10 minutes. People were coming over to see it, and I finally just had to get his attention so I could give it back to him. He was a real nice guy.

——**MIKE FREEMAN**, 37, Troy, Ohio

My dad and my mom went down to a take canoe trip on the Cuyahoga River. You get in a canoe, paddle it down, and they drive you back to your car. Dad arrived, and there was nobody in the office to take his money. He was looking around for an employee. He noticed a lot of Browns stuff on the wall. There was a container that held a number of autographed footballs with all the Browns players names and the coaches. They were just out where anyone could grab one. Finally, a woman came in, and as he was paying for the trip, he said, "Why do they have all the Browns stuff here? You must be big fans." She said, "This is my son's business, and his name's Dick Schafrath. He used to play for Cleveland." My dad says, "Oh, yeah, I know who he is." Dad said he saw him later bringing the canoes up, driving people around in a bus. My father was telling me that Schafrath would have teenagers working for him, and one of them would grab a canoe and try to drag it out to where it should be. Then, you would see Schafrath, and I don't know how old he was, and he would have one in each hand and be moving them.

——**MARK BLOOM**, 51, Akron native

I remember talking to Art at our dining room table—early '60s—when the Browns had a running back named Bobby Mitchell, who's in the Hall of Fame now. I used to tell Art Modell, "Why don't you let Bobby Mitchell be a receiver and be on the other side of the field as a flanker on one side with Ray Renfro on the other." There was no defensive backfield in the league that could guard them, could defend that. He would say, "Bobby Mitchell could never be a receiver, Robert, unfortunately, you don't know football." Paul Brown traded Bobby Mitchell very soon after that. Bobby became a receiver for the Washington Redskins and is in the Hall of Fame now.

Paul Brown traded Bobby Mitchell for the rights to draft Ernie Davis. He wanted to have a backfield like Green Bay had. They had **Paul Hornung** and Jim Taylor, these two big backs. The Browns had Jim Brown and he wanted to have this great running back out of Syracuse, Ernie Davis, to be right alongside him. Bobby Mitchell was my favorite Brown of all time. He was so fast—he was faster than Jim Brown, even. He made some of the most fantastic runs, but he never got the chance to be a receiver. I used to see him on these swing passes when Milt Plum would just flip him the ball. Just a swing pass to Jim Brown or Bobby Mitchell out of the backfield, and these guys would take it 70 yards to really add to Plum's statistics.

——ROBERT BRENNER, 66, "Hurricane Bob" on Sports Talk Radio

It's largely true that you don't cheer for the players, you cheer for the colors. The biggest thing that happened for Cleveland back then was that we traded Paul Warfield to the Dolphins. Paul Warfield! They traded him for the draft rights for Mike Phipps who did absolutely nothing. To think of a player like Paul Warfield leaving, and, these days, the guy we were going to build our franchise around, Tim Couch, is unemployed. Granted, he's made more money than you and I will ever see. Here's a guy who got booed by his own home town fans. Sometimes, I think there was a case for it. Unfortunately, that

> **At Notre Dame, 1956 Heisman Trophy winner PAUL HORNUNG played halfback, fullback, and quarterback; punted, kicked-off, kicked field goals; ran back punts and kickoffs; and was a starting safety. Against Iowa that year, he ran a quarterback sneak 80-yards for a touchdown.**

Sunday night game when people cheered when it became clear he had a concussion and couldn't get up was a little over the top, even for Browns fans.

——SAM CHAMBERS, 45, hospital consultant, Atlanta

There were other guys that I admired and respected very greatly. Of course, the great Paul Warfield was here when I came. What I admired about Paul was the gracefulness of his moves and his ability. He was poetry in motion. You think of Jerry Rice, but Paul, to me, was as smooth as there ever was at running routes and catching passes. I remember, unlike today, I'd watch him in a ball game or on film, and for whatever reason, the ball didn't get thrown to him on many occasions, and Warfield had got his guy beat by five or six yards. Yet Paul never came back to the huddle to moan and complain. I respect him for that. Certainly, Jerry Sherk, I admired greatly. He was a gentle giant on the field. He was a great nose guard on defense, and his speed and his ability were really hard to beat, but, off the field, he was a gentle person.

——DON COCKROFT, 60, former Browns kicker

I wrote a talk show for a couple of years—and people never understand what you write for a talk show, but, believe me, there's a lot of work that goes into it. One of the guests on the show was **Don Meredith**, whom I enjoyed greatly. His parents, Jeff and Hazel—he always referred to them—were there that day, and I went over and met them. He was a lot of fun. I had Lynn Swann one time. It was the off-season when Paul Warfield had been traded back to Cleveland. Of course, I told him immediately that I was a Browns fan. When I mentioned the Warfield thing, he said, "You know, they always say nobody comes back to the ball like Paul Warfield. This year they're going to see it face to face." He was looking forward to

> Frank and Kathie Lee Gifford have the same birthday, except they're twenty-three years apart age-wise. They were married in 1986. Frank Gifford was a grandfather at the time. Cody and Cassidy are uncle and aunt to Frank Gifford's grandchildren. When told that Kathie Lee was pregnant, **DON MEREDITH** said, "I'll hunt the guy down, Frank, and I'll kill him."

that match-up. He was a real good guy. I liked him a lot. I had Muhammad Ali, Ken Norton. Alex Karras came in because his girl-friend, now wife, Susan Clark, was on the show. They were doing a sit-com together at the time in '76. After the show, we chatted for a few minutes. When I told him I was a Browns fan, he looked at me and said, "You've got a tough way to go, pal." Basically, he was saying, you've got a long wait till they get back.

———EMIL DAVIDSON, 68, writer, Los Angeles

The biggest surprise to us was how small Brian Brennan was. He was the wide receiver, position guy, unbelievable hands. The guy is not real big. He couldn't be more than 5'8". I don't know what they listed him in the programs, but 5'8" would be generous for him. He couldn't have weighed 145 pounds. It was almost startling how small the guy was.

When we went to Houston, the last game before the team moved, we got in the stadium early and had front-row seats in the end zone—90 front-row seats in the end zone. We're on the field, because that's where our seats were, almost three hours before game time. Who comes walking across the field—but Ozzie Newsome. My son, who did not get his autograph earlier, was wearing an Ozzie Newsome jersey. So, what's Ozzie gonna do? He autographed the jersey my son was wearing…*but it was a borrowed jersey*. The guy he borrowed it from wouldn't let him keep it—wouldn't sell it to me—wouldn't do anything. So, no Ozzie autograph.

———DON DAVIE, Ohio U grad, San Antonio

I had a big crush on Bill Nelsen. He was the quarterback and was #16. He had terrible knees and would always have his knees drained before the game. My dad knew his doctor, an orthopedic surgeon. My dad said, "Well, how would you like to go and watch Bill Nelsen have his knees drained?" The doctor could do that then. I was really excited. But, poor Bill Nelsen, the last thing he wanted to see is some kid fawning over him while he's getting his knees drained. It was absurd. But, I did it.

———CARLA TRICARICHI, 42, Cleveland

Before I worked for Saks Fifth Avenue, I worked for a company called Higbee's, which was an old, old department store in Cleveland that turned into Dillards. They were throwing away this expensive

mannequin because it was busted so I brought her home. I actually have a mannequin sitting in front of my house on a park bench. She has a Browns flag and is wearing a Bernie Kosar jersey, long underwear and orange sweat pants, which is pretty funny because she looks real. I have a wig on her.

My husband and I are in our forties. A good friend of my husband is first-cousin to Hanford Dixon. We were having a barbecue over here one day, and Derek, my husband's friend, said, "Well, Hanford's going to come over." I thought, "Oh my God. I should clean the house. Hanford Dixon is coming to my house!" I was like a little kid—like the Pope was coming. It turned out that he's the nicest guy.

Once we went to Hanford's house for a barbecue. I actually have a *real* Browns helmet, one of the Riddell helmets. I've had it for years. I took it with me and put it in the back seat of the car. My husband said, "My wife has her Browns helmet in the car, and she was hoping that you would sign it for her." It happened that Ozzie Newsome was there as well. I got really embarrassed about it. But they went, "You have a helmet?" Well, they thought it was some queer helmet so said again, "You have a *real* helmet?" I said, "Yeah, I do." They were totally amazed about it.

——PAULA FOGEL-DUCKSWORTH, Bedford Heights, Ohio

The only thing Earnest Byner is known for is The Fumble, which is unfortunate, because he is a very personable, kind-hearted, big-hearted guy…he was a heck of a ballplayer. He would block, run, whatever. I hate the fact that his career is always going to be noted by The Fumble. I hate that rap on him because Earnest was better than that. I always tell everybody, "You can say what you want to say, but, first of all, he didn't fumble the ball, he was stripped. Second of all, if Webster Slaughter had completed his route and not wanted to be a cheerleader, Jeremiah Castille wouldn't have been there to strip him of the ball."

I was watching ESPN, and they were reshowing that game. Jeremiah Castille said "Webster Slaughter broke his route off." That's what made him realize it was a run 'cause Webster had been burning him all game. He said Webster cut his route short and turned around to be a cheerleader. Earnest was maybe a foot away from being in the end zone. Castille said, "Byner had been running people over all game, and I had to make a decision. Do I hit him head on, or do I just try to go for the ball and hit him on the side. With him running people over all game long, I'm going to the side and hit him." When he saw Slaughter cut his route short, he was able to see Byner coming, where if Webster had run his route completely, by the time he got there, Byner would have scored, and the Browns would have gone on to the Super Bowl.

———CURTIS FRANKLIN, 48, Cleveland

Years back there was a Cleveland Browns Touchdown Club. Just before the players flew out to play their last away game of the year, they'd have banquets at the airport where there is a huge banquet room. After the banquet was over, the players would hop on the plane and go to where they were playing their last game. They had the last one in 1992, and all the players were there. I was running up to the tables like a little kid to get autographs from them. My wife said, "What are you doing? They're eating." I said, "I don't care." I was able to get a lot of autographs, including Modell's. I asked him if I could take a large pennant that was hanging behind the table, and he said, "Sure. Take it." I got Belichick's autograph. The funny thing about Belichick's autograph was that he prints his name, so I thought that was very, very odd.

———BILL GILLAN, Rochester, New York

You want a summer camp story? I have the best. I've told it before, but it was the coolest thing that ever happened to me. For a couple of hours in 1964, I was friends with Jim Brown, the greatest running back of all time.

I was eight-years old and visiting my dad, former *Plain Dealer* sportswriter Chuck Heaton, who was staying at the Browns training camp at Hiram College in Portage County. One afternoon, practice was over. My dad was filing a couple of stories on deadline. I was bored out of my skull, throwing stones from the gravel parking lot into the woods. Brown came walking down the hill. "Want to take a ride into Garrettsville?" I said I had to ask my dad. "Well, go ask him," Brown said. Minutes later, I was riding in Jim Brown's metallic lavender Cadillac telling him all about myself. We rolled into town, where he bought me a grape soda and some comic books. For the rest of the week, whenever he saw me, he called me "little pardner."...

Equipment manager, Morrie Kono, frequently put us to work. With two-a-day practices, there was always laundry to be done. We washed clothes, made bundles of socks, jocks and tee shirts and carried towels, water and footballs. But, it was cool just being around the Browns. They were the biggest stars Cleveland had back then. For the most part, they were fun, funny and friendly guys. And, they liked us kids. Over the years, I got to know a lot of players. Frank Ryan told me about his son's experimental freezing of frogs. Ben Davis turned me onto the Isley Brothers' music. Gene Hickerson from **OLE MISS** was always trying to get me involved in some mischief. Holding footballs for kicker, Lou Groza, and returning Don Cockroft's punts in front of the crowds that gathered daily for practice made us feel like players ourselves. Kono always told us not to get too attached to any player. Fifty-five players reported to camp, but only 33 made the roster. Anybody could be cut or traded....

Players got bored, too. Veterans with secure slots on the team were known to race into Garrettsville after the afternoon practice and guzzle pitchers of beer in the hour and a half before dinner. They could be fined for being late. The veterans liked to harass the rookies at the meal. The standard routine was to make them stand on their chairs during dinner and sing their college fight song. But, sometimes the pranks were a little more elaborate. Linebacker Ross Fichtner was famous for his mongoose box. Rookies would be told that Fichtner was a little strange and he kept a pet mongoose—a vicious little thing. Eventually, curious rookies would ask to see Fichtner's mongoose. They were taken to his room individually where Fichtner would be sitting by his mongoose box, talking lovingly to the animal through a small caged window on the side. He would beckon the rookie forward. As the player strained to see the animal, Fichtner would hit a switch that released a spring-loaded

> The speed limit on the University of Mississippi campus is 18 MPH in honor of Archie Manning's uniform number.

door. A long, bushy raccoon tail would fly out. The screams echoed down the dormitory hallways.

——MICHAEL HEATON, sportswriter, *Cleveland Plain-Dealer*

What's really neat, though, is we're not far from training camp now, which has moved to Berea, and a lot of the players and their families come into the store. They'll come in, and they know that we're fans, so they just say, "Hi," and talk with us and bring their families in. Then the word spreads that we're a store that will do things for them and help them out. So they shop here a lot, but if they're in the mall, they'll just stop by and say, "Hi." That's really fun because you get to know them on a personal level.

Kellen Winslow, who was our first draft pick in 2004, came into the store. This was long before the motorcycle fiasco. He was a pretty popular guy, and everybody knew who he was. He was very cordial, signing autographs, being very nice to everybody. I usually don't ask the players for autographs, but this one I did, because I wasn't sure if I'd ever get to see him again. I asked for an autograph, and he signed it "#80." Number 80 happens to be Aaron Shea, who is not only a customer of ours, but a good friend, and a very nice guy. I said, "Why are you signing #80?" The story was that Winslow was supposed to buy the number from Shea. That's pretty typical in the NFL, to buy other players **numbers**. He wanted that number because of his dad. He said, "That's the number I'm going to have." I said, "That's Aaron Shea's number. Did you buy it from him yet?" He said, "No. Word is he won't be here this year." I said, "Oh, I hope you're wrong because he's my favorite player." Well, as it turns out, Winslow got hurt, and Aaron Shea went and took another number. It got me a little ticked when he said that.

It seems like the Browns players really appreciate their fans. When we went out to training camp at Lakeland, it was totally different. It was a whole different era, and the players were just so interested in the fans. They would stop and talk to them. They wouldn't

> Former Northwestern running back and TV color analyst, Mike Adamle, was the last NFL running back who wore a **NUMBER** lower than "20"…his number was "1"….His father, Tony Adamle, starred at OSU and played six years for the Browns.

just sign something and run. They'd actually stop and have a conversation. Or, "Hey, you were here last year." They would actually remember. It was pretty amazing. The fans just eat that up. It's great. A lot of the players are like that.

——SUE NAUMANN, 52, Parma, sporting goods store executive

I've got an authentic Jim Brown jersey, autographed and framed, hanging on my wall here in my home. I met him in '98 at a Joe Morgan Charity Golf Tournament in California. He was wearing the jersey out on the course—it was the year **Mark McGwire** was setting the home-run record. We were on the first green, Jim looked up and saw me wearing a Jim Brown jersey, and he said, "Hey, number 32." I said, "Hey, Jim, you're the man...not Mark McGwire." The people in the crowd all started barking. Then when we got to the second green, he came walking up and I said, "Hey, Jim, can I get your autograph? Will you autograph this jersey?" He said, "Sure." He autographed the jersey so I brought it home and had it framed, and it will never get worn again.

——PATRICK NIEDER, Jacksonville, Fla., originally from Erie

One of my favorite players was Edgar 'Special Delivery' Jones. I liked him because he had also tried out as a pitcher with the Cleveland Indians. Unfortunately, he didn't make the Indians. I got to meet Paul Brown. I know he is hated at Ohio State because when he formed the Browns, he had five players on the Browns team who still had eligibility at Ohio State. Three of them are in the Hall of Fame....

I was working for Harrah's, and we had a celebrity golf tournament with seven quarterbacks, Gabriel, Plunkett, Namath, Unitas, Hadl. I was working with a photographer taking pictures of the celebrities as they played. My wife was at one of the places where lunch was being served, so I go to meet her. There's

MARK McGWIRE's brother, Dan McGwire, a former #1 pick of the Seahawks, is the tallest NFL QB ever at 6'8". Former Celtic and Toronto Blue Jay, Danny Ainge, is the tallest second baseman in Major League history.

Unitas bringing her a plate of food. It turned out he thought she was one of the hookers that Harrahs hired. She didn't realize it, fortunately. He apologized profusely.

——*GOLDY NORTON*, California resident since 1944

We have a banquet every year here in our little town, and we usually bring a player in. Two years ago, we had Dennis Northcutt. It was so funny because he had never been in a rural setting like this. The man had never seen farm animals. He kept calling his mom on his cell phone. He'd say, "You're not going to believe this, Mom. We're going to Hicksville." We're so used to living around here, and he's like, "Well, you don't understand. I went from south-central LA to school in Arizona and from Arizona right to Cleveland. I've never been in a little tiny town like this." He was so friendly and was really a good person.

——**KAREN HOLSAPPLE**, bartender, Versailles, Ohio

Jim Brown's personal checkered past is what it is. It's a matter of public record. I was born the year he won the championship. I remember talking to my dad, who is a sports fan, but not a fanatic like me who really dies with it. He said, "I remember watching Jimmy Brown. There's nobody better." Every time I see something on Jimmy Brown, I just sit there and think that we'll never see a guy like Jimmy Brown again. Barry Sanders came close. Gale Sayers came close. **Walter Payton**. I still say 'came close,' because I obviously never saw him live, but that was the most graceful, powerful, punishing runner I have ever witnessed. I would defy anyone to say that God's going to grace us with another runner like Jimmy Brown.

> **Two of the greatest quarterbacks of all-time, Johnny UNITAS and Dan Marino, have the same middle name, Constantine, and both are from Pittsburgh.**

> **In the last 30 years, the record for the most touchdown passes thrown by a non-quarterback is held by WALTER PAYTON, with eight. In football pileups, Walter Payton would relax at the bottom and untie his opponents' shoelaces. That's why many defenders currently put tape over their laces.**

Bernie brought me so many great memories. I still remember his first pass in the game in December of '86 against the Bengals in Riverfront. It just shut the crowd out. Is there anything better than for a visiting team to go in, and on the first play from scrimmage…. And, of course, his double overtime win against the Jets. If you talk to Bernie, say, "Hey, Bernie, there is a fan that brought up, in overtime, you threw a throw-away pass into the left corner of the end zone, and the Jets cornerback actually almost picked it off." Instead of really throwing it out of bounds, he half-assed threw it out, and had that Jet cornerback not dropped the ball, that whole melodramatic double overtime, second longest game in NFL playoff history, would have never transpired. That was the game where NFL referee threw the flag on Gastineau. He said, "Fifteen yards for giving him the business." That was the Jets-Cleveland game in the playoffs. That's classic NFL folklore. Whoever heard of an NFL referee saying "Fifteen yards for *giving him the business.*"

———JOHN KARLIAK, 40, Cleveland

Bernie Kosar is a hometown guy. The fact that he wanted to play there—he planned it—kind of worked his way in the draft to make sure he came there. That was his dream…to play for the Browns. That meant so much to us. He truly, truly wanted to be there. He loved the team. There's the way he left Cleveland, too, when Bill Belichick waived him. I've never gotten over it, and I know he hasn't. It broke our hearts. He didn't want to leave, but he was waived, and there's something about it that makes him special to us. He's always been very good to the fans.

One thing I've learned about the Browns. We're like Cubs fans. There's always tomorrow…always next year. We've gone through some horrible times with 'The Drive' and 'The Fumble' and not having a team for three years. But, there's something about loyalty—team loyalty—that I've just learned from being a Browns fan. I try to define my life, and Bernie was the best example of that loyalty. That's why he's very special to us.

———MARILISSA SALYER, Nashville, Tennessee

Some other more positive memories—Greg Pruitt, Number 34. It has a two-fold meaning—because, if you're familiar with Cleveland sports, and my age bracket, there is also a great Number 34 in

Cleveland now doing commentary, **AUSTIN CARR**. So, Number 34—Greg Pruitt and then Austin Carr for the Cavs. To this day, I still wear number 34.

Back in Cleveland, one of the guys who was very nice to me—I used to manage a health spa in Westlake, where the Browns worked out—was Reggie Langhorne. When he was playing, he would work out in my health spa. I was just a pup then—21-22 years old. I would always ask Reggie questions like, "Like, you make X number, 700,000 dollars, how do you just go to the mall and not buy everything you want?"—and stupid questions like that.

The thing I remember most vividly, and I tried to mimic, as a little kid, was the tear-away jerseys that just reminds you of Greg Pruitt. I used to make paper-towel jerseys so they would tear away. I always wanted to be Greg Pruitt. I would do silly things, as a kid, like hike myself the football. We had a rec room with the old davenport, they called it then, which you would call a couch today. I would run and pretend I got hit and just dive headlong into that couch. Those were the tacklers. Then, I would bounce off and hit the floor. That whole time—I was Greg Pruitt.

Greg Pruitt was my idol of all time, I thought he was awesome. I got to meet Greg at the Cincinnati Browns Backers tailgate two years ago. Joey McGregor is the president of GCBB, Greater Cincinnati Browns Backers, a super, super guy. Greg still looks the same, but he's a little heavier. We had a great conversation. He asked me for a Dallas area Browns Backers tee shirt, and I gave him two, one for him and one for his wife. He was my superstar, childhood hero. But, he's a guy like you and me—just a normal guy, and a nice guy. As you get older, sometime, I think, we lose perspective on sports.

———<u>RICK RIZZO</u>, native of Elyria, Ohio, now of Dallas, Texas

The fact that Brian Sipe was a 13th round pick and was an MVP, is amazing. The quarterback I grew up with was Bill Nelsen. His nickname was Bill "No Knees" Nelsen. He had many surgeries on his knees. The quarterback in the championship game was Dr. Frank

> **Of the top twenty individual scoring games in NCAA Tournament history, only one name appears more than once: Austin Carr of Notre Dame. He has the single game record, three of the top five and five of the top thirteen.**

Ryan, who had a Ph.D. in mathematics. These are all kind of weird things for professional football. That defines Cleveland quarterbacks. That's why somebody like Tim Couch never fit in. People who have athletic ability but don't have the mind....

Ben Davis was a defensive back for the Browns when I was in elementary school. I was in the Boy Scouts, and he came to Boy Scout Night at my elementary school to talk. Ben Davis is Angela Davis' brother. She was running for president for the Communist Party, so obviously she was far out there. She was a very nationally known, and, at that point, a lightning rod figure. He was there and was supposed to talk about sports to the boys, but he was talking about politics, telling how much he loved his sister. That took the meeting in a whole different direction. One of the fathers stood up and said, "We'd really like to hear you talking about football rather than talking about your sister."

I would say that Greg Pruitt is the most exciting running back the Browns have had in my lifetime. One unique thing about Greg Pruitt: They pretty much outlawed the tear-away jersey because of him. People used to think they had him, but he wore those tear-away jerseys, and they were standing there holding a jersey...and he was 10 yards down the field. It was pretty humorous.

There is an underdog aspect with the Browns. Besides Bernie Kosar, who you'll hear about over and over again, Paul Warfield, is part of what defines the Browns. What defines him as a player is his intelligence, the epitome of a current football player in terms of being very smooth, very fast, ran great routes, worked very hard—that aspect of it really impresses a lot of people from Cleveland. Most people grew up with a blue-collar background or their parents did. I remember the day they traded Paul Warfield to the Dolphins for Mike Phipps. They had a front-page story with a picture of Paul Warfield standing there looking really, really sad. He had gone to **OHIO STATE** and grew up in Ohio, and it was a real negative. He

In the 1976 Ohio State-Indiana game, the Hoosiers scored first. Indiana coach, Lee Corso, called a timeout. During the timeout, Corso had his team pose for a group picture with the scoreboard—showing Indiana leading Ohio State 7-0—clearly visible in the background. Corso featured the picture on the cover of the 1977 Indiana recruiting brochure. Ohio State won the game 47-7.

came back at the end of his career, and they talked about how he was always one of the first people at practice…and this guy was a superstar. He could have done whatever he wanted to. What you picture in a Browns player is someone who has talent but doesn't have a big mouth. Hard work beats talent that doesn't work hard. He's someone who just seems to really appreciate the fans. If you get a chance to go to a game, the different experience you don't see on TV is, especially on defense, after almost every play, players on defense look to the Dawg Pound. They're waving their hands up and are trying to get the fans on their feet. It's amazing, especially in a professional environment where players want to distance themselves from the fans. It's like—"we make our money, and we don't want to really be around people." The relationship in terms of what the expectations are between the players and the fans, the trite way to talk about it is it's a fan thing, but it's really like that. The players are constantly looking into the stands, which surprises me. You don't see that with other teams. When I went to the Ravens games, and went to a Bengals game, you don't see that. You don't see that same type of relationship.

——STEVEN SOLOMON, finance director, Fairfax, Virginia

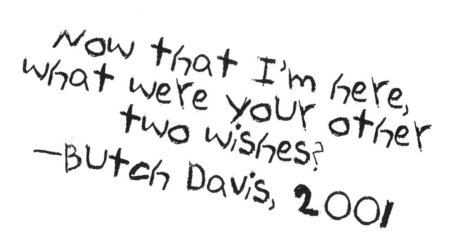

Now that I'm here, what were your other two wishes?
—Butch Davis, 2001

Chapter 7

Fandemonium

If There Were Sponges That Cleaned Up Broken Dreams, Woolworth's Would Still Be In Business

IT'S LIKE PLAYIN' HOOKY FROM LIFE

TOM CULP

When the Browns moved to Baltimore, Tom Culp, of Strongsville, had no idea the impact it would have on his life. Culp, 48, now owns four Sports Town stores in greater Cleveland.

T he way I started off in the sporting goods business was I had a design of my own back in '95. It was called 'No Barking.' Picture Marmaduke, the cartoon dog, standing up. He's wearing a Browns jersey that says '99.' He's got a hobo stick over his right shoulder, which has an orange bandana tied at the end of it with the dog bones sticking out, and a Browns helmet in his left hand—dragging on the ground. He's got this really sad look on his face. It says, "No Barking." Then on the back it's the same picture—really big—and says "No barking till the Dawgs come home. Kickoff 1999." I did the design and then manufactured it. We use it on sweat shirts, tees, hats, polos. We marketed it in little kiosks throughout malls. Then, we did trade shows. We went anyplace we could get into. It wouldn't even have to be sports related, if we could get in, we were there. That opened my eyes to how many people outside of Cleveland were Browns fans. I got orders from places outside the state and country.

When I was in downtown Cleveland in Tower City Mall, a lot of corporations had their headquarters and offices there. Sherwin-Williams, a huge paint company, is based there. They send people all over the world. Guys who would be moved out of Cleveland would come back in with orders for shirts. They had worn a shirt to the office—in Spain or France or wherever—and people would ask where they got it. They'd tell them they got it in Cleveland, and they'd want one. So when they came back to town, they'd be buying merchandise to take back with them for other people. It was kind of cool because my shirts were being worn all over the world. I've been in other cities, on business or vacation, and my wife and I would be driving down the street, it's really weird—I'll see the 'no barking' shirt on somebody. Even to this day, I'll be so surprised that I'll turn the car around and go back and if it's possible I'll stop the car and talk to them and ask them where they got the shirt. Usually, when I tell them I designed the shirt, they'll go, "Really? This is my favorite tee shirt."

After the team came back, we did a new design. It was pretty much the same thing except we changed the dog to look happy and it said, "Barking, again." That's all we did for years.

After the Browns came back, a buddy of mine said, "What are you going to do now? The Browns are back so your design doesn't work anymore." I said, "You're right." I hadn't planned that far ahead. Someone suggested to me that I should try to sell Browns stuff. So, I did some investigation and planning, and now we sell it all—NFL, NBA, college, NASCAR, hockey everything throughout Sports-Town locations. It's a great thing to do if you're a sports fan. For me, it's fun to go to work every day. As a general rule, when people come into my stores, they're in a good mood. They're not buying something they *need*. They're coming in to buy something for themselves or for a friend or family member—something they will enjoy having.

Why does the Dawg Pound drink chunky beer?

WE HAVEN'T SEEN ANYTHING THIS CRAZY SINCE THE MICHAEL JACKSON INTERVIEW

BRIDGET HUZIKA

The Browns Backers Clubs are arguably the greatest collection of fans of any sports team in the world. Their charity work, among other great activities, is what really sets the club apart from other fan organizations. Browns Backers are dedicated, loyal, passionate, fun... and crazy.

I am now a Browns Backers Coordinator, and it's my responsibility to maintain and grow the membership, participation and support of the Browns Backer fan clubs. I maintain and manage the entire fan club database, coordinate events and special offers to Browns Backers and assist with all aspects of the programs. The goal is to bring the fans in closer contact with the team and to embrace their support and passion for the Cleveland Browns.

As of 2005, there were 277 Browns Backers Clubs world-wide, representing 17 countries, including those in the U. S. and in Puerto Rico. This number changes based on new clubs forming and old clubs becoming inactive. Fans interested in starting a Browns Backer Club must complete a chapter application, including information about the potential president and officers, the club establishment location and a roster of interested individuals who will potentially be members of this club. Once an application is reviewed and accepted, the Club is chartered as an 'official' Browns Backer Club, and both parties sign an agreement that recognizes the guidelines and rules to follow. Each club is run by their elected officers who are responsible

> In 1941, Buff Donelli was the head football coach for the Pittsburgh Steelers and Duquesne University in Pittsburgh.

to maintain the membership of the club and to keep these members active and constantly connected to the Browns Backers Worldwide.

I interact and communicate with clubs and individual members on a daily basis, be it answering e-mails or phone calls, sending out mass e-mailings, and providing information and updates. It is very important to keep the lines of communication between the Backers and the Browns constant. Face-to-face interaction occurs as much as possible by welcoming Backers to Cleveland for special events and functions, or by attending specific Browns Backer Club functions locally and nationally throughout the year.

My experience with the Browns organization, as a whole, has been extremely positive. The unity and teamwork exemplified by the players and team personnel is unmatched. Each person brings something the table—personal skills, talents and/or past experiences. The organization is a family, and we continually strive together to succeed.

I had the privilege of being the Browns Backers Coordinator during the first ever Brown & Orange Weekend, a weekend dedicated to Browns Backers. This event brought in Browns Backers from all over the country for three days of exclusive events and activities. It was amazing to see fans come together and act as though they have known each other their entire lives. The expressions on faces, the 'barks' heard three days straight and the vivid life that glowed from each fan was priceless. It was awesome to see how a game of football, and one specific team, can affect the lives of so many people. It is an honor to be a part of this.

Ravens fans need braces just so they can hold their heads up.

SOME PEOPLE FEEL THAT ART MODELL WAS THE BACKBONE OF THE CLEVELAND BROWNS. OTHERS WOULDN'T PUT HIM THAT HIGH.

JOHN P. KARLIAK

John Karliak, 40, was born and raised in Cleveland. He graduated from Miami of Ohio and then traveled the country until 1995 when he moved back home. Karliak works for a psychiatric crisis team, a mental health agency, in the Cleveland area as a crisis counselor. He is known nationally on the Jim Rome Show as "John from C-Town."

For most kids, when they go off to college, it's the first time they are away from home. When you live in Cleveland, you're insulated. It's like, "It's us against the world." All of a sudden, you're away at college and meeting people from different parts of the country. I just thought, "I'll be damned if I'm going to take something off of somebody from Cincinnati. You wear those awful uniforms." I wasn't going to take that.

All Browns fans should be in therapy for the rest of our lives. The Drive. The Byner Fumble. Then really, since then, I was living out of state working as a federal agent for Uncle Sam, I remember Bud Carson coming back, and I remember being in shock when we beat the Steelers in Three Rivers in '89 —51-0. That lasted a year before Carson was fired. Then the whole Belichick thing.

The thing that really stands out for me right now is my total disgust and exasperation with the organization since they came back in '99. I can even entertain the fact that I would root for Pittsburgh due to the fact that Ben Roethlisberger, their quarterback, went to my alma mater. I half-heartedly did that.

I was one of the most vocal opponents of Butch Davis. Butch Davis will never be on the $25,000 Pyramid because he doesn't have a clue. I coined a term, "Hillbilly with a Headset." I called John Cooper that on the Jim Rome show. On a Cleveland radio talk show, I said, "We now have the second coming of the Hillbilly with the Headset— Butchie." If you were recruited by Butch in college, if you drove through Florida to go to spring break, if you had any affiliation with Florida, he looked past all your sins and would draft you on draft day. He collected a bunch of the most motley, inept, overpaid, under-achieving bunch of jackasses that I have ever seen assembled. That *gentleman* took 12 million to walk after what he did to this team— basically set us back by about four years. It makes it so hard.

There have been so many blunders and mismanagement of this team. This city deserves so much better. From the beginning, I think the late Mr. Lerner's heart was in the right place. I had no problem with him being the first owner since we came back. Carmen Policy was the wrong man at the wrong time. Dwight Clark should have never been given the position he had. Randy Lerner, Mr. Lerner's son, finally got it right by putting in a GM. I think Savage is a good pick.

If you read and believe what was in the Cleveland papers, it really crystallizes—the absolute, utter arrogance and the ineptitude of one Butchie Davis. In fact, Carmen Policy went to Randy Lerner and said, "We need a pro personnel evaluator who can get us back on the right track when it comes to draft day." Well, his first assignment was to evaluate the quarterback situation 'cause old Butchie wasn't sold on Tim Couch or Holcomb. He pushed for Ron Wolf to get hired. It was basically a stepping down of Butchie. It told him, "Look, you're not the omnipotent dictator anymore. We're bringing in another guy, and we're going to ask you to take his input." So, they hired Wolf with that consideration, and I believe he was paid $750,000. Wolf evaluated the quarterback situation, told them, "I think you're set between either Couch or Holcomb." This wasn't what Butchie wanted to hear. Butch said all the right things in front of Randy Lerner, but then, behind the scenes, he made that famous comment that made the papers, "I'm really not going to listen to whatever Ron Wolf has to say." That should have professionally insulted Ron Wolf because it made the media. Wolf had every right to say, "I'm not going to let this guy insult me. I'm brought in to help him, and he's going to talk me down like 'his opinion really means nothing to me.'" Wolf told Randy Lerner, "Thanks, but no thanks. You're on your own. I'm not dealing with this megalomaniac." We're the lesser for it. It obviously showed up again in this year's draft.

Maybe I'm romanticizing it, and maybe it's just as you get older, but since they've been back, it's irritating. It bothers you, but you just turn off the TV, or you turn to another game, and it's not that big a deal. I really wonder if other Clevelanders think that. Will it ever be the same? Will it ever be the Bernie Kosar, the Brian Sipe, the Cardiac Kids—those old enough to remember the '60s, with Jimmy Brown and Frank Ryan and Blanton Collier? Will we ever really, really fall in love? I've been to the new stadium several times. It's not the same as Municipal Stadium. I'm not saying I'd wish to go back to the old Municipal Stadium, but with the corporate suites and suits, and the hunkered-down security—is it ever going to be the same? I feel bad that kids who are growing up now are never going to experience what we experienced back in the '80s.

The Cleveland Browns have such a rich heritage. We have many things to be proud of. It's been very tough for us in the last few years. Hopefully, we're on the right track. I have so many memories. To feel this way about one team from the time you were a little kid—it does sort of mark your life. I used it as a barometer of 'where I was.' It hasn't been the same, for me, for my age group, since they came back. I can name almost the whole roster of the '80 team, and this year's team, I'd be lucky if I could name a dozen. I don't know what that means.

If Crennel let the entire 40-man roster go, there really is nobody the city is endeared to. There is no personal affiliation. When Belichick let Kosar go, my anger, my vitriolic reaction at Belichick was so bad. So, now, if everybody was let go, I wouldn't lose any sleep over it. There's not one guy on this roster who, if I heard he was going to be somewhere else, I have an affinity toward or any sort of personal bonding with. With a guy like Kosar, whom I met a couple of times by chance, you felt excitement to see him and thrilled to meet him.

That was cool and neat! These guys now, you know some of their names, but I really could not care less if they're on the roster next year. My mind just goes back to the days of Kosar, Byner, Mack, and the Webster Slaughters. Who could forget that game against Houston in '88? We used three quarterbacks that game, Kosar, Danielson and Strock—in the snow. It enabled us to play Houston again the very next week in a wild-card game, which we lost, on a crummy call because Clay Matthews recovered that fumble and ran it into the end zone. That idiot, referee Jerry Markbreit, said it was an incomplete pass. I still won't forget that.

I also want to go on record, without boring you, that I worked for a guy, who was a private investigator who was in charge of security for the NFL refs in the infamous 'Drive' game. He was guarding Markbreit and the referee crew to help them on and off the field. One night he and I were sitting in the car working on surveillance, and we were talking. He said, "John, as God is my witness, I was standing underneath the goalpost, waiting, in case the game ended, to walk the referees off the field. That field goal *did not go through the goal post*." I saw just a brief glimpse of that a couple of weeks ago—they showed Karlis' kick, and it did not go through the goal post. I was in a bar in Lakewood, Ohio watching that game live, and I remember when he kicked it saying, "Okay, he missed it. We're going to get the ball back." Then they said it was good, and I went, "No, it wasn't." That, to me, was the biggest conspiracy. Now, 18 years later, I'm not letting it go. My roommate at that time was a Giants fan, so it was so neat to sit there in his apartment and see the Giants take the Broncos to task. I took a vicarious thrill out of just seeing Elway get his a-- kicked. I mean that in a positive way.

Green Bay—
Come smell our dairy air

DO YOU KNOW WHERE VOLKSWAGENS GO WHEN THEY GET OLD? THE OLD VOLKS HOME.

LARRY KOPA

Larry Kopa is proud that "one man's trash is another man's treasure..." plus he's the only person who has ever "driven" a Browns helmet. Kopa resides in Riverside, Ohio, a suburb of Dayton.

My dad and my Uncle Joe, who lived in West 97th Street in Cleveland, would take me with them to games. They would be dressed up in their topcoats and top hats. Some years ago, after we had lived in the Dayton area for a number of years, my uncle knew that I was this avid Browns fan. One of his friends had died, his children were cleaning out the basement of his home and saw this football just sitting in a box. Also, there were some old game programs and other things in the box. He didn't realize the football had all these autographs on it. The ball had deflated and there's no way to know how long it had sat there. He said, "Larry, I've got this box with some Browns stuff in it. You can have it if you want it. I got it from a friend who was going to throw it away." I said, "Yeah, I'll take it." I took it home and it sat there for several weeks before I looked through it. I put some air into the football, and I went, "Whoa!" I saw all the signatures on it. I couldn't believe all those autographs. Then it became a task to search out when those autographs were done. By elimination and identifying players on rosters from the early 50s to the late 50s, I was able to key in that '57 was the year. One of the signatures there that is still fairly legible is Jim Brown, and that was his rookie year. We had a card show in Dayton. A former linebacker, Vince Costello, was there. He said a coach would take a few of these footballs every week and would require everybody to sign them. I really lucked out when I looked into the box and realized what I had. It's one of my most treasured possessions right now. To have that with these signatures and then just be connected that way with a part of history that was there in the early Browns era. The ball is not scuffed up, but over time just lost the air and stayed in that box and was forgotten about.

The Browns knew I had this old Volkswagen Beetle Bug. I had tried to get them to let me bring the Bug into the stadium for opening day. That didn't work out. So, then, I told them I had an old football, and they seemed very interested in that. Every year they change what they put in the display cases. They have a waiting list now of people who have old Browns memorabilia and are wanting to put it there on display. They told me just to send it up to them and they would display it. I said, "Well, I'm not going to send it. I'll bring it." The guy offered to give us a tour of the stadium, and we certainly weren't going to refuse that. At the end of the season, they offered to mail it back, and I said, "No, we'll come and pick it up."

When we brought that 1957 autographed ball to the stadium, the Browns put it in one of the Plexiglas display cases where they have a little Hall of Fame area. Afterwards, a gentleman gave us a personal tour of the stadium. We were able to get into Al Lerner's board room and some of the executive suites. Down underneath, there's a tunnel area, where you could almost drive a semi-truck around. They have two Puppy Pounds. There's a Puppy Pound for pre-schoolers, maybe two-three-four year old kids. Then they have a Puppy Pound for the grade schoolers which has computers, foosball machines and air hockey. The whole thing is for the players' families. They have valet parking set up for them. In the old stadium, they had parked outside, and the fans would be all over the players as they went inside. In the new stadium, the players actually drive into the stadium, get out of their cars, which are then valet parked. The wife can drop the kids off, and they're taken care of. There are three locker rooms we got to see. One is exclusively for the Browns. The other is for the visiting team, and then they have a third locker-room area. If the were to have a championship high school football game, for example, they would have a locker room for each of the teams, but the Browns locker room would never be used. There is a complete medical facility. They have whirlpools and saunas. It's totally mind-boggling to see what they do have, compared to some of the players locker rooms that are up in the Hall of Fame Museum area in the upper part of the stadium. There is an underground heating system for the field. Even with nobody there in the stadium, you can't go from one part to another without getting a clearance. Even the gentleman who was showing us around could not go from one part into another part without getting a clearance to go there. The press rooms, banquet rooms are great. If you wanted to have a wedding there, and could afford it, there are rooms available. There are huge portraits of all the Browns players from the past. There's no way to compare the new stadium to the old one. But, I did cry when they took the old one down. I have a little office room in my house, and it is decorated with a lot of Browns paraphernalia. I have a little jar with some of the dirt, and I keep the bricks here

The history of the Cleveland Browns football **helmet** is quite unique. You'll see today that all the other NFL teams have a logo of some sort on their helmets, with the exception of the Bengals, which just have their Bengal stripes. The history of the Browns helmet is the fact that it's never changed from when the Browns first came into the league back in the late 40s. It has the face mask and the face guard, but the orange part of that helmet has never changed. If you look at the history of the early Volkswagen Beetle Bugs, that car has never changed. The symbolism is there between them. There are new Volkswagens, but that's not the same. When I came back from Germany, where I had been with the Air Force, our first car was an old Volkswagen. That got me back and forth to work. I said, "How cool would it be just to make a car look like a football helmet. I thought about it for a while. I was at a flea market. I saw a little Volkswagen Bug, little car, and I bought it and took it home. Down in my little work area, I painted it orange and put a stripe on it. I told my wife, "I got the Bug, and I'm going to make the helmet out of it." She said,

> **The Los Angeles Rams were the first NFL team to wear helmets with a logo. The logo was designed by a player, Fred Gehrke.**

"Oh, you're not." Then, I showed her the model, and she was greatly relieved because she thought I had already done something. The more I got to looking at the model, I said, "This is something that could be done." I'd go out and look at cars and they would be rusted to pieces. I wanted something that had a good floorboard in it. I went to look at a car, and the one I went to look at was not the one I ended up buying. I turned a corner, going down to a street in a nearby town, and there was this orange Beetle Bug in this guy's front yard that had a 'for sale' sign in it. I stopped, went in, and made an offer for it. I bought it right there, just like that. The floor and the body were in pretty good shape. The motor needed a lot of work—it was probably only running on about three cylinders at the time. It was leaking fluids. I brought it home and parked it in the front yard. My wife goes, "Oh no." I went, "Oh yeah." She said, "All right, if that's what you want to do." That's what I did. I did a little bit of body work on it. It looked really good. It was a lot of fun.

After Modell took the team out of Cleveland, the helmet car sat outside for several years. The rust took its toll on the car. When I learned that the Browns were going to be keeping all of their history, their name, their records and colors and we were going to have the new stadium, I said, "Well, I need to get the car back in shape for the new Browns." A buddy of mine who lives nearby has done restorations on Volkswagens. He agreed to do it and kept it for nearly six months taking it all apart and put it back together. He did an awesome job with the repainting. The colors were custom-matched to as close to what you could see for the Browns helmets. Mathematically, I measured out—proportioned out—how big the stripe should be to be in proportion to those on the helmet. The last time it was done, it was put on with a laser-light. It stays in the garage. It's been to Cleveland half a dozen times. That's a long drive to take that little Bug that far—you just have to stay away from the semi-trucks. It's been in parades down here. We've done other parades and last year we participated when the 'Bone Lady' came down. We take it to car shows. I drive it to work. My big boss out at the base where I work is a Steelers fan We have this annual bet that if the Browns win, I get his parking place. So when you look at the directors' parking places at the building, you might see it there.

I was able to get 'Top Dawg' as my Ohio license plate. Hanford Dixon and I were talking about the license plate. He said he certainly would have liked to have that for his car. When Dixon and Minnifield started all the barking in the Dawg Pound back in the mid-80s, somebody in the state of Ohio had that plate. When the team folded, it appears that plate was given up. About the time I had decided to redo my car the second time, I queried the state asking if that plate was available. The lady said, "Yeah." I was so excited. Again, I was in the right place at the right time to actually get that plate. In all honesty, if I ever had a chance to pass that on to someone, I'd give it to Hanford Dixon. It should be his plate, but probably as long as I'll have the car, I'll just hang onto it. I plan on having the car for a long time.

Courtney Brown had an eye problem. He couldn't see reaching his potential.

CALLING BILL BELICHICK "BILLY" IS LIKE CALLIN' ATTILA THE HUN, "TILLY."

SUE NAUMANN

Sue Naumann moved to Cleveland from Pitts- burgh when she was nine. For the last five years, she has worked at a sports store in Strongsville. The married mother of three has been a solid Browns convert.

With our team leaving and then coming back, it's not the same. I would never transfer my allegiance. When they let Kosar go in '93, I got very frustrated with the team. I was not a Bill Belichick fan. I used to run into him at training camps, and I thought he was the rudest, unfriendliest guy. I know he's quite suc- cessful now, but when he was here, he was just a bear. When he let Kosar go, I just said, "That's it. I'm done with football." I followed Dallas, where Kosar went. Then I followed Miami the year after. It's funny because I said I'd never watch another Browns game, but that didn't last long because I couldn't stay away from it. I did go back to watching it…my heart wasn't in it like it was before. Then, when I heard the team was leaving, that was horrible. Even my daughter called me, "I can't believe this is happening." I continued to watch football while they were gone. It's just in my system. I never rooted really for another team. I would just watch a variety of games. Then, I heard they were coming back, and that was great, but we didn't have enough time to do anything properly.

Our reason for moving here to Pennsylvania was that my dad worked in the coal mines. He lost his job and Cleveland was the biggest city to come to find a job. A lot of Pennsylvanians have moved here for that reason—or did back 34-years ago. I think that's why there are so many Steeler fans in this area. When I'm working at the store, I'll ask them, "What made you a Steeler fan?" "My dad, or my parents, or my grandparents, was from Pittsburgh." They have roots there somehow.

When I became a Browns fan, my family was not happy…and still not happy. Every year my brother, who lives not too far from here in Streetsboro and is still a Steeler fan, and I normally get together when the Browns and Steelers play. When they play in Cleveland, it's at my house. When they play in Pittsburgh, it's at his house. It got pretty heated at some of the games, and we haven't done it in a couple of years.

A lot of Browns fans stay out in the Strongsville area when they come in for the out-of-town games. I have customers who will come for every out-of-town game so I've gotten to know them over the years. We tell them we'll do products for them and ship it for them. People routinely call me on the phone and say, "I need this. Do you have it? Can you ship it to me?" A lot of them come up and go to the games and will spend a weekend here for every home game. It's pretty amazing.

My husband and I both remember that when we were kids, for some reason, there were a lot of Cincinnati Bengal games on television. In those days, we didn't have cable so everybody just had to watch whichever game was on. That might be the reason for having Bengal fans who live here, along with Chicago and Green Bay.

I argue with people all the time about this team. People say, "Well, this isn't our team. Our team's in Baltimore." "Well, no it's not! Our history is still here." To me, this team that's in Cleveland is the Browns. The team that's in Baltimore is the Ravens. All the money and the free agency and everything makes it different. I have a Memory Book of the Browns, and I was just looking through it. You look at some of these guys who were here, and they were here for years. Those guys started with a team and stayed with that team. I miss that part of it. I know everyone says, "Oh, it's a business." I hate that part of it. I like when the guys really played because they really loved the game, and they loved the city they were in. A lot of people's attachment to Kosar is that he wanted to play here.

When they got this team back together, they used Bernie Kosar. Al Lerner and Carmen Policy knew the people of Cleveland loved Kosar. The story I heard was that Bernie was trying to buy the

Browns, too, but couldn't get enough money, or backers, together to do it. He went in with Lerner and Policy and they used him, in my opinion, to get the team. As soon as it was done, they just pushed him aside. I talk to his father often. I go to Bernie's Charity Classic Golf Tournament and one day when I was talking to him, I asked, "Why isn't Bernie in with this any more?" His dad said, "He wants to be, but they just kind of pushed him aside and won't give him a place." They've done that with a lot of the older players.

Now, that we have a new general manager, they say they want to get the older players back in. It's important to the players who are here now, to learn the history. If they're playing for a team, they should know the history of it. Since they don't stay with a team long, I don't know how important it really is them. I talk to them when they come in the store, "Now, you guys know you have to beat the Steelers. Do you understand what this is all about?" Some of them just look at me like…. I look at them and think, "You need to know. This is important to the fans, and the fans are backing you, and basically we're paying your salary." Some of them just don't have a clue and to them it's just another game. But the fans feel like they should understand that.

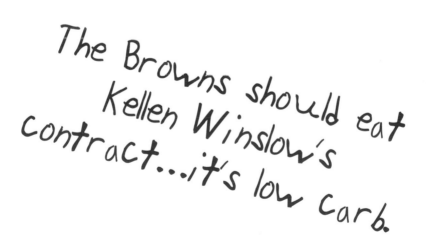

The Browns should eat Kellen Winslow's contract…it's low carb.

THERE'S NO "I" IN TEAM BUT THERE'S AN "M" AND AN "E"

RICK RIZZO

At the age of 38, Rick Rizzo has just switched careers. After 15 years with the phone company, starting in North Royalton, Ohio, he is now a rep for a biotechnic pharmaceutical company in the Dallas area.

W e had with the Cleveland Browns and with the Cleveland Cavaliers, back in the Bobby "Bingo" Smith and John Lambert days, teams that we followed. I wonder, as I'm chasing my 11-year old son around right now, if he'll ever have that. Today, it's not like that. It's not about the Los Angeles Lakers—it's about Shaquille O'Neal…and where does Shaquille O'Neal go. It's not about the Diamondbacks, it's who did Randy Johnson sign with last year. In fact, I have to tell you, I no longer buy any jerseys that are personalized. I put my own name on them now. I have three brand new—an orange, a brown and a white—Tim Couch jerseys that I can't wear.

I have two views on it. Either A—I've matured and grown up, and I'm seeing the business side of sports; or, B—it's the money and the greed. One of the two is tearing at the very fabric of the games that we see today. I sometimes worry; although, it's not at the top of my list, that our kids may never experience what we experienced in terms of love for our teams because of the free agency and the movement we see in the players. It's more about an individual than it is about a team. I think that's one of the cornerstones and building blocks that you had with the Cleveland Browns. You have a rust-belt area, high unemployment, terrible weather, but one thing you always had was your Cleveland Browns, and that was always the glue that kept the binding of the book together. You always had the Cleveland Browns.

I drove four hours to Houston last season, spent the weekend, and drove four hours back—why? My Cleveland Browns were in Texas, and I could see them. I'll give you an example—my buddy is a Texans fan. He goes, "You guys are going to get your butts kicked." "You don't understand, John, it's not about that. It's about coming down, experiencing football and watching the Orange and Brown take the field. We probably are going to get our butts kicked, but, you know what, when they run out on the field, and I watch them take a kickoff, the experience is done for me. I got to see my Browns play now. That's the key."

There's a book, *False Start*, by Terry Pluto. It tells about "why the Browns were set up to fail." A lot of it can be from excuses, but we even commiserate together. Here's what's going to be sweet. What's going to be sweet is there's going to be a day…some day…I don't know when—hopefully now with the arrival of my son…that we can enjoy together. The Browns are going to win. When they do, people like me, who have been fans for as long as we have—I don't want to blow it all too big out of proportion, but the only other thing I can think of is Christ's coming back. The resurrection—the Browns winning the Super Bowl —the two resurrections will probably be my two happiest days, man. That'll be about it.…

I travel around the country. I've been to the Arizona Cardinals, been to Cincinnati—that's just a cold, dark place. Reliant Stadium, in Houston, by far, is the nicest, most plushest, cleanest, neatest high-tech stadium I've ever been to. It's beautiful. Not only that, they do a great job at, what I call, *presentation*. Every stadium you go to, they're throwing footballs in the parking lot and grilling out—tailgating. That's a given. Well, at Reliant, they surround the stadium in activities, both pre- and post-game. It's a really, really cool experience, all the way through. The stadium is gorgeous. It's spic-and-span. Course, it's three years new. It's beautiful. Everyone was nice.

You've got to remember that we were 3 -12 at that time. Houston is fighting for .500. It's the last game of the season. You can't get any higher on the "this doesn't matter" scale. I bet you one in every twenty people we saw was decked out in Browns gear. The Houston guys invited us to eat with them. I had just a fantastic experience. For the most part, it's just that way. People have a respect for Browns fans, particularly from what we've been through, and the fact that we still show up in places like Green Bay and Houston and Arizona.

Not only the city of Cleveland hurt, when the team left, a lot of people hurt. In fact, the Pittsburgh Steelers—and I don't need to say anymore, other than Pittsburgh Steelers and the archrivalry—I'll root for the Pittsburgh Steelers if they're in the playoffs and the Browns aren't. How can a Cleveland Brown fan say that? Because the Steelers owner, the Rooney family and the Steelers organization and the Steelers fans, were some of the staunchest advocates that we not lose our name and we not lose our colors—as you know, the only team in any professional sport to ever retain their name and their colors. The Pittsburgh Steelers were a big reason for that. They said, "Hey, football, without beating up on the Cleveland Browns or vice-versa is not football." They advocated for us.

The place where I go, here in Dallas, we have our own private room. The Dallas area Browns Backers has about 175 families at two different viewing locations. My particular viewing location has about 60 people that come regularly, and we have our own private room. Just outside of our room sits the Steelers fans. They have about 20 that come regularly, compared to our 60. They come in, shake hands, send drinks in. We send drinks back. It's become a more respected, *friendly* rivalry. A part, too, is that we all hate the Ravens. We don't hate Pittsburgh as much 'cause we can transfer some of that to the Ravens. It's still one of the greatest rivalries in professional football, but the hate dissipated. When the bully that you don't like, stands and supports you in front of the principal, if you will, as an analogy, you get some respect for them.

The Bengal fans were probably the most vocal. I probably would be, too, because they have a lot of reasons to be depressed. That brand new stadium down there is just God-awful. If you could make anything more plain, by pouring concrete, that's it. It is just characterless. Cleveland Browns Stadium is beautiful, but my comments on that are much the same way there with the NBA today—it's way too corporate now, and that's unfortunate. If you go to an NBA game today, as a "regular" person, and we buy a ticket, we're going to be at the 200 or 300 level. You sit there and watch the entire lower section go half-filled with corporate seats and giveaways. I'm an executive, and I give those tickets away to people, too, but that sterilizes the environment.

I sure would like to tell you, sometime, about the Dallas area Browns Backers, about our makeup, about the things we do for charity, the money that we raise. Every one of these clubs is a not-for-profit organization. But, more importantly than that, we all do things. We do things here in Dallas. We raise over a thousand dollars every year for Christian Community Action, the SPCA—we've sent packages to the troops. We all get together for the camaraderie or to commiserate, but we also, every year, pick something of a greater cause and make sure that we do something to make a positive impact, even as Browns fans here in Cowboy Land in Dallas.

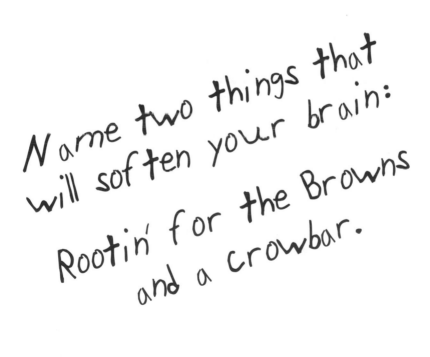

Name two things that will soften your brain: Rootin' for the Browns and a crowbar.

A ROCKYTOP TENNESSEE WALTZ WITH SOME NASHVILLE CATS

MARILISSA SALYER

Sissy Salyer is a school nurse for the Tennessee School for the Blind. A native of Dayton, she lives in Madison, 15 miles east of Nashville.

S ports were always very important to my family, and my brother was a Minnesota Viking fan. Our dog was even named Viking. My dad was always a Brown fan. I had never followed football very much until 1978—the Cardiac Kids days.

I fell in love with the Browns, and it hasn't changed a bit. Then, I started dating a fellow who was a die-hard Browns fan. I still remember a story he told me. He said, one time, when he was a kid, he didn't speak to his parents for about a week because they wouldn't let him change his name to Jimmy Brown. I knew right then that he and I were meant to be. We later married, and, of course, we planned our wedding around the Browns schedule. It would have to be an 'away' game weekend because we knew most of our friends would be going to a home game. We got married on a Saturday, and on Sunday, the next day, we went to Dayton to watch the Browns play the San Diego Chargers with Dan Fouts. The Brown got an overtime win. I still had my flowers in my hair from the wedding, and that was great...I didn't have to buy a drink or any food. If they know you've come from your wedding, the Browns fans will take care of you!

Shortly after we married, we moved to Tennessee—it was horrible. Here we are in Nashville, Tennessee, and all we had to depend on was the 10-minute ticker. Back then, they didn't have the constant changing scores all the time. *It was every 10 minutes*. We would sit in front of the TV, and all we got were the Dallas Cowboys or the Atlanta

Falcons. We never got to see the Browns except when they were in the playoffs. We lived by the 10-minute ticker.

Most of the people in our group are transplanted Ohioans. There are a few who were born here, but, for many, their parents may have come down here from Ohio. A lot of what happened in Ohio was that jobs were hard to find so a lot of people moved away. We've had several plants that have moved from Ohio to Tennessee so we've got a lot of people that way. Some of us just were looking for a change of weather or some other reason and just came South. We all found each other again. That's what is so amazing to me. When I go every Sunday for the game, I feel like I'm home. My home is really 325 miles away, but every Sunday—I'm home, and it feels wonderful. There's something about a Browns fan. I don't care where I go on all these travels when we go to different games, all you see is somebody with a Browns shirt on. There's a bond there. I feel like I've known these people forever, but probably I've just met them a few times, or, maybe, e-mailed a little bit. As soon as we get together, there's this sense of family, that sense of home. That's the fun of it.

The first road trip I ever made was to Indianapolis, a long time ago. I remember that I didn't like it because I felt like they were playing on a pool table. I like grass. It was inside a dome, and we were all going, "Oh, no, this is not the way it's supposed to be done." What I remember most about that game was there were more Browns fans than Indianapolis fans. That was a long time ago—before Peyton Manning. That was the day Eric Dickerson broke Jim Brown's rushing record. It was a terrible day for somebody to do that because it was mostly Browns fans there. I felt so bad for Eric Dickerson because nobody cared. In fact, some people were booing because he *dared* break Jim Brown's record.

We went to New Orleans one time, and it was fabulous. Kosar's magazine, *Bernie's Insiders*, has sponsored several Browns Backers Reunion Trips. Bernie Kosar was always my favorite player. I loved Brian Sipe, but Bernie was always very special to me. Bernie was there at the club. People were getting pictures and autographs. Here I am, a grown woman, and it was so sad, because when it became my turn, I just burst into tears, and I couldn't do it. So, I have no pictures—no nothing of him. I do have a postcard that I got from him in 1988. It was after 'The Fumble.' I wrote to him and to Earnest Byner. I got a postcard back from Bernie thanking me for my words of support. I've treasured that postcard and am saving it in plastic. I wanted to have him really sign it because it was typewritten. I'm sure his mother probably typed it, but still I felt like Bernie appreciated how I felt.

I remember my very first visit to Municipal Stadium. It was so cold, but that's the way it should be—you should be cold for football. They were playing the Cowboys, and some of their fans were sitting behind us. Every time Dallas scored—and they scored a lot that day—they screamed and sang, "The Eyes of Texas are Upon You." I thought, "If I ever go to another stadium, I'm not going to act like that." I always try to remember that.

During the Cardiac Kids days, 1980, was what I call 'my conversion.' I was working as a nurse in a hospital. This was when I knew I had it bad. I almost lost my job one time due to the Browns. I was working evenings on a step-down cardiac unit. I had to work one weekend, and it was Sunday, and the Browns were playing Green Bay. I was making my rounds. I made sure I was in a patient's room that had a TV on and who might be watching the game. There was this little man there with heart problems, and he was on a monitor. He was watching the game so I was in there straightening up his room. It was a Cardiac Kid day. Brian threw this beautiful pass to Dave Logan, last two seconds of the game—a lot of Browns fans remember this game—and we won. I'm hollering. I'm screaming. This little man, the patient, is jumping up, and we're all excited. Then I realized, "He's on a heart monitor." I guess his heart rate went really high—like to 140. We were clapping and saying, "Yea, go Browns." My charge nurse, a tall gal, was standing there, "What do you think you are doing?" I thought, "Oh my god." But the man went, "The Browns won. The Browns won." I just remember her waving her finger, like, "come with me," and I felt so bad. I said, "I am so sorry." The best part is that the little man's heart was okay. They thought it might have done him bad. But, his heart was fine, and he got to go home. Everything was good…and the Browns won. That was when I knew, "Oh, this is bad. I've got it real bad. I had just gotten out of nursing school, and I'm going to lose my job over getting excited about a Browns game, and I put a person at risk." But, at the time—he didn't care, and I didn't either. We were celebrating.

Everybody I talk to today says, "The Browns are going to turn things around." The first thing Phil Savage said, when he became the general manager, was, "There's a lost generation of Browns fans out there who haven't had anything to cheer about in a long time, and we've got to bring this back to them." I love that so much. Even the general manager knows who we are and knows how important we are. I said, "Yes. We're going to do it right this time. We're going to get a good coach. We have a general manager now who's gonna know how to do the draft and the salary cap and all those problems." We are just so full of hope right now. This is going to be a great gift to all of us.

I have never been more hopeful. Better times are ahead. We're gonna do it right this time. Our day will come…and I will be there. It's going to be great. Rootin' for the Browns is like a divorcee getting married again: Hope wins out over experience.

What's the definition of gross sports ignorance?

144 Steelers Fans!

SO SAY YOU ON, SO SAY YOU ALL

When Jan, my wife, and I first met back in '99, she invited me to her house to watch the Browns game. I told her "no" because I usually watched the games with my mom and dad. They are now 80 and 77, and they even went on the bus trip to a Browns game this year. Our first date was a Browns game against the Jets. The following year, as we were going up to the game on the bus, we were having trivia questions. The last question, as we were near the Independence exit, I asked her to marry me—while we were there on the bus. Last year, we took the bus trip to the Baltimore Ravens game. Before we got on the bus, at 7:30 in the morning, I had everybody get in front of the bus by saying I wanted to take a photo. Then, Jan and I got married right there before we got on the bus to go to the game. There were 73,000 people at the game, and I commented that it was the largest reception I'd ever seen. Also, I said if they would all just have given us $1 wedding gifts, we would have been all set.

——RANDY RINE, 46, Coshocton, Ohio

One of the years when I was struggling, I missed a couple of **field goals** in a game, and the Browns ended up losing. I remember, after the game, coming out of the locker room at the old stadium in Cleveland, to meet my wife. There was an old guy there, who was drunk and slobbering and looking for me. He said, "Cockroft, you suck. You couldn't kick the side of a barn. Why in the blankety-blank you're the kicker for the Browns, I'll never know." It was just humiliating. He was wiped out. Two weeks later, I kicked three or four field goals, and we win by three points. I come out of the locker room, same guy, but not quite as drunk…" Mr. Cockroft, I'm so sorry. You're the best kicker there ever was." So, either a hero or a bum!

Sometimes, we forget and don't even think about what our families go through when we're having a bad day. My wife sat up in that stadium many, many times. One guy always sat behind her, and every

> Twenty years ago, two-thirds of all NFL field goal attempts were made. Now, better than 80-percent are successful.

time I performed poorly—this went on for two or three weeks, "Cockroft, get that blankety-blank bum out of there." One day, she had enough. She turned around to this guy and said, "Sir, you're talking about my husband." Of course, the guy—what's he gonna do? That next week, she got the biggest bouquet of flowers I've ever seen from this guy, apologizing for the way he acted.

———**DON COCKROFT**, 60, retired Browns kicker

Butch Davis should be in prison. What a fraud! He leaves town with his skirts clean. He didn't get fired. He resigned. He pocketed twelve million dollars, and he leaves, in his wake, a smoldering wreckage that he created by firing all the good people in the front office. He finally resigned because he couldn't stand the pressure. Well, guess what, Butch, the buck stops here. You wanted all the pressure, all the reins, all the power—you got them. Now, what did you do with them? You left us a wreck, is what you did!

I just don't want another BS artist, which I thought Davis was from day one. He was too slick and oily. He's the guy who learned in Sunday school how to charm people. In a press conference, he would always say, "Well," and he'd call every reporter by name, "I believe…" He wanted to ingratiate himself. All he ever really cared about was himself. He thought he could pull it off, and he vastly overrated his own talent. Maybe Romeo can get it done.

Not only are the Browns an expansion team, but they're an expansion team created within a few years of the creation of two expansion teams that entered the league under much better circumstances. The Panthers and Jaguars had much better access to players, and they came along very, very quickly, and one of them was in the playoffs in two years. I'm sure the owners said, "Wait a minute. Next time we start a franchise, let's make it a little tougher to catch up," so, the Browns paid that price.

———**EMIL DAVIDSON**, writer and filmmaker, Hollywood

When my friend, Tom, was 65, he retired from the post office. They had a retirement party. Hundreds of guys were there. Tom's father at that time was 98 years old. There was a part of this party where he was opening up his birthday presents and his retirement gifts. The obvious question is, "What would a 98-year-old father give a 65-year-old son for his birthday?" Browns boxer shorts! I swear to God.

Here he is opening up this box. His father had wrapped that gift up in a bigger box so you couldn't tell what it was. He opened it up, and there it was—Browns boxer shorts. People just died! Everybody knew this guy was a die-hard Browns fan. 'Tis better to be over the hill than under it.

——DON DAVIE, 60, San Antonio

There's one thing about Browns fans—they just don't give up. Look at me. I've been a Browns fans in all the terrible years that we've had lately. And, we're all looking forward to the next game—we want to see what the new quarterback looks like, and what any coaching change is going to do. It's kind of a social thing…it's definitely a social thing. I have never seen this kind of loyalty to a city. When I was at NBC—West Coast, we had a Cleveland club there. NBC had about 48 people who had come originally from Cleveland. There are a lot of Cleveland people in the entertainment industry. You can't walk too far on any of the movie lots or any of the TV networks—or at least it was that way—without meeting someone. These people are so loyal, so loyal to their home town, and the team is representative of the home town. That's the way I feel, and that's the way a lot of the people feel. After all these years and years and years and years and years, and I talk to people who are from other towns, like Chicago or Detroit or wherever, and there's not that feeling. I don't know what it is. What is it about the northeast Ohio area—I have no idea.

Remember the era of the Cleveland jokes, "the Mistake on the Lake"—those were started by a couple of writers from Cleveland, of course. They got a lot of mileage out of it. A lot of writers, particularly sports writers who have no imagination, still do these, and they think it's funny. It's like Polish jokes. They think they can get a laugh. It still happens today. Why? I have no idea. When people attack your homeland, you tend to get a little defensive, and you tend to band together. I think that's one of the factors. Everybody felt it was unfair and that Cleveland was no worse than any other Eastern city. Thankfully, the Cleveland jokes are pretty much dying out now.

——RAY DEWEY, North Olmstead High, '51, Los Angeles since '52

I went from Texas to the Cleveland at Green Bay game on December 23, 2003 at Lambeau with a buddy of mine, a large African-American man named Derritt. He was an all-Packers fan, and I'm an all-Browns fan. In Green Bay, they don't have a lot of minority population so we made quite a pair. There was this large, black man, with this man all decked out in Browns regalia. I have to tell you—those fans at Lambeau were totally awesome. They invited us for brats, invited us for beer—we never heard a cross word. As you probably know, every seat in Lambeau, at least when I was there, was a bleacher seat. It was freezing cold—about 23 degrees. You walk down the bleacher line and everyone is sitting cheek-to-cheek. There's no seat, but miraculously, when you got to where you thought your seats were, they just kind of spread apart a little bit, and you kind of wedged yourself in, and everybody had a good time.

I'll paraphrase a Brett Favre comment. It's the only game he ever played in at Lambeau that it snowed from start to finish. The Browns lost. James Jackson ran for a big game. But, it was a really great experience to go to Lambeau and hang out with those fans and be treated as nicely as they treated us, given diversity in both person and team. That was real cool.

——RICK RIZZO, Dallas, Browns fan

Back when the Browns were in their heyday, there weren't 32 teams. The leagues were a third that size. Their television coverage was pretty extensive. They got into places like the southeastern part of the United States. Elvis Presley was a Browns fan. He was a friend of one of our fabulous All-Pro guards, Gene Hickerson, who was from Mississippi. He was a great guard, one of the best they ever had. The games were always on so Elvis started watching and became a Browns fan. The Browns have had some famous fans—**Condoleezza Rice**, Martin Mull, Drew Carey, Fred Willard, Patricia Heaton and Pat McCormick, who was originally from Rocky River. I live in Sherman Oaks, California…and I *still* have two season tickets to the Browns.

——RAY DEWEY, retired NBC executive

CONDOLEEZZA RICE's only long-term boyfriend was Ricky Upchurch. He was a star with the Denver Broncos and she was a doctoral student at the University of Denver in the 70's.

Maybe twice a season I make a banner, a sign, out of a shower curtain so if it rains it's gonna repel the water. I do it with permanent marker. In 1993, I wrote down, "Cleveland's Largest Fish Fry" when they were playing the Dolphins. **Marino** tore his Achilles tendon. I taped the game, and I try to look for my banner on TV.

In 2004, when the Browns played the Eagles, I used some spray paint to do my sign and wrote, "T. O. has B. O." I put the little stinky lines up next to the B. O., and I put "The Gillans, Rochester, New York." It was cold here so I laid it out in my front yard to dry so I could fold it up. I folded it up. We got to Cleveland, and it was messed up. We went to the store and bought another shower curtain and a big marker. I went back to the room and my son and I made the sign. We got up the next day, took everybody to the game and showed them around 'cause they'd never been before. We hung up the sign and Terrell Owens scored. I just had some weird feeling he's going to do something. What is he going to do? All of a sudden, he stood up and he started heading toward my sign. I didn't say anything to anybody but to myself I thought, "What's going on?" All of a sudden, he's pointing at it, and he got real close to it, and he threw the ball at it. I thought, "I can't believe this is happening." I'm in a fantasy football league, so I was switching around on the radio for scores, and the news about my sign was all over the radio. I thought this was cool. We stopped at Erie, Pennsylvania on the way back home. Sure enough, SportsCenter was on. Sure enough, they showed it on the program. It had gotten on the Internet. The *Philadelphia Enquirer* had it on the front page—Owens throwing the ball at my sign. I got a kick out of that, too.

——BILL GILLAN, Rochester, N. Y.

The year the team came back, my first child was born. She is now six years old, and I have a three-year-old son. They know that, every Sunday after church, during football season, we have to get out our Browns stuff. My son says he wants to be a Browns football player and my little girl wants to be a Browns cheerleader. During the Super

> In the 1979 baseball draft, the Kansas City Royals selected Dan **MARINO** in the fourth round and John Elway in the 18th round. That same year the Royals hired Rush Limbaugh for their group sales department. Limbaugh left in 1984 for a radio opportunity in California.

Bowl, my little girl asked me who we wanted to win. I said, "Well, your daddy wants the team in the white to win." She said, "Well, I want the Browns to win." I said, "Yeah, we do, too, but we're not playing today."

The husband of one of my co-workers is a big, big Steelers fan. If we lose, we get phone calls. I'm like, "Okay, don't answer the phone!" It's all in good fun. But, sometimes it is frustrating. You can always pride yourself that, as a Browns fan, you're with them thick or thin. You're not a bandwagon jumper. You're there. It makes you feel good about your state, and about your team…and there's always next year. We're hopeful. This could be our year.

——SHAWNA QUEEN, 27, Portsmouth, Ohio

I have a friend, Roberto Valenzuela, a little younger than me who grew up in a Hispanic migrant atmosphere in **south Texas**. When he was 10 years old, he got to go to town one day, after working in the field. His family didn't have a television, and he stopped in front of a store to watch a TV, something he never got to do. There was a football game on. He stood there watching for about five minutes, and the owner of the store came out. Roberto started to run because they usually shoo you away, but the gentleman said, "No, no, come here, come here. Do you want to come in and watch the game?" He said, "Sure." He goes inside. The man proceeds to tell him the team playing is the Cleveland Browns. The store owner happened to be a Browns fan. He sat the kid down, and they watched the game together. Because of that half an hour, from that day forward, sitting there with that man watching the game, he became a Cleveland Browns fan for life. To this day, he's never been to Cleveland.

——DAN JARVIS, 56, Albuquerque

We're an hour and forty-five minute drive from Cincinnati. When the Bengals went through all those bad times, and they still are, you would not see a Bengals shirt—you would not see a Bengals hat. It was like, "Gosh, are you not a fan anymore? What's going on?" Then

> **Coach Jimmy Johnson and Janis Joplin were high school classmates at Thomas Jefferson High School in Port Arthur, TEXAS. Jimmy Johnson didn't know she sang. They hated each other. She called him "Scarhead" and he called her "Beat Weeds."**

they start winning, and they come out of the closet. I always tease them, "Aw, I smell the mothballs, man. That thing's been in the closet for a while." I'm always right on their case because I wear my Browns stuff. Win or lose, I wear it all the time.

My friend Sharon and I became friends in '85 because of the Browns. She was always coming into Creekside, the place where I work. Football was on television one day, and I was there watching. She said, "Oh, you like the Browns?" I went, "Yeah." "Who's your favorite player?" "Bernie Kosar." We became very good friends just because of the Browns. We used to joke about our criteria for a date—had to be a Browns fan! She actually met a guy at a Browns party, and she married him. They named their first dog Felix Wright, after a former Browns player from the '80s. He passed away—the dog, not Felix Wright— and they got a new dog. Their new dog's name is Winslow, aptly named for a dog.

——**KAREN HOLSAPPLE**, bartender, Versailles, Ohio

During the three years the Browns were gone, I just didn't watch football. A lot of people became Ravens fans, but I chose to just not follow football. For me, the most important thing was the Browns— the players come and go—the owners come and go—coaches come and go. It really didn't bother me that the team came and went, as long as we got to retain exactly what the Browns are about—the helmet, the logos. Why would you want to fight for somebody to stay who doesn't want to be there? At that point, it's "You go ahead, but leave us with who the Browns really are." I think the majority of Browns fans felt the same way, "Just go ahead, take the team, do whatever, just leave us the name. That's what it is." There are certain cities that you can't imagine not having football—all the iron-belt cities, Detroit, Chicago, Cleveland, Pittsburgh—all the Midwestern blue-collar towns. All the Midwest teams are comprised of blue-collar fans who live and die by their team. They refer to the team as if they were on the team—my team. Everybody I know who is from the Midwest, roots for a Midwest team. It's just part of the nature of growing up in the Midwest.

——**SEAN SAMUELS**, Clevelander, now living in Arizona

In the military I was stationed on the West Coast, but I was always able to keep up with the Browns. In the early '80s, I was introduced to the Browns Backers group, and I joined immediately. At that time, we were over 2,000 members strong. We were doing everything by hand and by mail, folding all the letters and sending them out to everybody, every week. We had to write the articles for the weekly newsletter and run off all those copies and fold and put the stamps on it to get it out. We didn't have the access to the Internet then. People would just hear about us—word of mouth—or they just found you. You ran into Browns fans everywhere. I was working at a print shop at the time, and a guy walked in and saw the Brian Sipe jersey I had on. He said, "You're a Browns fan? I'm a Browns fan." He was from New Jersey. I don't know what the attraction is…maybe it's the forbidden fruit, the inability to win. All the fans are just people who are real down to earth and enjoy having a good time. It's the whole atmosphere. Cleveland is a very family-oriented town. That has a lot to do with it. You can go down to visit the neighbor's house and just walk in.

——**KEVIN WHITE**, 43, Los Angeles area

When satellite TV came out, about '87, we found a way to watch the games. We started getting together at the Ramada Inn/Damon's in Indianapolis, on the south side near Beech Grove. We would cross our fingers at game time that they would be able to pick up the game. We would pray that they found the feed of the K2 band on NBC. It was funny because most of the time they would end up finding it, but sometimes they came up dry. In our area, we didn't really have a radio feed. Finally, we bought a device that, if we didn't get the game, there was some product that you could hook into the phone line and play it over speakers. We only ended up using it twice. Worst case, we would plug that into the phone lines and pick up the Browns radio broadcast on WJM or WWWE.

——**PHIL TEMPLE**, 40, Indianapolis

Two years ago, a bunch of us from the Canton area were tailgating pretty frequently. So, twelve of us brought a school bus. We painted it very similar to the helmet, took all the seats out of it and replaced them with five couches. A buddy's brother-in-law owned a local Coors distributorship, and they give us $1,000 just to put their logo up on the bus. We ended up putting a urinal in it with a stall. Every game, we pack that thing up and head up to the stadium. For our group, we have anywhere from 45 to 60 guys tailgate every week.

Our menu depends on who we're playing. I own a catering company, and one of the other guys owns a meat distributorship, so if we play Baltimore, we'll have crab cakes. If we play Washington, we'll do pork, in honor of "the Hogs." For Philly, we did Philly cheesesteak sandwiches. When we're playing Pittsburgh, we do some pirogues. Every game, we have the hot dogs and Stadium Mustard, of course—no other mustard but Stadium. It's the one that has been served in the stadiums for years and years and years.

At Browns' games, we park in what was once an active area known as The Flats in Cleveland. Now, a lot of the night clubs have left the area so it's more or less deserted, but we park there—probably about a mile from the stadium. You take the train in, or we'll walk, or we can take a cab up to the stadium. In Cleveland, there are designated parking lots that the Browns do. But it's just sort of easier for us with the bus, getting in and out of the traffic, to park where we do. We could probably park closer to the stadium. When we drove separately, we used to park right by the stadium. Then, they outlawed grills where we were because some guy who was parked in a tiered garage put their hot coals down next to a car, and it caught the car on fire, and blew it up.

We haven't taken the bus out on road games because we are little fearful of it being destroyed. We thought about Cincinnati, maybe, because there are probably more Browns fans in Cincinnati than there are Bengals fans. We've gone to a Pittsburgh game over there a couple of times, and it's very brutal going into their stadium. We decided to leave the bus at home.

———CHUCK SCHUSTER, Penn State grad, Canton

We really are die-hard fans. We can take the jokes. I heard a joke today and pulled it on my husband. I said, "Did you hear that today down at the Cuyahoga County court, they were trying to take away custody from a kid's parents 'cause they were beating him?" He said, "No, I didn't hear that." I said, "Yeah, so the judge was going to award custody to his aunt." The kid stood up and said, "No way, my aunt beats me worse than my parents." So my husband was like, "Oh, that's horrible." I said, "Then the judge said she was going to award custody to the grandparents." The kid was like, "Absolutely not. My grandparents beat me worse than anybody." So they officially awarded custody to the Cleveland Browns 'cause they knew they couldn't beat anybody.

That reminds me of the one where a drunken Browns fan is sprawled across four seats, face down. An usher comes over and says, "Hey, buddy, get up. Where's your seat?" The bloody-faced, drunken Browns fan lifted his head and said, "In the upper deck."

——HEATHER GREENE, 29, Cleveland

I've been to San Diego for a Browns game, and their fans were pretty calm. In fact, I think they were sleeping. I went to the New Orleans game a couple of years ago when the Browns won. Those fans weren't all that bad either. One thing that impressed me about **New Orleans** was that immediately after the game, almost every restaurant and every bar in the French Quarter had signs up saying, "Congratulations Brown Fans. Come on in." We thought, "Boy, they really know how to market." In Arizona, we had a street not too far from Sun Devil Stadium completely blocked off for a party just for Browns fans. There were thousands of us. We had a band playing. We had give-aways. We had all the regular tailgate stuff. We had a DJ who was playing a lot of Cleveland songs. We flew in Vince Costello, former Browns player, to be at the party. Big Dawg was there for the party and the game. After the party, we all went into the game, and we had more fans than the Cardinals had.

If you are a Browns fan, and you are a true Browns fan, you understand loyalty. It's kind of like a family. All the people here at work know I'm a Browns fan. I took my door name plate out and had a little Browns helmet engraved on it. One time I was checking out at Petsmart and happened to have my Browns tee shirt on. There was a lady and her son standing in line behind me. The son was about five years old. She had a Steelers shirt on. I thought, "Oh no." She looked at me, and I looked at her and said, "Obviously, you're a Steelers fan." She goes, "Yeah." I said, "I'm a Browns fan." Her son starts jumping up and down and says, "See

At half-time of a **NEW ORLEANS** Saints game in 1968, Charleton Heston drove a chariot and rode an ostrich while filming a scene for the movie *Number One*.

Mom, I told you. There are Browns fans all over the place." Then her son looked at me and said, "I'm a Browns fan. For Christmas, I got a Browns tee shirt and Browns socks." I looked at her, and you could tell she didn't really want to tell me, but she said, "I don't understand it. My husband and I are both from Pittsburgh, moved here…and he loves the Browns." I'm like, "Well, your son is smarter than you or your husband." I said, "Way to go, kid. Keep it up." He was all excited!

——JOYCE WILLIS, Phoenix, Canton native

It was fun at half-time to go into the bathroom in the old stadium and huddle around the pipes to get warm. We would drink hot chocolate. And, I really liked the band. It was a fun old stadium but it was sort of gross in many ways. There are great memories there. When we were in those championship games, there was just an electric quality—a quietness you could hear. It had such an intensity. Even the next day, it would sort of color your mood—whether or not you'd done well that week….

Since the new Browns have come, there's a little different level— at least for me and my husband—of feeling. My husband also went to the games when he was growing up. I maintained my season tickets, but he has no interest. Some people just lost interest when the new group came. A lot of people really did not like Modell. I didn't like him either, but the whole thing was blown way out of proportion. I don't think they had to leave the way they did. "Misunderstanding" is maybe too weak a word, but there were a bunch of egos—Mike White's ego and Art Modell's ego. There's no question Modell had some estate tax problems then.

When they came back, I bought the personal seat license, and my husband just about killed me. I didn't even consult with him…I just automatically bought it. It was pretty expensive although supposedly it was half price of what it would normally have been. Such a deal! But, it wasn't such a deal. It was still pretty expensive. I initially bought the club seats, which were really expensive. And, then he said to me, "Do you just want to mortgage the house for these tickets? Are you out of your mind?" I keep them, but I don't go to that many of the games. I either give them away or sell them. I just feel a different level of connection with this group.

——CARLA TRICARICHI, Cleveland lawyer, mother of two

I've been a Browns fan since I was 13 years old, watching Jim Brown every Sunday on an old black and white TV when Carling's Black Label was the game sponsor. I've been to only one game—the last game Bernie Kosar played.

It was great growing up watching those guys play. Jim Brown, Leroy Kelly, Dick Schafrath, Frank Ryan and all those guys played good, old hard, smash-mouthed football. There was none of these high-fives. They just did their jobs—none of this bumping-chests or fancy dances.

Maybe that three years was a good thing health-wise. Before that, every Sunday night, if the Browns lost, I wouldn't sleep. I'd go to work and suffer the abuse. Maybe that vacation from that helped the fans out, health-wise. The Browns always found a way to lose in the most extraordinary way there ever was. If there was a way to lose, the Browns found it. There was The Drive and The Fumble and then we had this guy take his helmet off—we find a way to lose.

All my friends who are Bengals fans like to tell me, "We've been to the Super Bowl. Have you been to the Super Bowl?" I say, "Hey, you lost. You lost. We *have been* on top. We were the champs in '64. We *were* on top. Can you guys say that?"

———BOB WITTENHAGEN, 56, Carlisle, Ohio, south of Dayton

When I heard the team was leaving Cleveland, I was totally depressed, p----- off, blood-boiling angry. I just couldn't get over what was happening. I pretty much swore off of football after that. I would not watch the Super Bowl at the end of the year. I had no reason to watch. I'm not really a football fan—I'm a Browns fan. That's what it is. If it weren't for the Browns, I couldn't care less—these overpaid, pampered, spoiled athletes, and these millionaire-billionaire owners! Football is so big in Ohio—kind of like basketball is in Indiana.

Even when Modell did all that he did and the team left, a lot of those Browns players still claimed allegiance to Cleveland, not Modell. In New Orleans, Steve Everitt, who played for the University of Michigan before playing for the Browns—the way he would sign his autographs for the fans, was "F--- Modell, Steve Everitt."

The whole NFL basically got off the ground in Ohio. If you take any year's roster for the Ohio State Buckeyes—they usually dress a hundred or more for every game—you might find five guys who weren't born and raised in Ohio. You go to Michigan, and there will be as many guys from Ohio playing on Michigan's team as there are guys from Michigan. To paraphrase O. J. Simpson, you can beat the heat and you can beat your kids, but you can't beat Ohio.

——BUZZ BUZEK, 60, Phoenix, originally Akron

Remember when they first took on the persona of being the dogs with the barking and all of that? They had a poster out with Hanford Dixon, Don Rogers, Al Gross and Frank Minnifield, basically defensive backs. It was funny because these guys had on suits. They were dressed real sharp. All of them had a different breed of dog. They were standing there with the dogs, and Hanford dubs himself as "Top Dawg." I guess he was the leader of the defensive backs. They turned it into a defensive back thing. It's funny because a lot of people don't realize that's not what it really started out to be. I always tell Hanford, "You may be the top dog, but you're not the original dog." He says, "What you mean, man?" I said, "You're not the original dog, and you know you're not. I'm upset because you didn't give credit where credit was due. The original dog was Eddie Johnson." He acknowledged that I was right. Eddie was in practice one day, and he just started barking. If somebody made a good hit in that practice, Eddie would go into his bark mode. Then, they just kind of moved Eddie to the side and they took on the persona of being 'the Dawgs,' and they just left Eddie out in the cold. When I see Eddie, I always say, "Hey, you know, and I know…you're the original Dawg."

That defensive backfield was probably one of the best in the NFL at that time. Don Rogers, God bless his soul, reminded me a lot of Jim Brown. You could see him in the community. He would be involved. You could see him riding down the street or see him go on appearances and involved in fundraisers. He liked dealing with the inner-city kids because he was an inner-city kid himself. When he died, it was really rough.

——CURTIS FRANKLIN, 48, Cleveland, Indiana State '79

My mood is around the Browns. When they win, I'm in a good mood. If they lose, there's just this kind of mellowness inside that you can't control. I swear there's nothing like a Browns fan—nothing.

I was at the game—It was my first game— where Turkey Jones almost pulled Terry Bradshaw's head off. Actually, if you run that tape backwards, it looks like Jones is just helping Bradshaw to his feet and showin' him on his way. There's just something about football that's so fun. You get to scream. The Dawg Pound was pretty scary when I was little. I remember it always smelled like pee and alcohol. That area was like the pee-pee zone.

I'm eternally optimistic. Every year, they're always *going to be good!* It's interesting because I hate Baltimore a lot. My sister worked for Art Modell so you hear a personal side to the man's character, which was very, very wonderful in many ways, from what I heard.

There's a line in some movie that said, "I'm like the country I'm from." Sometimes I always feel like I'm like the city I'm from. There's just a certain mentality about being from Cleveland, especially when you leave Cleveland. I don't know what it is. There are tons of comedy writers, for instance, out here that are from Cleveland. There are a lot of people in Los Angeles from Cleveland. I'll always be a Cleveland girl, which, by the way, is the name of a script I'm writing. It is about three fanatic Browns fans.

It's so ironic—the team goes to Baltimore and they win the Super Bowl. It's like the girl that got dumped for the 50th time, and you just can't take it anymore. You find this perfect guy, and he gets married—to somebody else! It was really painful. Art Modell finally achieved the mountain he had been climbing—he got to the top. There was probably something unfulfilling for him, as well. It's a sad thing. People make these choices in life.

———**MICHELLE SHACK**, Los Angeles, aspiring writer

Last winter, in Waynesboro, Pennsylvania, 15 miles from the underground Pentagon—coming back from the dentist—I felt like eating breakfast or grabbing a doughnut. I see this place with a big parking lot so I pull in and park, get out of the car, and look up and down the street. It's almost surreal. There's nothing moving. Nobody is driving. It's very white and stark. Maybe a block and a half away, there's a man with a cane walking slowly toward me. This was like a foreign movie—bright light. I'm fascinated. Across the street is the restaurant, but I delay going over there. The guy approaches. I see he's very old and wizened and has an old Browns hat on. He's coming along at a terribly slow pace. I wait. Any time I see a Browns fan, I have to talk to them. I said, "Oh, you like the Browns?" He said, "Yeah, I've been a fan since they started." Right away he went into the litany— Dante Lavelli, Lou Groza—I didn't even have to prompt him—Otto Graham. He said, "Yeah, we should be pretty good this year." We looked at each other and talked for a couple of minutes. Then he started to move on, "Okay, I'll see ya." Then he turned around, looked at me backward, and said, "Hey, Jim Brown was the greatest." What's nice about this is that Waynesboro is like a 'Klan' town. The Klan is really alive—they march. It moved me to think that somebody, an old-timer, could plug Jim Brown. This guy looked like a redneck. I was speechless.

——GENE BEECHER, retired antique dealer

I was one-year-old when the Browns started. My father said they held a contest to determine the name of the team. The name they chose was already taken, and they decided they wanted a name synonymous with a champion. At the time, the biggest name was Joe Louis, called The Brown Bomber. That's where they got it. They've since said they named the team after Paul Brown and everybody has accepted that. But, as I got to thinking about what my father said, I thought what owner would name a team after a guy that he might have to fire.

A while back, they showed the first contract Paul Brown signed when the team was formed in '46, and it was for four years. You don't name a team after a guy you're not even sure you want to keep after four years. This solidified it with me. No owner would ever name a team after a coach. What do owners normally do when they try to be immortal and are trying to be bigger than everything? They would name the team after themselves, but *never* after an employee. In any field, I've never known anybody that owned anything to name something after an employee.

——HARRY WRIGHT, 60, Cleveland

When Paul Brown started the Cincinnati Bengals, my home town became half-and-half—half were Cincinnati fans and half were still Cleveland fans. My family has always stayed Cleveland fans. They're the first team…they're the only team. "The Real Men in Orange" is what we used to call them. My mother, who just turned 78 still calls them that. A lot of people sprained their ankles jumping on that Bengals bandwagon, but they have had a lot of years for the injury to heal.

Going to games at five years old was extremely cold. We would have a stadium blanket. We wore huge jackets, putting socks on our hands, and then mittens on over the socks, and we'd have a big old quilt over us. I'd usually sit in between my dad and one of my brothers. When everybody else would stand up and cheer, I felt I had to stand up and cheer. My dad would say, "Sit down. You're pulling the blanket off everybody else." There was such excitement being around all the other people.

I was flipping through the TV channels recently and Larry King had Elvis's 'Memphis Mafia' on there. What was so funny about it was that I just decided to stop and hear what they were saying. They were talking about **Elvis Presley** and were trying to decide what was one of the most eccentric things he did. They got to talking about when he watched motorcycle races on TV, he would wear a motorcycle helmet. If he would watch football on TV, he would wear a football helmet. One of his very early girlfriends was on the show. She was asked what she was doing now and said, "I married a football player who played for Mississippi State and the New Orleans Saints and Cleveland Browns." Then his business manager said, "The Cleveland Browns was his favorite team." My family was all sitting there, and we looked at one another, "Oh my God, Elvis was a Browns fan." They said he would sit with a helmet on while watching the televised games. We knew Elvis was the King—he died on the throne, ya know—and now we find out he was a Browns fan....

My mom got me a tee shirt that said, "Count down to '99." She said, "Well, what are you going to do? Are you going to get back into it?" I said, "Mom, I don't know. I don't know if my heart's into it. I don't know if I can do it again." Then the Hall of Fame game came, and all got together to watch it. I still had my doubts, and then I saw the helmets come out—I saw those orange helmets on that field—it just gave me goose bumps. I just went, "Oh my gosh. We're back!" I said, "I don't care how bad of a season we have, I'm just so thankful I finally have a team." People were saying to me, "How can you like them—they went 2-14? I said, "Yeah, but that's *my* team!" My dad

Do you know what Jerry Garcia said to Elvis when he first saw him in heaven?
"Hey, King! Guess who your daughter married?"
That's a true story...give or take a lie or two.

always taught me that you stick by them, win or lose, 'cause when they finally do go all the way, you're going to be able to say that you were with them the whole way—that you didn't jump on their bandwagon—you were there with them the whole way…and I've been hooked ever since.

My boss is a Titans season ticketholder. He travels a lot overseas to **Scotland** and Ireland to play golf on the different golf courses there. He came back from one of these trips and said, "You're just not going to believe this story." He said while they were in Scotland, they had golfed all day, and they decided to go to a pub to get something to eat. He said, "We walked into this pub, and what's hanging behind the bar? A big Cleveland Browns flag! I can't get away from these people for nothing."

———JULI WATSON, 43, Nashville, native of Portsmouth, Ohio

Sundays are special in Cleveland. You wake up early. You have your breakfast. You go to mass, and then you get in the car and go downtown. That's just the way it is from week-one through week-seventeen.

The Drive. My mom and dad are already trying to get hold of a travel agent—we're going to the Super Bowl! What a lot of people don't know is if we had just a little bit of luck on that drive…. Elway was in the shotgun at about their forty-yard line. He sent Steve Watson in motion. The center snapped the ball a split second too soon. It hit Watson on the hip. Elway had to scramble to fall forward to get the ball. If that ball's on the ground, I believe Carl Hairston or one of our guys up front like Reggie Camp, falls on that ball. People don't remember that. If someone's got film, I'd love to watch it again. If we fall on that ball, we're going to the Super Bowl. But, Elway, being such a great athlete, was able to reach down and grab the ball, literally, off his shoe tops. He ended up completing a pass on the play, and the rest is history.…

The *Plain Dealer* had an essay contest every year for a chance to become the next Cleveland Indians batboy. My brother bet me that if I entered it and won, he'd give me a car. I dropped the letter in the

> While playing golf in 1567, Mary, Queen of **SCOTS**, was informed that her husband, Lord Darnley, had been murdered. She finished the round.

mail on a Sunday night at midnight. About four days later, I got a call from the *Plain Dealer* and a representative of the Indians that I was among 25 finalists. They brought me down to the Stadium and interviewed five groups of five kids. Out of each group, they took a finalist. Then, they interviewed the final five, and I ended up winning.

It was a blast. I wasn't cocky or arrogant, but I was confident. When they were interviewing, the one thing that struck me was a lot of the kids, when they were asked questions, would look down or they would look up or look sideways. I kept my nose and my eyes right in the face of the people who were asking the questions. That's just the way I was. That's how I was brought up.

I ended up being the batboy for two years. That first year, I was paid $15 an hour. The second year I got $17-$18. Next to my children being born, that was the greatest experience of my life. I was a huge sports fan to begin with.

As a batboy, I saw the journalists come to the park. They'd get there about three o'clock, and they'd mill around on the field, or in the clubhouse, then they'd watch a game. I saw these guys get paid to watch ball games. I said, "That's something I want to do." I ended up going to Cleveland State and, also, to broadcasting school. I wanted to become a sports guy, but the first job that came open was a news job in Cleveland in late '91. I come from an extremely blue-collar family. Right after World War II, all my uncles got jobs in the mills and coal mines. I feel guilty going to work—I don't have to put a hard hat on.

———CARMEN ANGELO, St. Edwards grad, Cleveland newsman

I had been in Paris on business for Apple, and it was my last night there. I hadn't seen or done much, and I had one night, by myself, to go do something. A couple of the travel books had said that it was interesting to go visit the grave site of Jim Morrison from **The Doors**. The guidebook said because of all the attention to that grave site—it's only open during certain hours of the day—they have a guard

> The band, Pearl Jam, was originally named Mookie Blaylock, after the NBA player, and they recorded their first album, "Ten" under that name. In 1992, the band Mookie Blaylock changed their name to Pearl Jam after a hallucinogenic concoction made by lead singer Eddie Vedder's great-grandmother, Pearl.

standing there so you can't get close to the grave. I didn't think too much about that, but then that last night, I decided I was going to go see the grave, no matter what it took. I figured I would have to climb a wall or something to get in, but I had no idea what I was in for.

I got on the Metro—the train—with a couple of beers and rode for about 20 minutes out to the suburb where the cemetery was located. It's a very famous cemetery in Paris where a lot of notable people are buried. I walk up to the cemetery. There is a wall around it that is easily 20 feet tall, with metal spikes on the top. The gates at the front of the cemetery are imposing—you can imagine the gates from the original King Kong movie—giant, iron gates that are all locked up like a fortress.

It was about midnight when I got there so I decided to walk around outside the wall to see if there was some other place to gain access. I didn't want to try to be a criminal but was just wanted to get in and look at the guy's grave site. Now, I was determined to see it since I had wasted my night to get there. I walked around the entire cemetery which was probably two miles. The wall went the entire perimeter, and there was no entry point at all. I was getting tired, and I was kind of disillusioned—it was getting late. The second time around, I'm walking back around toward where the train had stopped. It had stopped running by then, but I noticed there was a courtyard in an apartment building right adjacent to the cemetery. There was a wall that was like a 'T' off the main cemetery wall which was enclosing that courtyard in the back of that apartment building. It "T"-ed up against this other wall.

I was able to get into the gate—don't ask me how—of the courtyard at that apartment building. I walked all the way to the back. It was dark and shadowy. I realized that the wall that "T"-ed up against it was probably hundreds of years old. It had odd, uneven bricks that looked like a rock-climbing wall. I managed to get up to the top. At that point, I was just thinking that I wanted to look over into the cemetery.

I get up to the top, and there's razor wire going across the top in both directions because this is obviously an entry point that has been identified for people trying to sneak in. I was exhausted by the time I got to the top of the wall so I decided I would just hang out up there. After a while, I realized that the razor wire would not be that tough to deal with as long as you're not trying to run through it or crawl through it. If you just go slowly, you can step through the loops and if it gets caught on your jeans, you can just pull it loose and step through it. I was doing that and looked down. There was a very large crypt built close to the wall—about 20 feet away. One side of a cross at the top of that crypt is about four feet from the wall. I thought that if I could get to that part of the wall, I could reach across. Sure enough, I was able to drop down into that cemetery. It was just the creepiest cemetery you've ever seen. The moon was starting to come up and it was all covered over with trees.

After I had dropped down, I knew I had to go find the grave. The cemetery was all laid out with these crooked, weird streets that were all named in French. It took me another hour and a half to find the grave. When I first dropped in there, I took off my shoes and was trying to walk softly because I felt sure there would be dogs or security of some kind. After about a half hour of that, I just said, "To heck with it," and put my shoes back on. It's really dark so I'm using the light from the cellphone display, holding it up to signs so I could read them.

When I finally got to where it was, I found that there were crowd-control barricades around the three graves on the other side—that's how I knew I was at the right place. I had a nice little moment there. I stepped over those barricades and went right up to the grave. I had my iPod playing "Riders on the Storm." I was just sitting there, chilling out. The moon comes out bright at that time, and I had a nice little introspective moment there—at three in the morning—in France—with the spirit of Jim Morrison.

To commemorate the visit to the grave and to celebrate that I actually made it there—actually got there—I had some stickers of Cleveland Browns helmets in my wallet. I didn't really want to deface the grave, but I did want to at least put a mark of some kind there and take a few digital pictures. I peeled off one of these stickers and put it on the gravestone marker and took some pictures. I just thought, "I don't think Jim would mind." With the pictures, I could show everybody that I really was there. When else are you going to see a Browns helmet sticker on Jim Morrison's grave?

That was quite an adventure for me. I'm usually pretty law-abiding and don't do stuff like that, but I don't know what got into me that night. I assumed that if I could go back to one of the gates that I would be able to get out. I figured that, from the inside, there would be some way to unlock them…but, no, I actually had to end up crawling back up onto the top of that crypt and reach over across and pull myself up onto the ledge that had the razor wire. I had to go back out the way I came in—which was not easy. Long live the Cleveland Browns!

——DAVID ZBIN, Berea native; Video Production, Apple Computer

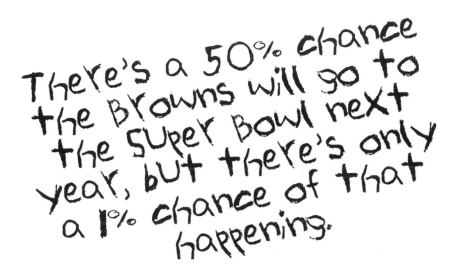

There's a 50% chance the Browns will go to the Super Bowl next year, but there's only a 1% chance of that happening.

When he dies, Modell's friends are going to bury him ten feet under. Deep down they think he's a good guy.

TO BE CONTINUED!

We hope you have enjoyed the first edition of *For Cleveland Browns Fans Only.* You can be in the next book if you have a neat story. You can e-mail it to printedpage@cox.net (put "Cleveland Fans" in the Subject line) or call the author directly at 602-738-5889.

Also, if you have stories about Ohio State, the Indians, Notre Dame, or nasty stories about the Steelers or Wolverines, e-mail them to printedpage@cox.net (put the appropriate team name in the subject line). On any e-mails, be sure to include your phone number.

For information on ordering more copies of *For Cleveland Browns Fans Only,* as well as any of the author's other best-selling books, go to www.fandemonium.net.

In '89, the Browns beat
the Steelers 51–0.
The Steelers were lucky
to score 0.

There were no actual Ravens fans harmed during the making of this book.